PRAISE FOR A HEALING JOURNEY

"In *A Healing Journey*, we follow Gilda Morina Syverson as she guides us through her own intimate journey of trials and errors, successes, and awakenings - teaching us along the way to open our eyes to our own paths in front of us. Gilda's spiritual connection, stimulating curiosity, and culture-rich wisdom inspire us to embrace each day as it comes and accept our unifying truths in our own experiences of life. From Healing Touch to sacred manifestations, we see that healing on a soul-deep level is within reach for us all."

~ **Lisa Mentgen-Gordon**, CEO/Owner of Healing Touch Program

"Gilda Morina Syverson is a woman of high energy, creative intelligence, and scintillating curiosity. In *A Healing Journey* she uses these gifts to explore her deep Italian roots and the healing powers of her ancestors. Determined – no compelled – to heal herself, she offers her own hand as she guides us along an ancient footpath toward restoration and inner peace."

~ **Dannye Romine Powell**, author of *In the Sunroom with Raymond Carver*

"It is abundantly clear from the very first chiseled sentence of Gilda Morina Syverson's crucial new memoir, *A Healing Journey*, that she is a poet, a very fine one, who not only feels, but witnesses everything and has the courage to forge it into inimitable language. With absolute candor and breathtaking cinematic imagery, at once aching and epiphanic she illuminates the emotional core of what it's like to stand on the earth with the abiding questions of all who have preceded her."

~ **Joseph Bathanti**, North Carolina Poet Laureate (2012-14) and author of *The 13th Sunday after Pentecost*

"*A Healing Journey* becomes an elusive plunge back into time and place within the space of Gilda Morina Syverson's own personal history and eventually her family's history. Little does she know that her search leaves us eager to peek back with her at the discovery and values of not only our generational past, but a past that had been left behind in Sicily long before her birth."

~ **Delia De Santis**, editor of the Anthology *People Places Passages, An Anthology of Canadian Writing*, author of *Fast Forward and Other Stories*

"This is an encouraging, deeply human, accessible memoir of one woman's desire and search to find "the still point of the turning world," as T.S. Eliot expressed. *A Healing Journey* offers hope and clarity to all of us interested in demystifying the process of keeping the promises we've made to ourselves. What a gentle and compassionate guide Gilda Morina Syverson is!"

~ **Judy Goldman**, award-winning author of seven books, including *Together: A Memoir of a Marriage and a Medical Mishap*, and *Child: A Memoir*

"Artist, writer, mystic, seeker Gilda Morina Syverson takes the reader on an intimate journey through the sacred spaces of the heart. She travels both a metaphysical and grounded path, letting her keen intuition guide her towards finding a Spiritual Director, learning about Healing Touch, and discovering her life's purpose. Using these tools, she maps the flow of energy that courses through her - from the healing abilities entwined in her mother's ancestral lineage to the here and now where she deals with wide ranging questions relating to the soul, her health, and her frustrations about the political and pandemic situation. Gilda's awarenesses awaken both herself and the reader to the potential of deep, expansive healing."

~ **Ann Campanella**, former magazine, newspaper, and award-winning author of two memoirs, *Motherhood: Lost and Found* and *Celiac Mom*

"Through her own deep, unwavering heart- and spirit-led Healing Journey, which memoirist, poet, artist, and wellness practitioner Gilda Morina Syverson shares in illuminating detail, we fortunate readers are gently led on our own journeys to discover our gifts and passions and use them to heal ourselves, our loved ones, and our world. What a beautiful, generous present Syverson's book gives us to unwrap."

~ **Maureen Ryan Griffin**, founder of WordPlay, author of *Spinning Words into Gold* and *Praying You Goodbye*

"The takeaway from Gilda's unique spiritual journey is that unless we dive into the deepest parts of our soul, we cannot launch ourselves to where that soul wants us to be. Her journey began with warm memories of her Italian grandfather and how his touch had healing powers and ended with her becoming a Certified Healing Touch Practitioner. Full of twists, turns and risks, I found this book to be compelling and thought-provoking."

~ **David Figura**, retired newspaper journalist and award-winning author of *So What Are The Guys Doing?*

"*Healing Journey* is a true tale that leaves the reader completely captivated as vivid scenes come alive and each spoken word presents new meaning. With an innate story telling ability, Gilda Morina Syverson takes the reader on a transformational journey of self-discovery with mystical experiences that evoke compassion while toggling the practicality of a fragmented world desperately searching for love.

~ **Laura Ponticello**, award winning author and publisher of Divine Phoenix Books

A Healing Journey
From 9/11 Beyond the Pandemic

Gilda Morina Syverson

THE BRIDGE
Cornelius, NC

In conjunction with
DIVINE PHOENIX

Published in North America by The Bridge in conjunction with Divine Phoenix LLC, www.TheBridgeBooks.com, Cornelius, NC

This book is a work of creative nonfiction. The events are portrayed to the best of Gilda Morina Syverson's memory. This is the Author's story since each person may remember incidences and occurrences differently. While all the stories in this book are true, Syverson sometimes condensed conversations, summarized scenes, or changed names. Additionally, given the topical matter of *A Healing Journey* this book offers no medical advice. The story is a perspective based on the author's experience. So neither the author nor publisher can be held liable by any person for any loss or damage arising from this book or any information therein.

Library of Congress Cataloguing-In-Publication Data
Gilda Morina Syverson
A Healing Journey, From 9/11 Beyond the Pandemic/Gilda Morina Syverson—1st ed.
p. cm.
Library of Congress Control Number: 2023912316
ISBN - 979-8-218-23778-3

1. BIOGRAPHY & AUTOBIOGRAPHY/ Women. 2. BODY, MIND & SPIRIT / Healing/ Energy (Qigong, Reiki, Polarity). 3. BIOGRAPHY & AUTOBIOGRAPHY/ Personal Memoirs

Author photo credit © Kevin Shank
Book Cover Design by Chris Moebs

Comments about *A Healing Journey, From 9/11 Beyond the Pandemic* and requests for additional copies, book club rates, and author speaking appearances can be directed to Gilda Morina Syverson at www.gildasyverson.com

10 9 8 7 6 5 4 3 2 1

Printed in the United States of America

Dedicated to:

Mom

Mary Morina

for the gift of my dear mother
and her
"matriarcale" lineage

NOTE TO READER

Welcome to *A Healing Journey, From 9/11 Beyond the Pandemic*. My hope is that in reading my story, you'll go in search of your own direction, follow where the energy leads, discover your purpose for living.

My journey was as unexpected as the shock of 9/11 and the changes that ensued in the decades that followed.

Each morning upon awakening, if a dream appears, I capture it in my journal, meditate, maybe write a poem, and maybe not. I focus on following my own curiosities while paying attention to coincidences that surface throughout the day, and I listen, intently, to the still small voice within.

Peace & Safe Keeping,

Gilda

TABLE OF CONTENTS

PART I

PART II
AFTERWARDS

I

II

III

IV

V

ABOUT THE AUTHOR

PART I

"Things falling apart is a kind of testing and also a kind of healing.
We think that the point is to pass the test or to overcome
the problem, but the truth is that things don't really get solved.
They come together and they fall apart. Then they come together
again and fall apart again. It's just like that. The healing comes
from letting there be room for all of this to happen:
room for grief, for relief, for misery, for joy."

Pema Chodrin
When Things Fall Apart

PROLOGUE

My body floats above Taormina, the shimmering city on a hill in my family's beloved Sicily. Blue-green waters of the Adriatic Sea sparkle. In the distance, light-gray smoke hovers above snow-capped Mount Etna. My ancestors lie in graves below this active volcano in Linguaglossa, the village where my mother's parents were born. Like a bolt of lightning across the sky, I land and stand in front of the small triangular piazza in front of the Chiesa di Sant'Egidio Abate. After trying multiple times during numerous visits to get inside this church, colossal wooden doors now open. Why now? Why not the times I'd visited Mom's cousins on both Nonna and Nonno's side? I walk up the stairway, enter the open portal. In front of me, a red carpet covers the diamond-shaped marble floor leading down the nave past remnants of frescos peeling away from the surface of the thick Gothic walls on either side of me. Ahead lies the altar I walk towards. I am finally in the church where generations of my mother's family worshipped.

I had a special bond with my mother's parents, *Nonna* Egidia and *Nonno* Francesco Stagnitta. Living as a child in the flat above their home, on the Italian Northside of Syracuse, New York, reinforced my relationship with them.

Nothing called attention to the stories of my Linguaglossa relatives more than the power of living in the shadow of an active volcano. One of my favorite tales was of *Nonna* and *Zia* Concetta, *Nonna's* sister and my great-aunt, carrying umbrellas to protect themselves from the ashes and spurts of lava spitting overhead.

My maternal line wielded a powerful energy, and I wanted to return to Linguaglossa, dig deeper, find out why. I had spent much time on an earlier trip to Sicily with my parents and husband, Stu, where I learned, through the eyes of my father, about my patriarchal lineage. Something was needling me to go back again and find out more about my mother's ancestry.

Although *Nonna* appeared to have all the influence and power, it was *Nonno*, a quiet man, who held a certain intrigue. My grandfather was the person who had done healing on my siblings, cousins, and me when we were growing up. *Nonno* was also the one his *paesani* (those who came from his village in Sicily) would seek out whenever they had health problems.

One or another would show up at the door with any number of items—bottles of wine, vegetables, fruit, a plucked chicken. They were mostly gratitude payments but sometimes they brought healing items, such as eggs for the whites *Nonno* used to dip cloth into for setting broken wrists, ankles, or other broken bones.

Nonno Francesco and *Nonna* Egidia would escort the person who came, and often the accompanying spouse, into the front room of the house. I loved the dark tones and mood of that room. It was where the fireplace was located and where I loved playing church in front of the hearth, setting up an altar, pretending to say Mass while imagining angels all around.

Even as a little girl, I knew I would never be allowed to perform any kind of church ritual. Only men could become priests in the Catholic Church I was raised in.

Once the door closed behind my grandparents, who were entering into the front room with the people who had come to see *Nonno*, it would leave us kids on the other side wondering what was going on behind those walls. Sometimes I would put my ear up against the door and could hear a voice sighing or even calling out in pain. My grandfather would be doing something to help heal whatever ailed the person. That's what my mother told us, anyway.

After we moved away from my grandparents' house, out of the Italian Northside, if one of my siblings or I had a health concern, my mother would drive us to see her father. *Nonno* didn't limit his healing abilities to humans. He also tended to dogs, cats, and even birds.

My older sister, Nicki, once found a wounded sparrow in the backyard. *Nonno* set its tiny broken leg somehow, then put a string around the good leg. When its leg began to heal, my sister walked the little critter around the yard.

Over the years, I closely watched *Nonno's* demeanor—the way he gently moved among the vegetable plants and the roses in his multiple gardens, how he communicated in a quiet, caring manner with the *paesani* who came to see him, and how mindfully he took care of each of us when Mom took us to see him for healing.

At the time I didn't think that what my grandfather did was out of the ordinary. I scraped my knee and *Nonno* cleared it up, making the scratches that had been there disappear. He would also help reduce the soreness that one of my siblings or I had from a fall off a bike or the porch, or when we were pushed by some neighborhood roughneck.

I remember once when *Nonno* took my sprained foot in his hand and turned it gently side to side. His hands moved up and around my ankle, foot, and the bottom of my calf. Unprepared for what was to come, I gasped as my grandfather made a quick twist of my ankle.

Something inside my foot fell perfectly into place. He asked me to stand up and walk. Whatever had created my pain was gone. Then *Nonno* softly rubbed the place where the wound had been and put me at ease.

My Aunt Barbara loved to tell the story of her youngest, my cousin Frank, having terrible pains in his stomach for a number of days when he was around four. *Nonno* sat down and laid Frank on his back on top of my grandfather's legs. He covered my cousin's eyes with one hand, took his index finger, placed it lightly in Frank's navel, made circles around his tummy, quietly recited words in Italian that my aunt clearly did not remember, since she didn't speak the language.

Then *Nonno* pulled an imaginary line from stomach to midair, uncovered Frank's eyes, gently stood him up. The pain was gone.

If my grandfather's healing held such fascination, what might I discover looking deeper into *Nonno* and *Nonna's* lives by visiting their village again? Going back to Linguaglossa was the only way I could find out, or so I thought.

Trying to lure my parents back to Sicily the year after we had been there, mostly in Dad's hometown of Gualtieri Sicaminò, didn't go well. When Dad realized that I wanted to spend more time in Mom's family's village, he wouldn't hear of it.

At one point he bellowed, "I am not going back to Sicily and spending my time in Linguaglossa. I'm just not doing it."

"Let it go, Nick," Mom said. "I don't need to go back. Stop worrying about it."

I knew I could still go to Sicily on my own. But I wanted to be there with my mother.

In the end, our discussion was for naught. Less than a year after we returned from our original trip together in 2000, during the Catholic Church's Jubilee year, the Twin Towers in New York City collapsed, after terrorists hijacked two Boeing 767 flights and flew into the skyscrapers.

Close to 3,000 people were killed and more than 6,000 injured. There were additional deaths of people at the Pentagon, plus victims of another hijacked plane that crashed in a field in Pennsylvania.

The catastrophe convinced my parents they would never fly abroad again. It changed Stu's and my mind about traveling, too, at the time. For how long, we didn't know.

The way we once traveled would never be the same for any of us—Mom, Dad, Stu, me, and the world, really. For a while, even hopping on a plane from Charlotte to Syracuse, or the other way around, was out of the question. If Stu and I didn't drive to Upstate New York, we didn't go.

During the years following 9/11, I spent much of my time writing the story of my original journey from Rome to Sicily with my parents and Stu. I pushed away any thoughts I had about getting back to Linguaglossa in the near future.

Instead, my patriarchal line, and especially the experiences I had with Dad on our earlier trip, preoccupied most of my writing hours. I loved my dad, but we'd had our issues over the patriarchy I'd been raised under.

After years of my own internal struggles, I came to accept my father for who he was. The resolve came for me by writing the story of our trip where I had the opportunity to observe my father as he moved through Italy and especially the Sicilian village where he was raised.

It was not just the relationship with my father that I ruminated about each time I sat down to write. It was also the recognition of the rampant male dominance in our culture that many women like me had navigated throughout our lives.

Lingering in the background now was the desire to learn more about my mother's heritage. Little did I know that I would eventually, in a way I could never have expected, find out more about my matriarchal lineage.

Chapter 1
September 2001

The Spring Before 9/11

The dream, never written
or remembered, buried deep in
the psyche, until the shock
of planes flying into Twin Towers
and she, hundreds of miles away,
stands in front of the television
thrown back to an image of herself
looking through invisible walls
at skyscrapers engulfed by scorching
flames reaching into dark. People
wail and thrash, sleepwalkers move
through city streets, and from her side
of the wall, all she can do is watch, like
a prisoner in Plato's cave facing
the rear, while fires burned behind
captives casting shadows.[1]

I have always been drawn to mysticism and spirituality. Even though I hadn't majored in theology or philosophy in college, those themes had impacted my life and work as a creative person.

It had been close to a year since I'd stopped seeing my therapist and, during that time, I had been asking colleagues and friends if they knew a good Spiritual Director. I wanted to shift from a therapeutic

---

[1] Syverson, Gilda Morina, "The Spring Before 9/11," *Quiet Diamonds*, edited by John P. Kristofco, The Orchard Street Press, Ltd., 2018, pg. 48

approach and talk with someone who came from a spiritual perspective.

I jotted down names but never followed up on any suggestions. After 9/11 and the many sleepless nights of worry over relatives, friends, and all those living, along with people who died in the Twin Towers, the Pentagon, and the farmland in Pennsylvania, I needed to be more assertive about finding someone who could help me move through this present world.

Although I'd been doing art for decades, over the last ten years I had been particularly focused on drawing angel forms surrounded by various colors and gold-leaf surfaces. Part of my process included periodically turning around from my drawing table to my laptop and writing a poem that appeared at the moment, or about a dream from the night before that came back to me, feelings on death and dying, struggles with living in a patriarchal world, and other thoughts that would surface in my day or night meanderings.

That's why, after the tragedy of 9/11, I knew it was time to find a different kind of support. I pulled out my hanging file marked "Spiritual Direction" and looked over a list sent to me by a nun—a spiritual counselor by profession—whom I'd met a number of years earlier on a retreat at The Oratory Center for Spirituality in South Carolina.

Even though I was born and raised Italian Catholic, finding a nun or even a Catholic counselor was not a priority. A priest was definitely not an option. The sexual abuse scandal in the Catholic Church was just coming to light.

Plus, my issues around the patriarchy, still loud in my head, excluded not only a priest but also, at this point in my life, any male voice. I needed someone who understood living in a woman's body and experiencing life with similar female roles—wife, daughter, sister, niece, friend, teacher, and more.

Ten days after 9/11, I headed down to the old Charlotte Merchandise Mart on that Friday to participate in the Woman's Expo for *Today's Charlotte Woman*. The magazine had published a number of my articles and its booth was located in an area with other vendors related to women's publishing and spirituality.

Behind the table where I sat stood a woman whom I'd met a few times at Well of Mercy, another retreat center, situated on 110 acres of farmland fifty minutes from where I lived in North Carolina. Jan and I started talking about Well of Mercy, writing, publishing, and, most of all, about the weight that hung heavy from this national disaster the country was moving through.

"I've been wanting to find a Spiritual Director for quite a while," I said. "Do you know of anyone?"

Jan told me about her Spiritual Director. "Her name is Betty White," she said, and I immediately went silent.

Aware of my sudden hesitation, Jan stopped and asked, "What is it?"

"This is the third time someone has given me Betty's name."

The first time was a few years earlier, when a student-turned-colleague mentioned a Spiritual Director whom she thought I would like. I wrote down Betty White's name but it got shuffled aside, and I never contacted her. The other time I saw Betty's name was on the list tucked away in my file sent from the nun I'd met at The Oratory Center for Spirituality.

Everything Jan told me about Betty fit my own profile—educated, well-read, married, (although, unlike me, recently widowed) with a family and a professional life. Betty had children, another thing we did not share, but it didn't matter. Being the second oldest of a large Italian American family with so many sisters, brothers, cousins, nieces, nephews, and more has been like having a family with the same expectations as a woman with children.

A certain appeal to Betty's association with the Episcopal Church felt comfortable since I'd attended St. Martin's Episcopal in Charlotte for a while because the pastor was a female priest. Having seen a woman behind the altar was not something, it appeared, I would ever experience in the Catholic tradition I grew up in. Meeting with someone whose religion allowed women to perform its main ritual appealed to me.

Jan had no idea if Betty would take on any new directees but she gave me Betty's phone number.

On Monday morning, I phoned Betty. We talked and she asked why I thought it was time for me to find a Spiritual Director. I told her how I'd been thinking for quite a while that I needed to talk to someone about my thoughts on spirituality, mysticism, and various life experiences. I mentioned that my interests did not follow typical topics of conversation in most social circles and that meeting with a woman seemed important at this juncture of my life.

"The final straw," I said, "were the events of 9/11, and when I heard your name for the third time, it felt like a clear message."

"Well," Betty said, "the number three, the trinity, seems significant."

I also warned her about my sensitive, artistic, intuitive nature. But nothing seemed to shock her.

"I hadn't planned on taking on any more directees," she said, "But I never know what God sends my way, and I feel prodded to say yes."

The first available appointment was a few weeks away at 11:30 in the morning on Wednesday, November 2, 2001, in uptown Charlotte at St. Peter's Episcopal Church.

During my first meeting with Betty, it was clear we were kindred spirits, not only educated, literate, and sensitive women, but women not afraid to question the dictates of a church or look beyond man-made dogmas. To my surprise, Betty never flinched when I mentioned my interest in astrology, numerology, archetypes, dreams, Rumi, and animal medicine cards.

"They are all tools to access the Spirit," she said with no reservations.

Since I've always been a bit cautious about mentioning my alternative interests, finding Betty was a godsend. We discussed the logistics of our relationship—meeting once a month at St. Peter's Episcopal, no socializing.

Then she gave me an assignment to complete before we'd meet again. "Write down who God has been for you throughout your life."

Being a writer, I was not afraid of taking on the task of putting words to paper on my thoughts and feelings. Finally, there was someone I could talk to about spiritual and life questions, concerns, struggles, and joys. On top of all that, I could include my alternative interests without someone looking at me cross-eyed.

Betty also mentioned that it would be easier to refer to God as "God" rather than trying to identify all the other various names attributed to him, her, or both. For clarity, I went along with it, at least for the time being.

I was especially relieved that now, in this new world of post 9/11, I didn't feel stranded with my own anxieties, worries, and the unknowns of the future. Betty and I would have our second meeting after the holidays.

But before I would meet for Spiritual Direction again, I decided to call Well of Mercy right after the New Year and schedule a time for my own self-directed mini-retreat.

The first time I'd ever gone to Well of Mercy was soon after it opened in the autumn of 1997. I drove up one September afternoon to Hamptonville for a couple of hours to meet Sister Donna, whom I'd read about in a bulletin at St. Peter's Catholic Church. Sister Donna Vaillancourt, along with Sister Brigid McCarthy—two Sisters of Mercy from Belmont, North Carolina – had begun a retreat ministry.

These nuns were not like any I'd ever met before. They dressed in casual slacks or jeans, shirts and sweaters, and were open to questions about life, God, religion, and all their facets. They felt like peers, contrary to my past experience with nuns who acted like Mother Superiors.

That afternoon on my first visit, I had a long passionate conversation with Sister Donna about my struggles in a male-dominated church. I felt no judgment coming from her. She listened quietly with what felt like great empathy over my concerns about the spiritual constraints I had experienced being a woman in the Catholic faith dictated by men.

Sister Donna admitted that she had her own patriarchal experiences. Her kindness and facial expressions made me realize that she understood me. Toward the end of the conversation, I asked what made her stay in the church.

"I feel called to religious life and can only make change from within," she said.

Sister Donna and Well of Mercy were safe ground for me.

Four months later, on a cold January day in 1998, I returned for a two-night stay, arriving minutes before a winter snowstorm blew in. I drove up to the large two-story, gray clapboard, Williamsburg-style house flanked by two guest houses and a spacious covered porch that connected all three buildings. The first person to greet me that afternoon was Julia, the administrative assistant, who showed me to my room upstairs in Sunset, the guest house on the right.

Julia explained the protocol: dinner at six and lunch at noon in the main residence. Everyone did breakfast on their own. Each guest house was equipped with a kitchenette stocked with breakfast foods—muffins, cereals, yogurts, fruit, cream cheese, peanut butter, jams and jellies, along with milk, juices, teas, and coffee—regular and decaf.

My room was cozy and warm. It was my first self-directed retreat—something I was a bit intimidated by at the time. I jumped in anyway.

Besides the two Catholic nuns, the rest of the staff, both women and men, consisted of people from various religions—Moravians, the Bahá'í faith, different Protestant sects: Baptist, Methodist, Presbyterian, and others. Well of Mercy appeared to have attracted every kind of seeker.

For the next four years, when I needed to get away and be by myself, I'd head up to what I affectionately referred to as Well.

Chapter 2
On Retreat

In January 2002, four years after my initial visit to Well of Mercy, and after finding a Spiritual Director to whom I could speak openly about what was going on in my life, I scheduled a retreat for the end of the month. The first person who greeted me when I arrived late that afternoon was Julia. After settling my suitcase, books, and other belongings in my room, I slipped out for a quick walk down to Hunting Creek before dinner.

As they've always done, the nuns, staff, and guests gathered in a circle, and Sister Brigid offered a blessing. It included a huge welcome to everyone, especially new arrivals. I sat with Julia for dinner, and that's when she told me that Sister Brigid was participating in a program in something called Healing Touch.

"Maybe you'd like to experience it," Julia said.

I had a sense of Healing Touch because my sister Nicki, a nurse, had gone to workshops on Therapeutic Touch when we were still single and roommates in Boston. Plus, there was my maternal grandfather, *Nonno* Stagnitta, who had done his own type of healing work on my family and me while I was growing up—those customs he brought over from his hometown of Linguaglossa in Sicily.

So the idea of a practice having to do with healing was not all that foreign to me. I asked Julia what exactly it was Sister Brigid did. Julia told me that Healing Touch was new to her, too, and that I'd have to get the details from Brigid.

It didn't matter what Brigid had to say, something was tugging at my heart and I blurted out, "Can you ask her if she has time to do Healing Touch on me?"

Once I asked the question that was it. All I could do that night was wonder whether Sister Brigid would say yes. My intention for this particular retreat had been to journal and delve into questions about my true purpose in life, especially after having found a Spiritual Director to guide me through this changing time.

Even though I didn't know the full extent of what I would be getting into, all I could think about was whether or not Brigid would be willing to do Healing Touch on me. During the night I woke to a memory.

It was almost ten years earlier when my sister Nicki and I went to a Medjugorje conference in Worcester, Massachusetts. (Medjugorje is in Bosnia where there were accounts of Mary, Christ's mother, appearing to six young people.) I drove the car into the large parking lot where the conference would be taking place and made a quick turn to the left with my head.

"Ugh," I moaned. "I twisted my body funny, and now I have a stiff neck."

No matter how I rotated my head, I was in deep pain. Nicki told me to turn the car off and to sit still. She placed her hand over the right side of my sore neck, where the ache was most intense. I forced myself to calm down from the frenzied feeling of having just thrown a monkey wrench into our time together.

My sister centered herself immediately and rested her hand gently on the area of my neck that was hurting. We sat in total quiet. After a few minutes, Nicki slowly lifted her hand away.

"Stand up," she said, and pointed to outside the car.

I pulled my legs around and stood up, turned my head from one side to the other a number of times. No pain.

I twirled around right there in the parking lot and rolled my head. I turned my neck side to side a number of times, tipped it up and down. Still no pain.

"Nicki, what happened?" I asked, excitedly. "What did you do?"

"Therapeutic Touch," she said, nonchalantly stepping from the passenger seat of the car.

At the time, my mouth dropped open, but my sister acted as if it were a normal, everyday phenomenon and began walking toward the arena for the conference on Mary, Christ's mother.

That had all happened almost ten years earlier.

Now, at Well of Mercy, after a quick bite of breakfast in the Sunrise guest house, I continued to obsess about Sister Brigid and Healing Touch. Patiently trying to wait until I heard from either Julia or Brigid, I headed off toward my favorite trail bordering the creek that winds slowly through the property. It was the path where I'd walked the previous night after first arriving, and where I've often begun my conversation at Well with God, the Beloved, or whatever one calls the Divine.

Having found a Spiritual Director, it felt only right to say thank you for Betty. Then, while looking up into a few white clouds, I started thinking about how I'd seen God over the years, since that was what Betty had asked me to write about and bring in to her the next time we met.

God was no longer a big, white man in the sky for me. But I didn't really know what God was anymore, especially since I'd always envisioned God as male. Now that I had particular struggles around the patriarchy, the idea of a male deity was becoming a challenge.

What I did know was that there was another way of seeing the Divine that was different from the way I'd been taught to believe. In between my internal meanderings around one question or another, I still thought about Healing Touch and if Sister Brigid would agree to see me. On my walk back, instead of feeling the calm I've often had on my return journey by the creek, I was fixated on the idea of Healing Touch.

Finally, after arriving at the main house for lunch at noon, Julia sought me out. She sat next to me. "By the way," Julia said, "Brigid would be happy to do Healing Touch on you. Can you make it at two this afternoon?"

Hell, I would go in the middle of the night if it were the only time Sister Brigid had available. I was ecstatic, overjoyed really, that my burning desire had been answered by whatever it was that would not let me stop obsessing about this thing called "Healing Touch."

Chapter 3
Healing Touch

I left my room on the second floor of Sunrise and headed two floors down to the renovated and decorated walkout basement, used as the common area, The Peace Room. As I entered the large living-room setting complete with wrap-around couches, chairs, large comfortable pillows, tables, and lamps, Sister Brigid greeted me with a hug.

Brigid's whole being emanated peace. We walked together through the large space. Off to the right were two rooms—a bathroom and a small kitchen; against the back wall were shelves of books and in between the shelves were doors to four private rooms.

Sister Brigid and I made small talk as she directed me into the second room from the right. "This is my counseling room," she said, extending her hand out in a welcoming gesture. "I thought we could talk a few minutes while I explain Healing Touch."

The walls were painted a soft mint green. Two comfortable-looking, white rocking chairs faced each other, and a six-foot-tall glass shelf sat against the back wall. There were books resting on either side of the shelves with breathing space in the middle and where a small lit candle sat. On a corner shelf, a contemporary sculpture of a cross next to small angelic figurines were positioned with obvious care.

Brigid pointed to the white rocker on the left. "Have a seat," she said, and gently closed the door before sitting in another rocker across from me.

"I'm not sure what Healing Touch is," I said, "but the minute Julia told me about what you were doing, I was totally enamored. I haven't been able to stop thinking about it."

Brigid told me she understood and that she'd felt the same way when first introduced to the process. I mentioned that my sister Nicki does Therapeutic Touch and told her about our time at the Medjugorje conference when Nicki placed her hand on my sore neck and healed it. Then I shared with Brigid a few stories about how my grandfather, *Nonno* Stagnitta, who used to heal us when we had any kind of ailment or childhood mishap.

"This is wonderful!" Brigid said. "It appears you have already had some experience."

"I suppose so," I answered, "but I'm not sure I know exactly about Healing Touch."

Brigid told me that Healing Touch was an energy therapy used in balancing one's physical, mental, emotional, and spiritual well-being. She talked about working with the energy fields in and around our bodies to support our natural ability to heal.

"Healing Touch doesn't necessarily take the place of traditional medicine, but it can," she explained. "It can also work in harmony with other medical care you might be receiving."

When Brigid started talking about Healing Touch's ability to reduce stress, I was intrigued. Heaven knows I've been a rather anxious person a good deal of my life. Brigid continued explaining that Healing Touch also helped to release anxiety and depression, and effected pain reduction, along with strengthening the immune system. Each descriptor she added pulled me in deeper.

"Do you have any specific questions?" she asked.

"I don't think I do, or at least not at this minute," I replied. "I just want to experience the feeling of having my energy moved around."

"Well," Brigid said, "when we go next door into the Healing Touch room, there's a massage table. You'll lie down on it fully clothed. I keep that room a little cool because once I get started and the energy begins to move, I can get really hot. I'll cover you with a light cotton blanket, and if you need any more cover, there will be extra blankets available. Just let me know."

Brigid continued to explain the process. She would first turn on soft meditative music and then begin working on me by connecting the chakras.

"Do you know what chakras are?" she asked.

"I do," I said. "A number of years ago, a friend introduced me to a book on chakras and the whole concept intrigued me."

Even though I was excited to begin, it had been a while since I'd read about chakras. When I let Brigid know that, she gave me a quick review:

The first chakra is the root chakra located at the base of the spinal column. It's about material security, stability, primal trust.

Right on top of our base is the second chakra, the sacral. It rules our reproductive organs. It's also about feelings, relationships, creativity, money.

The third chakra is the solar plexus, the stomach. It's our personal power point.

It helped me to review the chakras with Brigid, almost as if revisiting old friends that I hadn't connected with for a while. Next, she led me right to the heart. The fourth chakra, in the middle of all seven chakras, is about love and the language that surrounds divine love.

We moved up to the throat. The fifth chakra rules anything to do with communication and self-expression.

Above the throat is the sixth chakra, the third eye, positioned on the brow between our eyes. It rules the pituitary gland along with other parts of the body around it. My favorite part of the third eye is its connection to intuition.

The seventh and final chakra is the crown at the top of the head. It's associated with the pineal gland, the chakra of integration, unity, divine wisdom.[2]

"I'll begin by checking all of your chakras," Brigid said, "by doing a hand scan over each one to see which are open and which are congested and can use a little help."

"I'm not exactly sure what that means," I said, "but I trust you."

I did trust Brigid and had since the day I went up to Well for my fiftieth birthday, three years earlier. At lunch, I quietly shared with Brigid what day it was for me, and that I'd pulled the plug on a birthday celebration my husband was going to have in New York City with my parents, seven siblings, their spouses, and children.

The anxiety of bringing together all those people, at least thirty of them, seemed overwhelming to me. The longer Stu put off planning the event, the more tense I became.

When he left for the Daytona 500 a week and a half before my fiftieth birthday and still hadn't made arrangements for our travel from

---

[2] Blackburn, Elizabeth, *The Chakra Tune-Up Chart*, Victoria, B.C. Canada: Onwords & Upwords Inc., 1992.

Charlotte to New York City nor had he chosen a restaurant where we would be celebrating, I stopped answering my phone, called Well of Mercy, and booked a reservation for myself.

When Stu came home, I told him that I wasn't going to New York and he could notify my family. I was going to Well of Mercy.

Even though Stu was disappointed, in late February 1999 I was at Well, secluded in my favorite upstairs corner room in Sunset House. I had thrown myself into my own private retreat—resting, journaling, writing, and responding to the questions that I had about life.

On the day of my actual birthday, when I would be leaving to go home, I shared with Brigid that I was actually turning fifty that day. She flew upstairs in Well's main house and came down with a book by one of my many favorite writers, Sue Monk Kidd, *When The Heart Waits, Spiritual Direction for Life's Sacred Questions.*

Brigid understood fifty. It turned out we're the same age, born the same year, both raised in the Catholic Church. Inside the book Brigid inscribed a note to me, "For Gilda~~Happy 50th!! Way to go!! Well of Mercy. We Love you!"

Chapter 4
On the Table

Now, three years later in 2002, I was ready for whatever Brigid had planned for my Healing Touch session. "When do we start?" I asked.

"Let's go next door," she said, and I followed her into what she called the Healing Touch room.

I stopped in place before entering. The lights were dim, soft, almost night-like. A massage table was in the center covered in a quilt checkered in shades of beige and off-white. At the head of the table was a pillow with a fresh clean pillowcase.

As if stepping onto holy ground, I took off my shoes and left them at the door. Brigid told me to lie down face up on the massage table. I rested my back end against the table, pushed myself up, swung my legs around, then laid my head on the pillow. Sister Brigid tucked a bolster under my knees and covered me with a light cotton blanket.

"Are you comfortable?" she asked.

"I am."

"Would you like an eye pillow?"

"That would be nice," I said, and Brigid took a piece of tissue, placed it over my eyes and positioned the pillow on top of the tissue.

"Does it feel okay?" she asked.

"It does," I answered, and the next thing I heard was Brigid fiddling with the CD player.

"I'm putting on the meditation music," she said. "It's called *Chakra Suite* by Steven Halpern."

"Nice," I said, then relaxed.

Despite my years of frustration with the Catholic Church, there was something comfortable, calming, trusting about having a sister of the church performing Healing Touch on me—especially Brigid who was always open and understanding about the shared issues women our age had moved through while living in a male-dominated culture.

Some of those issues included receiving less pay than men, the devaluing of housework as "women's work," contending with the limited professions in which we were allowed to participate in our younger years—teacher, nurse, secretary—with little potential for any leadership positions. In the case of nuns such as Brigid, they were allowed only to be sisters in the church versus clerics, such as priests, bishops, or cardinals.

And as women, we had little control over our own bodies until *Roe v Wade* was passed in 1973. (Little did we know at the time that the U.S. Supreme Court would call *Roe* into question fifty years later.)

I'm not sure I would have been quite at ease with anyone else. Sister Brigid knew where I'd come from spiritually, had always accepted me for who I was, and encouraged me to be exactly the way I was created.

I sensed Brigid standing behind my head at the top of the massage table. She placed her hands on my shoulders and asked me to set an intention for this Healing Touch session. All I could think of was asking God, Spirit, the Divine to show me what this experience was about.

Then Brigid said, "Focus on your breathing," before she spoke the words, "Mother, Father, God, I call in all angels and guides, Gilda's and mine, as I ask for Gilda's highest and best good."

Brigid pulls her hands ever so slowly from my shoulders,

then moves over to my right side. The sound of the music pours into

my body. I know she is doing something above me, which I can't see.

That's okay.

Awhile later I feel Brigid at the foot of the table. She holds

my feet, and I am off somewhere. I don't know where …

it doesn't matter.

I'm floating around in a fog, a very, very, very comfortable,

gray, soothing, serene fog.

In time, I see it around, above, and over my body.

A diagram.

Small dotted lines — green, I think.

It's like a graph, a grid, a grid of lines connecting parts

of me from one spot to another.

I am a diagram of energy swirling around and through

and in between.

Am I a hologram? I wonder.

No matter.

Whatever I see

feels perfectly right.

I did not know how long I'd been in this other dimension when Brigid whispered in my ear, "Stay put. I'll be right back."

I lay there ever so quietly. Not a thought crossed my mind.

Silence.

Brigid returned to the room. "I'm taking the pillow off your eyes," she said, and she did, gently.

The room, still fairly dark, left me feeling serene and relieved. Daylight would have been too much to see. I opened my eyes, looked at Brigid standing by my right side. She was holding a glass of water, placed it on the shelf behind me.

"How did it go?" she asked.

"You won't believe what I saw," I said, and spurted out, "a grid, a series of small, short hyphens interwoven across and above my body, like an entire energy grid planned and always there."

Brigid smiled. She waited a few more minutes before saying, "Are you ready to get up?"

"Yes," I said.

"Let me help you," she said, and supported my right arm, as I sat up slowly. "Stay sitting," Brigid said. "Let your legs and feet dangle over the massage table. Don't stand up yet."

Then, she reached for the glass and handed it to me. "Drink this water," she said calmly.

I did.

We were quiet. Eventually Brigid told me to come next door to her counseling room when I was ready. Relaxed, I stayed sitting on the table for a few minutes. Nothing was going on in my mind. How nice. I wasn't used to my mind being this quiet.

When I finally got myself next door to the counseling room, I asked Brigid about the grid, the hologram-looking web that appeared to be surrounding me. We talked briefly about the energy fields that encircle our bodies.

"There are physical, emotional, mental, and spiritual fields," Brigid said.

I had this knowingness she was right, that there are fields, information, and knowledge hidden in the background. I could see that Sister Brigid knew this, and now I knew it, too.

There was something bigger than words that occurred in that Healing Touch room. Brigid and I talked briefly about her apprenticeship in the Healing Touch program, and she asked me if I'd be interested in being a case study for her.

"I'd love to," I said, and asked what it would entail.

Brigid and I set up a plan for me to come to Well of Mercy about every two weeks to receive Healing Touch. The thought of receiving more energy made my inner soul jump for joy. If I had to cancel or if Brigid had to cancel, for whatever reason, we were both in agreement that it would be okay. We closed our time together with a warm hug. I went back upstairs to my room in Sunrise and fell asleep.

Two weeks later, I returned to Well for my second session. Brigid and I talked quite a bit. When we got into the Healing Touch room, I felt tired. I slept through most of the energy work that Brigid gave me. Even though I came out feeling relaxed and cheerful, I did not experience all the wonderful details and have the awareness that I'd had the first time. It felt like I went somewhere. I'm just not sure where.

After my session, Brigid told me that most of my chakras were at least partially open. But when I told Brigid how little I remembered, she suggested that I receive Healing Touch next week rather than wait two weeks.

We also decided that the next time there would be little talking beforehand. We'd go right into the Healing Touch room, and Brigid could get to work with whatever energy needed attention.

In between my Healing Touch sessions, I pulled out different books that I wanted to explore, including *Sacred Contracts* by Caroline Myss. Having looked over the Contents page, I saw three subjects close to my heart: archetypes (unconscious models in our lives) which I learned about in my freshman year of college; chakras, which have appeared now in a broader way with Sister Brigid and Healing Touch; and astrology, which I'd been studying on my own for decades.

I have always been attracted to systems that I could relate to like astrology, as well as the Myers-Briggs (Personality) Type Indicator, the Strong-Campbell Interest Inventory, Animal Medicine Cards, Oracle cards, Rumi cards, and other alternative approaches. I've discovered along the way that they've helped me stay focused on who I am versus what outside forces tell me who I should be.

For years I've been a member of the Charlotte Friends of Jung. I studied Carl Jung decades earlier when I was still living at home in Syracuse and attending Maria Regina, a small Catholic junior college about ten minutes from my parents' home. I have a memory of sitting on the floor of the library hidden in the stacks pulling one Jungian book out after another. It was Carl Jung's work that intrigued me and where I first learned about archetypes.

The Jungian archetypes that stayed in my consciousness were those that I learned in those foundational years –The Persona, The Shadow, The Anima/Animus, and The Self. There were others, many others, and I became intrigued by those archetypes that reflected someone in my life: Lover, Jester, Sage, King, Queen, Mother, Seeker, and more.

Since the *Sacred Contracts* book starts with exploring archetypes, I decided to begin by looking at the author's method of selecting them. That's when I started listing characters I identified with.

Jung had been part of my life for so long, choosing archetypes was a natural fit. Being a creative person, I knew I'd add a twist or two of doing my own exploration along the way. No harm in being imaginative. After all, the Artist was clearly one of my archetypes.

With each consideration, I enjoyed seeing myself in relationship to one character or another. Eventually, I would write so much about each archetype that my words would spill into multiple journals.

In the end, I knew I would be choosing only twelve archetypes, but I was determined to explore as many as I could. The one unexpected challenge in the *Sacred Contracts* book was that no matter what archetypes fit my life, after reading "The Four Archetypes of Survival: Child, Victim, Prostitute, Saboteur[3] including these characters in my list of archetypes was a must.

To me these four represented the shadow side that Jung talked about. I wasn't going to back off from facing the hidden parts of who I've been. I was determined to be totally open and honest with myself as I entered this journey.

---

[3] Myss, Caroline, *Sacred Contracts, Awakening Your Divine Potential.* New York: Harmony Books, 2001.

Chapter 5
Valentine's Day: Session Three

Despite the fact that my husband was out of town, it was going to be a busy day ending with my third Healing Touch session at Well of Mercy. Stu called me from Florida before I left home in the morning to drive into Charlotte.

For many years, Valentine's Day fell on the same weekend as the Daytona 500. Stu and I always hid Valentine cards for each other. We chatted about the two cards he had left for me—one funny, one romantic. While we talked, he dug through his suitcase to find the two that I'd hidden inside one of his folded polo shirts.

I spent a few extra minutes on the phone telling Stu about the raccoon that tried to get into the crawl space around 1:00 a.m. I also told him about my dream of having had a massage two days in a row.

"It felt wonderful," I said.

"I'm sure it did," he replied, "and you deserve an extra massage even in a dream."

"Oh, you sweet talker, you." I said, and we both laughed as I hurried off the phone.

The extra-long conversation was why I was running late for my nine o'clock poetry group in town. I'm sure it didn't help that I stopped to read about Raccoon in my book, *Medicine Cards, The Discovery of Power Through the Ways of Animals.*

"Raccoon asks that you honor yourself and others equally. Provide for your own needs, or your well will be dry when you choose to give generously." [4]

When I finally arrived at my poetry group meeting at my friend Tootsie O'Hara's house, she and my other writing friends and colleagues, Irene Honeycutt, Mary Wilmer, and Naomi Myles, were still chatting over coffee before we sat down to critique each other's work. I have loved having my work critiqued and scrutinized for clarity.

---

[4] Sams, Jamie, & Carson, David, *Medicine Cards, The Discovery of Power Through the Ways of Animals,* Revised, Expanded Edition, New York: St. Martin's Press, 1999.

But near the end of the meeting, I started to get anxious when our conversation moved from our individual poems to the Literary Festival. Irene was the founder, director, and organizer of the festival at Central Piedmont Community College (CPCC) and was a long-time instructor in its English Department, where she had taught creative writing classes and other innovative writing courses.

Irene had brought amazing writers and poets to the festival from all around—Stephen Dunn, Anne Lamott, Dana Gioia, Sue Monk Kidd, Mary Oliver, Li Young Lee, and even the Czechoslovakian poet Miroslav Holub, among many others. Irene had this intuitive gift of inviting a writer to be a keynote speaker soon before the person, unbeknownst to him or her, was about to get a special honor.

No one, including the recipient and Irene, ever knew this was about to happen, but it did time and time again. It was one of many reasons the festival was so extraordinary.

At one point, I'd participated more in helping with the event at the college. CPCC is also where I had taught fine arts for over a decade and a half. I had also taught fine arts in other schools, colleges, and universities.

But a few years earlier, I began to feel stifled about spending time being a helper or even a teacher at the college. Deep in my heart, I needed quiet time to write stories and poems, draw angels, and take a self-imposed sabbatical. Even though I loved my classes and students when I was there, after I arrived at my poetry group, all I wanted to do was keep my head in the writing process for as long as I could and not talk about anything related to teaching or CPCC.

Was I not listening to the message of Raccoon about not letting my well run dry? Did I just need a temporary break from teaching? Supporting my students' work and helping with events, for example the festival, had always inspired me.

At this point in my life, though, what I wanted to do more than anything was my creative work.

During my poetry group, I tried to keep our conversation on the creative process of our poems. When it veered off, I didn't have the courage to speak up and share with my colleagues and friends my need to stick to the topic of our own poetry. Instead I participated, all the while trying to steer the conversation away from talking about the college. I never was effective at achieving my goal.

As a fire burned in the fireplace, my attention was pulled to the flame. I thought of how the animal medicine message from the raccoon encouraged one to provide for their own needs first. I excused myself early, something I rarely do, opting instead to stay put almost anywhere even if I am uncomfortable.

I drove back up Interstate 77 toward home to meet a friend for a cool February walk in the nearby park. The barren trees opened to the gray, still water of the lake on the right of our path. Hiking through a natural setting in deep winter, or any time of year, often clears my mind.

Instead of taking in the quiet nature, my friend and I talked more than usual. I wasn't sure how much mental debris I actually cleared away about having left my group early or what it meant to be awakened by a raccoon.

After the walk, I drove home for a quick lunch. Soon after, I left for my third Healing Touch session with Sister Brigid.

I got back on I-77 and headed further north. When I'd awakened this morning, I was full of myself, cheerful, and excited about the day, despite the raccoon incident. I have not always been that optimistic, although I'd been this way for the last three weeks.

The big difference in my life had been the two Healing Touch sessions with Sister Brigid. Now I was ready for a third. If I'd not had this upcoming session, I might have been home fretting about any number of things—this morning's poetry group or the fact that Stu was away every Valentine's Day for the Daytona 500 race.

Once off the highway, I followed the route that led toward Harmony, North Carolina, through the rolling farms. Mercy Lane came up on my right, and I turned my Honda Accord onto the gravel path that led to Well.

I chugged up a short incline and was surprised when tears began to roll down my cheeks. There wasn't anything consciously wrong, but I was emotional over the euphoria I was feeling about soon being back on the Healing Touch table.

If it hadn't been for last night's dream about having a massage two days in a row, I might have even felt overly extravagant driving up here again this soon. Truth be told, it did feel a bit lavish, but I couldn't help it. I loved receiving Healing Touch.

After cresting Mercy Hill and passing the Labyrinth on the right, I was thrilled to see the three gray houses of the retreat center. I drove my car to the far side past the last guest house, Sunrise, took a right down and around the small incline, and parked near the door that led into the Peace Room.

Sister Brigid greeted me when I entered. We walked through the common area, bypassed her counseling room, then headed directly to the Healing Touch room. Brigid asked me what ailments I'd been having. I told her my stomach, my ovaries, and my busy, busy mind.

Then I lay down on the massage table and Sister Brigid turned on the same relaxing meditative music, Halpern's *Chakra Suite*. She didn't offer the eye pillow this time and I didn't mention it.

Chatter in my head still prattled about what it meant when a raccoon entered one's life, my poetry group in Charlotte, the walk with my friend in the park, and other thoughts still whirling around.

And then a moment of clarity came. I had to be honest with myself. I was focusing on all kinds of minutia to avoid the guilt I felt for having walked out early on my poetry group.

Sister Brigid laid her hands on my shoulders, told me to focus on my breath, and started the same prayerful words she'd used twice before, "Mother, Father, God...."

This time when she moved around to the right side of me, rather than keeping my eyes closed or even letting myself slip away into a peaceful state, I peeked and saw that Brigid was suspending her hands over the parts of my body that I told her were troubling me — my stomach, ovaries, and eventually my head.

Lying still, I let the thoughts of the day whirl around until finally my mind shifted, and ...

I am somewhere, that feels like the same place as last week,

    I think,

except, I did not know then, I was there.

But now in this place of stillness,

I feel quiet, calm, no mind chatter.

And I break into nature,

rest under barren trees like those

in the winter scene outside

surrounding edges of the landscape I visit.

I'm not afraid of barren, I love winter a deep, deep, deep

time of year.

Chapter 6
Session Four

Two weeks! Two whole weeks since my last visit. Dust billowed from the wheels of the yellow school bus that I followed down Hunting Creek Road. It reminded me of the tunnel in the tornado that swirled around Dorothy in one of my favorite childhood movies, *The Wizard of Oz*.

As the bus headed straight, I turned left onto Dash Road, then right onto Mercy Lane. I remembered tears welling the last time I drove up this road. But today only a smile. I was happy to be returning.

"I'm at the back end of a cold," I said to Sister Brigid, as I walked into the Peace Room. "You may not want to hug me."

We kept a distance, both mimicking a hug toward each other. I took off my coat and pulled out the picture of the "Liberty Christmas Angel" that I brought to show Brigid. It's the one I drew after 9/11 for my 2001 Christmas card.

After using the restroom, I stepped out to find Brigid in her counseling room rather than in the Healing Touch room. At the end of our last session, we had decided that we would, again, get right to work on the energy. I was surprised to see Brigid sitting in her chair. It appeared we'd be talking first. I walked in and closed the door behind me.

Brigid had been in Atlanta the previous week studying under Janet Mentgen, the founder of the Healing Touch program. I asked about her workshop with Janet, and Brigid told me that she'd asked questions that came up during one of our discussions.

The most important was how does one maintain clear and open chakras once they leave the Healing Touch room and enter back into the world. We hammered that out for a while, and eventually Brigid said that the more times an individual received Healing Touch, the more centered he or she would become. She asked how I'd been feeling since my last session, after she had worked on a couple of my chakras.

"I spent a good deal of time on your root chakra—family and tribal issues," she said.

"I'm feeling much better. But now my left eye is irritating me, and, although I rarely have sinus problems, they are feeling full-blown today."

It's amazing how one part of the body heals and another condition appears elsewhere. Sometimes I've wondered if I'm a hypochondriac.

Brigid and I talked about my upcoming trip to see my family in Syracuse—a surprise seventy-fifth birthday party for my mother, as well as the closing of my father's barbershop after fifty-five years in business. Before I realized it, I was in tears, crying about the barbershop being the only consistent building in my life.

Worse yet, I had an underlying fear that my mother was losing her will to live. Brigid encouraged me not to get too far ahead of myself and to wait until I saw how my mother was doing.

My old therapist used to tell me something similar. "You are jumping way too far into the future and scaring yourself half to death," she would say.

My talk with Brigid slipped from my family to a larger family— the Catholic Church and my struggle with the male-dominated institution. Since Brigid and I were the same age, fifty-three, both raised Catholic—she Irish Catholic, me Italian Catholic—we reminisced about the Church and what it was like during those years in our schools, our towns, our country.

We also shared our feelings about the changing world and our thoughts mostly about God, energy, and the work around Healing Touch. Our conversation went for well over an hour before Brigid or I noticed the arms on the clock.

When I finally lay down on the Healing Touch table, we both acknowledged that my time would be short. I focused on my breath as Brigid had directed me to do at the beginning of every session.

Instead of Brigid saying a prayer aloud, she said, "Let's pray quietly this time."

My breathing changed almost immediately, becoming harsher as it

moved in and out of my nostrils. It shifted a few times before I heard a voice in my

head that said,

"You still have some time."

I knew the message was about my mother,

I still had time with her. The voice didn't say a lot of time or a short time,

just that I had some time. My mind settled, I relaxed.

The next thing …

a tunnel, a wide tunnel, close to me, at the beginning of a passageway.

Further down it narrows. In between, white smoke at the other end

something blocks the way, like a door.

Was it a cervix across the lower end of the uterus?

Then, a dark void.

Total calm, no words, no voices.

I feel a sensation - Sister Brigid's hand over my left eye.

She repositions her hand. Same eye.

Then that voice again, then

nothing.

I was startled back into the room, when a voice called my name. I quickly opened my eyes, looked up, saw Brigid at the end of the table, then looked overhead on the wall at the clock behind her. Wherever I was before my eyes opened, I'd been there for almost forty minutes.

"Where was I?" I asked Brigid. "I can't remember."

"It doesn't matter," she said. "Don't think. Come next door when you're ready."

She touched my forehead lightly.

I lay there wanting to remember where I'd been. Brigid said not to think. Thinking has gotten me into trouble in the past—migraines, worry, anxiety. I slowly pushed myself up from the massage table, swung my legs around and dangled them for a minute or two.

I stood in the doorway of Brigid's counseling room. She wasn't there. The most I could do was rest my body against the door frame. Brigid came up from behind and handed me the cup of water she wanted me to drink after each Healing Touch session.

It must be for grounding because she's always asked me if I'm grounded before I leave. I'll have to ask her one day.

Brigid sat in her chair, and I sat across from her.

"Where was I?"

"You let go more than you ever have before," she said.

We talked briefly about my breathing, about the energy she pulled in for my left eye, about our meeting the following week. I forgot to tell her about the voice that said I still have more time.

The next morning my sinuses were clear but my eye was still a bit sore. The pain continued on and off throughout the eleven-hour car ride driving north to Syracuse with Stu. I tried to ignore my eye, pulled out my journal, and continued writing about different archetypes.

The more I wrote, the more I realized which of those unconscious models were ones I'd been living. The Writer, of course, was obvious. Writing keeps me sane. I was also pulled to the Angel archetype. After all, I'd been drawing angels for almost ten years.

I didn't stop with just Writer, Angel, Artist. Oh no, I kept pursuing more and more archetypes, even though I knew I wouldn't be using them all. But I didn't want to be haphazard in my choices before covering all ground.

I wanted to be sure to choose wisely when deciding on my personal archetypes. I knew there were different ways of approaching this. But for now, I enjoyed reading up on all sorts of archetypes, especially those that reminded me of characters in my life.

Lucky for me, I can read while Stu drives. He doesn't mind one bit, and I have always gotten a lot written and read while traveling up I-77 to I-81 into Upstate New York. During the drive I was still able to keep my attention on reading and journaling, and away from my sore eye.

My mother was truly stunned when she walked into a private room at a restaurant to find Stu and me among other siblings and their families.

Mom never suspected that there had been a party for her in the making that my sister Teresa, the only one of us eight siblings still living in Syracuse, planned with my father. The rest of us who drove in were quite a surprise for my mother.

Why was I amazed that the pain in my eye disappeared after my mother's celebration? Of course, Sister Brigid was right. Once I arrived in Syracuse and saw my mother in person, I was able to *see* for myself whether she was giving up on life or choosing to stay around with all of us.

Dad's barbershop? Well, it turned out that he couldn't bring himself to close it quite yet. When we left Syracuse, Dad was still standing in the same spot behind his barber chair cutting hair.

For Mom, her whole demeanor had changed from the gloomy conversations I'd been having with her on the phone this winter. My mother was her jovial self again. She would be around for a while longer. I did indeed still have time with her.

Chapter 7
Five Weeks Later

When I walked into the Peace Room, I saw the door to Sister Brigid's counseling room cracked open. She struck a match, reached over, lit a candle, then turned around and saw me. Brigid smiled and we greeted each other with a hug.

I was not only relieved to be back at Well of Mercy but delighted that I'd be staying the night and not rushing back down I-77 after my Healing Touch session. It had been five weeks since I returned to Well for energy work.

A lot had transpired. After Stu and I drove to Syracuse for my mother's seventy-fifth birthday party and what we thought would be the closing of my father's barbershop, I went to Central Piedmont's 2002 Literary Festival. Despite my earlier reservations about being back at the institution where I once taught, I enjoyed attending all four days of writing events and activities.

I have to admit, being around a crowd of people, now that I was used to spending more time by myself in the studio, was a bit overwhelming at times.

There was also Easter and the taxes that I had to pull together. How I hate doing taxes. I attended a Jungian workshop on *Silence*—thank God. All the while, I had been in turmoil over the previous number of weeks with the amount of news that had been revealed about the uncovering of sexual abuse of children by Catholic priests.

It was hard to face having been raised so Catholic, going to parochial school from kindergarten through twelfth grade, then onto a small Catholic junior college, before making the break and continuing my education at Buffalo State College, one of the State University of New York's (SUNY) institutions. I knew I had taken steps away from the church, but the thought of men abusing young children was beyond my comprehension.

So much had already been going on. Just before I'd left to drive up to Well of Mercy, a phone call came about Mary Wilmer, one of the members of my Charlotte poetry group.

"You look tired," Sister Brigid said.

Minutes earlier, before walking into the Peace Room, I'd pulled down the visor over the driver's seat in my car and looked into the vanity mirror. I hadn't even noticed the stress in my face. Brigid must have sensed how frenzied I felt as soon as she saw me.

I settled in the rocking chair where I always sat in the counseling room. Brigid closed the door and sat directly across from me in her rocker.

"What's going on?" she said.

"Did you know Mary Wilmer?"

But Brigid did not know Mary. I remember having had a conversation about Mary with either Sister Brigid or Sister Donna. I told Brigid it must have been Donna who knew her.

"Just as I was walking out the door to drive up here," I said, "I received a call that Mary died last night."

Mary Wilmer was a vibrant seventy-eight-year-old poet. She served countless hours in various ministries across the city of Charlotte. One place was at St. Peter's Catholic Church. She also worked with alcohol and drug dependency, sponsoring people who struggled with addiction.

Mary and I had been in and out of various writers' groups together over the years. Mary was also a member of the Thursday morning poetry group that I met with in Charlotte.

I'd been invited to join the group about two years earlier at the memorial service for our eighty-five-year-old writer friend, Katherine McIntyre. Mary was a wise woman, an elder, a striking example of a sage, a spiritual crone, someone I wanted to emulate in my later years. Katherine had been that for me, too, and her death a few years earlier had been a huge loss. It had been a gift to be back in a writers' circle with Mary.

Besides participating in the same writing group, our paths had crossed often. Mary and I shared similar interests: The Charlotte Friends of Jung, The Oratory Retreat Center in Rock Hill, South Carolina, alternative health care, and lectures on spirituality at different locations throughout Charlotte.

In fact, Mary had been at the Jungian workshop on *Silence* the previous Saturday, just five days earlier. We had eaten lunch together and talked about our Thursday morning poetry group's attempts to come up with a date for a weekend away at Well of Mercy.

With great sadness I learned that Mary had been found dead the night before from a heart attack in the sauna after her workout at one of the YMCAs in Charlotte.

Sister Brigid and I talked more about death after I mentioned bringing flowers over to my accountant's office on Monday. Her husband had died at fifty-eight years old. Then I told Brigid that a friend's father had been pulled off life support. The last I heard, before heading up to Well, was that he had barely been hanging on in Hospice care in Florida.

After talking with Brigid about the people around me who had died and those dealing with death, I shifted to the anger I could not shake off about priests' sexual abuse of young people. I hashed out thoughts and feelings surrounding the hierarchy.

Then I switched to my disappointment with the local NPR station for not having accepted the commentary I wrote on the pedophilia problem in the Catholic Church, and the need for the hierarchy to include women in its leadership. I was all over the place rambling, talking. My own energy spread thin, real thin.

I tried to get away from talking about myself and asked Brigid about how she'd been feeling. My appointment four weeks earlier had been cancelled because she had come down with a terrible cold and flu hours after our previous meeting.

A thought flashed in my head. Oh God, I hope I didn't give her that cold that I was sure I was over the last time we were together. It couldn't have been me, I told myself, if she got sick within only a few hours after my leaving; plus I never had the flu.

Brigid pulled me back from thoughts leading me into a dim and murky tunnel. She told me that when the influenza hung on for weeks, she focused on how energy works and how to protect oneself when performing energy healing on another person.

Brigid decided to clear the Healing Touch room after each session by lighting candles or using aromatherapy, which would avoid her taking on someone else's problems. Lemon was her preference.

"I think I have an interest in doing energy work beyond receiving it," I said to Brigid. "But I do have a way of taking on other people's stuff."

We talked for a few minutes about my interest and about not taking on someone else's problems. Then we agreed that it was best I let my interest in energy unfold in its unique way.

Before we headed to the Healing Touch room, Brigid said, "I'm going to try and pull your energy in today, ground you, and pull you back to center."

"Grounding," I said. "Is that what you do at the end of each session when you press down with your hands from my knees to my feet, and then bring me a glass of water?"

"Yes," Brigid replied, "but this time I want to make grounding the intention of the session. Then afterwards your energy will be totally present in the here and now."

The Healing Touch room felt cooler than the counseling room, or perhaps I'd worked myself up from rambling about my recent disturbances and felt the temperature shift when changing locations. Five weeks with no Healing Touch must have caught up with me. I was not even sure I'd be able to settle down once I laid on the massage table.

Sister Brigid put on calm, soothing music. Light instrumental strings led me to think of my workshop on *Silence*. Oh, did I yearn to go into that quiet place—wherever it was.

I feared that I was too riled up and it would never happen. Once on the table with music floating around my head, I was hardly aware of Brigid's hands moving over my feet, above my body, and onto the seventh chakra at the top of my head, the Crown.

I forgot to tell Sister Brigid, "Hey, it's my head I need to shed." The reeling, spieling, all the goings on, and then ...

Cool air ... blows in, and a smell of lemon clears

the space, I assume.

In the background, calming music soothes my soul.

I've been here before. In the void.

Silence.

A slight breeze. A slim figure, radiant, smoky blue.

Is it Mary Wilmer's spirit floating above, toward my right?

Behind her and in the distance Katherine?

The spirit is here long enough to peek through, then

my dead friend Mary's energy comes forward, center.

"This is what you've been doing up here," Mary seems to say,

whooshes away, leaves with a notion she has somewhere to be.

Her condo back in Charlotte?

Her children gathering after the news of their mother's death.

She'll get back to me later.

I usually struggle to enter the void.

Not this time.

Happy to have been in Mary's presence, sensing Katherine,

the quiet …

At this very moment I know the session is over.

Within seconds Brigid took my hand. I nodded my head—a signal letting her know that I know.

"Take your time," Brigid whispered.

Chapter 8
Intention

Back in the counseling room, Brigid told me that she had concentrated on my head, trying to get me to not think as much.

"You must have read my mind," I said. "I forgot to mention that I wanted you to work on my crown chakra."

We both smiled. These coincidences have happened often over the last few months, like the time I told Brigid that I couldn't make the next scheduled session right before she had a chance to say she wouldn't be available.

We were both excited about the synchronicity and slapped our hands in a "high five" like two athletes making a good play. Then Brigid suggested I do two things before leaving Well the next day.

One was to go up behind and to the right of the buildings and walk around the grassy field counter-clockwise for at least fifteen minutes. The purpose was to pull myself back into my body instead of being far out in my head. The second thing she asked me to consider was walking the Labyrinth sometime before leaving.

"Set your intention," Brigid said, "It's all about intention, you know."

She also talked about me trying to stay with myself and not get pulled into conversations at dinner.

"That's not always easy for me," I said, knowing that I'm a person who cares about others and has a hard time not responding to people's needs.

"I know that," Brigid said.

I was surprised, but then again, why should I be? She's an energy worker and energy workers are intuitive by nature.

Brigid continued, "I noticed your concern for others the first time you came here."

Walking the perimeter of the large grassy field, it took a while for me to pick up momentum. Once I settled into an even pace, I didn't want to stop. I kept going around and around like my mind did before the Healing Touch session.

It wasn't until I started walking that I recalled how just before my session was finished, Brigid floated her hands above my heart. She whispered that my heart chakra was wide open.

Looping the circle, I felt I could walk forever. My head, oh my head! I loved what the rounds were doing to my head. I stopped thinking, went into neutral, concentrated on taking one step after another.

I must have hiked around that circle for at least forty-five minutes and completed at least fifteen rounds. I lost track until all of a sudden my body started to get tired. It was 5:50 p.m. before I looked at my watch again. Dinner would be in ten minutes.

I hiked down the path toward the houses and could see others waiting out front. From the backside of the buildings, I climbed the stairs to Sunshine House to avoid the laughing and carrying on of other visitors sitting on the covered porch in the front. I wanted to stay in the calm place that I'd built up in my walk.

At dinner, I sat peacefully and enjoyed every morsel of food I put in my mouth. Afterwards, in the chapel room in the main house, I told Sister Donna about Mary Wilmer having died.

I didn't want to drop the news on her before or during dinner. It turned out that it was Donna who knew Mary, and she seemed as shocked as I had been when I received the call. She told me that the last time she saw Mary was out in front of St. Peter's Catholic in downtown Charlotte on a Saturday night before Mass.

"Mary looked thinner than usual," Donna said, "and she seemed to be in pain."

I shared with Donna that Mary was scheduled to be operated on for her shoulder in a week and a half. I also told her about the *Silence* workshop that I'd attended with Mary the Saturday before. Then I quietly mentioned that Mary and I were in a poetry group together. Donna reached over and squeezed my hand.

"I'm so sorry," she said, and I realized then that I'd been holding back, reluctant to feel my own grief over Mary's death.

Energy works in ways I would never have suspected. I didn't believe that the visions I had on the Healing Touch table were just my imagination. I trusted that Mary, her soul, her energy had been present. I'm sure that Katherine McIntyre's energy was there, too.

Katherine always echoed Wisdom to me, as did Mary. I loved them both—Mary and Katherine—dear friends, sisters, mothers, mentors.

Before Sister Donna began the evening prayer service, she looked across the room to a woman sitting against the left wall adjacent to me and asked her if she knew Mary Wilmer. She did and said that she'd also been to the Oratory in February with Mary at the annual Newman Lecture. The woman was shocked to hear of Mary's passing.

Then another woman directly across from me said she recently saw Mary. Even more unusual was a woman sitting at the fourth and final wall of the chapel. I'd met her at dinner, and we'd talked for a few minutes then. She spoke up and said that she didn't know Mary but had been at the YMCA when she heard about a seventy-eight-year-old woman found dead in the sauna.

On each of the four walls of the chapel, at least one person had some connection to Mary. Even a stranger was present who'd been at the location where Mary died.

As the evening prayer began, Sister Donna said, "I believe—no, I know—it was Mary Wilmer who told me years ago that coincidences are manifestations of little miracles sent by God. I feel sure that Mary is with us at this very moment," Donna continued, and in my heart, I agreed.

After chapel, Donna and I chatted for a few minutes. I hadn't talked to Donna for a while. She was the person I initially came here to visit when I first heard about Well of Mercy.

Years ago, someone suggested I track down Sister Donna because she was a person in the church who would understand my concern about the Catholic Church's reluctance to let women be more involved in the hierarchy.

That first day I'd driven up here it was to check out Well of Mercy and to meet Donna. She had generously let me know that, for the most part, she'd backed out of being overly assertive about pushing women's rights in a tradition not yet receptive to that.

Sister Donna decided to do her own ministry work through the retreat center. I, on the other hand, did not keep my opinions about the church to myself, and I'm not sure I ever will.

Then again, I am not a nun who has a community and a church to answer to. I still find it necessary to write articles on my discontent with the church, the priesthood, and other discrepancies that I've seen in such a restricted institution.

When I first started coming to Well over four years ago, Donna and I used to have a lot to chat about, and I knew she accepted me and my feelings about the church we were both raised in. But over the last few years, Sister Donna seemed to have had other responsibilities here at Well and with her community. That's when I began to have more conversations with Sister Brigid.

Donna invited me down to see her counseling room and the bright yellow walls that she'd painted. When we returned back upstairs to the kitchen, Brigid was there and I sensed an odd discomfort.

It was the first time I'd ever picked up on that with her. She'd always reached out in a cheerful, kind, and joyful manner. I asked Brigid if she wanted me to get the commentary I wrote, "Pedophilia & The Red Sea," but she looked at me, her brow furled.

"You can get it for me tomorrow," Brigid said.

Something didn't feel right, but I didn't say a word and let it go. I had things to do during my short twenty-four hours there.

I was not in the room I initially fell in love with at Sunset House, upstairs on the right side of the building. The one I was in now, Sunrise 6, was almost a complete duplicate. This room was tucked upstairs, too, but in the left corner of the second floor.

Once in the door, a twin bed was positioned on the wall straight ahead, bed stands on either side, wonderful reading lamps that I knew would come to good use, since I read late into the night. There was a bathroom to the left of the door only a few steps away from the bed.

The room had an extended section on the right beyond a wide opening off the main bedroom. Here in Sunrise, there was a twin bed in the extension rather than the double bed that had been at Sunset.

All the rooms were comfortable and homey with contemporary and modest quilts covering the beds. Also available in all rooms was the same style lounge chair I'd grown attached to.

I settled into the comfortable recliner and looked across the room toward the light of the moon shining through the windows. The trees outside rustled gently in the breeze. After sitting and just being for a while, I flipped open to the bookmarked page in my journal and began writing.

After all these weeks, I was still reading, exploring, and writing about archetypes, in relationship to my life. I identified with characters such as Networker, Rescuer, Poet, and still the Artist and Writer. But there were others that certainly were not me: Joker, Seductress, Intimidator.

When I read about the Knight archetype, I remembered someone telling me once that I'd been a Knight in a previous life. But after cross-examining the character on paper for a few minutes, I wrote on the side of the page, "I don't think so."

As I kept journaling and exploring, I was reminded of a novel I'd read awhile back, *The Celestine Prophecy*, by James Redfield. He had come to Charlotte for a reading at an auditorium in a church hall that had been rented by the metaphysical bookstore I frequented. The reading was packed with people who, I assumed, were seekers much like myself.

Redfield's story was a spiritual adventure, a hero's journey, reminding me of Joseph Campbell, the American writer and mythologist who wrote extensively on the Hero's Journey. In Redfield's book, he describes nine insights. Insight #4, Human Control Dramas, felt to me like its own unique family of archetypes: Intimidator, Interrogator, Aloof, and Poor Me.

I talked Stu into going to the reading with me. Sometime after that, we were lying in bed and I was chatting away about one thing or another. I imagine it was about the four control dramas from Redfield's book that I was enamored with during that time.

"Stu," I said, "let's play *The Celestine Prophecy*. You be me and ask me a million questions," (I've always been a classic Interrogator.)

Stu chuckled

But I wasn't finished, "And I'll play you and not say a word." (Stu is a perfect example of Aloof.)

We laughed and laughed. We know each other well.

In my journaling, I began recognizing people in my life that for me clearly fell into certain archetypes. My own mother lived her perfect profession of Mother archetype. Her mother, *Nonna* Egidia, was a Matriarch archetype. Then there was Dad.

King had to be one of my father's types. Not only was he treated as a king, but he expected to be waited on in such a manner, having labeled himself many years ago "The Supreme Commander" of the household. His expectations included being waited on at the dinner table, during family gatherings, even at the barbershop by his employees, who served him well. In fact, my father always told my siblings and me when we were growing up that he was sure that his family came from royalty.

Who knows? That energy may have been passed onto someone else, like my brother Anthony perhaps, first born son, astrological sign of Leo, the leader.

When I came to writing about the Healer archetype, I thought of my sister Nicki, a nurse, who studied and comfortably practiced with great success another form of healing energy, Therapeutic Touch. That brought me to writing and thinking about my grandfather, *Nonno* Stagnitta.

My goodness, he was the first and most obvious healer in my foundational years. All those times my mother brought us to see him when there was a health issue or a minor accident or mishap.

It was wonderful to have this opportunity to delve deeper into archetypes and Jung again, and revisit different memories when these characters wove in and out of my life. I also couldn't help but recognize the strong archetypes of those from my childhood.

Of course, I could go on with all the relatives that I have and my recognition of many of them in reading the various archetypes. But my goal was to focus on my own experiences so that I could get more clarity on myself and on moving forward in this new world we had entered after 9/11.

At home it was impossible to read as much as I'd like without the distractions that so many of us live with each day. Here at Well, I had the time to be quiet, explore, discover all the different kinds of archetypal characters that have affected my life.

Periodically I stopped for one thing or another, including calling Stu around nine. There was no answer on the home phone or on his cell. I continued writing in my journal, reading, dozing off until close to 11:00 p.m., when I tried Stu again. He still didn't answer at home or on his cell. I hate when that happens.

We've established a calling system when either one or the other of us is away. It started two years after we married and when we first moved to Charlotte. We had no relatives or close friends nearby initially. Since Stu traveled a lot for his race business, we finally came up with a plan for touching base at least once a day to be sure we were both okay.

Stu had mentioned that he might have dinner with some business associates, and I counted on that being the case. I tried again around eleven-fifteen. This time Stu answered his cell phone while driving home from dinner at his partner's farm not too far away from Well of Mercy. Sometimes the service in the farm area of this county can be spotty.

I was relieved he was in a place where his phone worked. After we talked and said, "Goodnight and don't let the bed bugs bite," I continued to journal before eventually falling asleep.

The next morning was more of the same—reading, sleeping, writing. My room became a sanctuary, where I felt comfortably tucked away. By noon, I was in the main house for lunch. It was the second time I sensed that Brigid was not so happy with me.

"You're working too hard," she said. "You need to take a break."

I was taken aback, especially since I'd spent the evening and morning quietly in my room writing and relaxing. Healing Touch with someone watching what I was doing? This wasn't what I had expected. Maybe I wasn't reading this right?

I had already gone through almost ten years of therapy and now had my own Spiritual Director. At one point I had considered asking either Sister Brigid or Sister Donna to be that person but decided on Betty mainly because she was a layperson.

I hadn't told Brigid about Betty yet. But now I was glad I had Betty. I didn't want anyone watching over my shoulder.

Growing up in a large extended Italian Catholic family everyone knew what everyone else was doing. Each person had their own thoughts and weren't afraid to express them. Over the years I realized I needed more breadth, more breathing room, more freedom.

After lunch, I took a lengthy walk behind the retreat house. Along the way I talked to myself and to whoever God was, as I struggled with how to handle this feeling of someone watching me.

Just like the last time I'd been here, and almost in the same spot, I heard a voice in my head. This time it was saying, "You have to talk to Brigid about your feelings or you won't be able to go on working in such a personal situation."

If Brigid was in the house when I was leaving, I would approach her. Otherwise, I would wait the two weeks until our next meeting.

Donna was in the main house and she told me that Brigid was giving a Healing Touch session. Something seemed odd about the energy, even though it was hard to pinpoint. With Brigid not available, it would give me time to sort out exactly what I needed to say.

I packed my car and drove up to the Labyrinth. It seemed important that walking the sacred circle was the last thing to do before returning to the outside world.

Chapter 9

Spiritual Direction: Who Is God for You?

Healing Touch and Spiritual Direction were both clearly important for my spiritual growth. But I spent more time on Healing Touch with Brigid since she had asked me to participate every other week as a case study in her apprentice program.

My schedule with Betty was once a month. I hadn't talked much about Spiritual Direction with Brigid and only a little bit about Healing Touch with Betty. A few days after my first experience on the Healing Touch table, I met with Betty for the second time. That was when I shared my excitement of having received energy work.

At the time, I told Betty I couldn't stop thinking about Healing Touch and that the experience of receiving energy seemed to shift me, although I couldn't explain how. Betty and I had things we were planning on doing, so both of us decided that in time I'd be able to explain just what the shift felt like.

I had given Betty my essay on who God was to me and, before I left, she gave me the Myers-Briggs Type Indicator personality test to bring home. "Take this test when you feel most like yourself," I remember her saying.

One night around midnight, when the house was quiet, the phone had stopped ringing, the television echoing from Stu's cave was silent, and he had gone to bed, I sat down and began answering the questions on the test. They were not the kinds of questions one could study for. Basically, they were statements from which I had to choose the one I most agreed with, for example, "You are almost never late for an appointment" or "You enjoy having a wide circle of acquaintances." For each question I'd select one of the following: *Strongly Agree, Moderately Agree, Neutral, Moderately Disagree, Strongly Disagree.*

After I brought the results to Betty, I learned I was an Introverted, Intuitive, Feeling, Perceptive type, INFP.

I'd actually taken this test twice before, once when I was teaching at the community college surrounded by my colleagues. The second time was when I went to a career counselor. I had the notion that I might have been better off investing in a suit, stockings, and heels, before heading out into the business world to make more money by selling insurance than having become a writer, artist, and educator.

But every test I took with the career counselor directed me right back into the fine arts, writing, and poetry. The Myers-Briggs indicated that I might even be good at some kind of performance work.

Since I was way too old to be the ballerina I had wanted to be when I was young, I realized that standing in front of a group—reading poems and stories, teaching classes and workshops, giving talks about the importance of capturing one's story—would be a form of working as a performance artist.

Both times I took the Myers-Briggs, at the college and then during career counseling, I was identified as falling between Extrovert and Introvert, and Judging and Perceiving. Betty assured me that as I got older and spent more time going within, I would discover more of who I really am.

That was how it became clear I am the Introvert, not the Extrovert, strong in Perceiving not Judging.

Once we established my personality type, Betty gave me a slew of handouts to help me understand myself as a person and how I would function best in life. In addition, Betty and I planned to work on the paper I wrote, "Who Is God for You?", which she had asked me to do the first day we met.

Last time, when I'd handed Betty seventeen full pages, I noticed she held back from letting her mouth drop open.

"I can't help myself," I said, almost apologetically, "I'm a writer, a poet, an artist. I automatically thought in terms of making something creative out of what you asked me to do."

"That's perfectly okay," Betty said. "It reflects your INFP nature."

Betty told me that over time I would get a better handle on what it meant to be an INFP.

Now, at this month's meeting, Betty brought my essay back in and asked if I would begin reading my story aloud. As I did, she periodically stopped me to make a few observations about my life experiences of God, church, and the way I explained how I had been raised as a Catholic.

"Who Is God for You?"

From my early memories, when I think of God I think of church, of walking with my maternal grandmother, *Nonna* Egidia. *Nonna* would march my older sister, Nicki, younger brother Anthony, and me through Our Lady of Pompeii Church directly across the street from where she lived on the Italian Northside. It's not that I think of my grandmother as God. Nonna was no divine being. Heaven's no!

But I do think of how *Nonna* presented God to my siblings and me, and how she took us into the church— God's house. "La casa di Dio," she called it in Italian. It was apparent that God was a "he" to me back then—a large white figure of a bearded man, suspended and outstretched above the altar. That was the God of my childhood.

The figure I connected to, more than the big white man in the sky, was Christ's mother, Mary. It's not to say that I had no attachment to the "he" God as a divine being. But it was Mary's spirit with which I felt a special bond.

When I walked around the inside perimeter of Our Lady of Pompeii Church with *Nonna,* along with my sister and brother (and later on my younger siblings and cousins), I would stare at all the statues of different saints. Mary, of course, was tops on my list, then the twin martyred saints Cosmos and Damian, (I was always intrigued by twins. Two of my closest friends in elementary school were twins.) and Saint Egidio—the patron saint of Linguaglossa, Sicily, where my grandmother came from.

For years I have repeated the story of my name. It's obviously one of my abiding images. Egidia, *Nonna*'s name, was the female derivative of the male saint's name, Egidio, (Giles in English), whom my grandmother was named after. And I was named after *Nonna,* a Sicilian tradition my family continued in this country: first daughter, named after my father's mother, Nicolina, my sister Nicki; second daughter named after my mother's mother, me.

The name Egidia is on my birth certificate, but Mom always called me Gilda. She even signed me up using the name Gilda for kindergarten, ballet, Brownies, Girl Scouts, and every other undertaking I was involved in.

Mom always thought the name Gilda was the English derivative of Egidia, even though her younger brother, my Uncle Alex, had researched this and told her at the hospital the day I was born there was no female derivative of the male English name Giles. My mother respected the family's Sicilian tradition by placing her mother's name on my birth certificate, and followed her own heart after she brought me home.

Now at Our Lady of Pompeii Church, there was an array of sculptures of other saints set inside alcoves of mini-altars that had been constructed against the walls on both sides of the building. But it was always Mary, up in the front right-side altar, whom I would look for first. Her female form with outstretched arms and hands seemed gentle, nurturing, loving. Her heart opened wide calling me to enter.

I loved seeing the other statues, too, including Michael the Archangel with his take-charge stance. He held a sword, as if defending any one of us if need be, a youthful man of action. But Saint Michael wasn't God. Even at a young age, I knew that.

I knew that Mary wasn't God either. Mary had been human and Christ's earthly mother. Period. Whether Mary was God or not, she was the force for me. I related more to her soft facial appearance embodied in marble, her fine-featured nose, warm eyes, slim hands, gentle smile. She stood on a mound stomping out the snake wrapped around her feet.

Betty stopped me and we talked about the images I saw as a child—God, the snake, Mary. Betty pointed out the sculpture of Mary "stomping" out the snake was held in a particular religious environment that created a certain atmosphere, as this living, limbless creature was kept underfoot.

Betty even suggested that perhaps the snake was being held back from having any more power. "You might want to explore the snake," Betty said. "Its ancient archetype was once known for healing."

Healing, I thought. Of all things, *healing*. The idea of Healing Touch flashed through my mind, as did her use of the word *archetype*. After all, I'd been spending a great deal of time with the archetypes. What coincidences!

Betty asked me to continue reading my vision of God.

Now God's son, Jesus, hung on a cross over the main altar of the parish where I'd been baptized and raised in my early years. But his father—God—was a figure who looked like an older, middle-aged man with white hair, his head and upper torso extended over the apse, above the altar, even higher than Jesus on the cross.

God dominated the sky, as if he hung ever present everywhere, like Santa Claus, I suppose. But the image of God the Father was much more serious than the jovial character who appeared every December in a red velvet suit with a bag of toys for kids everywhere, including me.

I don't know why I imagined God suspended, as a reviewer and critic. Maybe it came from my religious education in a parochial school that emphasized a patriarchal deity or perhaps it had something to do with my relationship with my own father. Nonetheless, God was everywhere (I'd been taught.), watching my every move, evaluating all my thoughts and words.

Because of that, I was self-conscious of anything I ever said. I had to use the right words: kind, giving, loving, accepting words. If my language was not all of the above, God was watching from his perch, keeping notes in a large white book with long, flowing pages.

Even though, as a Catholic, I could go to the sacrament of Confession and confess my sins to a priest—the intermediary between God and me—I still felt I had to be as good as good could be. After all, if God was watching, I was forever being scrutinized.

Betty stopped me and pointed out my self-consciousness over every word I spoke as a child, and then she took me by surprise when she said, "This is you trying to live into your personality as an INFP."

I always saw my self-consciousness as a negative. Is it possible that there is a real purpose for being that kind of a person? As Betty continued talking, it appeared that this self-consciousness was rather typical of Introverted, Intuitive, Feeling, Perceptive types.

"And there is only a little over one percent of the population that are INFPs," Betty said. "Your desire to be sure to say the right words—kind words, giving, loving, and accepting words—fits into your INFP personality. A personality, by the way, with a strong sense of values."

I could see that this process of understanding my Myers-Briggs Personality Type, at least in this new way that Betty was explaining, would take me awhile to comprehend. Thankfully, I had begun. Betty kindly pointed to my story and I continued reading.

By the time I got into high school I was vomiting every morning of life. I wondered why a God watching over me would let me be sick one, two, three, or more times a morning without doing anything about it. But, honestly, most of the time I was too ill to think of God.

It's not that I didn't think of him. At that point, God was definitely a man, a father, everything that my religious instructors—mostly nuns—had taught me. Well, the priests at the altar referred to God as "he," too.

If "he" was such a loving father, why didn't he just let me die rather than get sick every morning, leaving me feeling humiliated in front of old and new classmates, on the bus, at the side of the road when I would get off the city bus going to school, in various classes where certain nuns would not allow me to leave the room.

I'd gag back the bile or, when I felt almost faint, I'd get sick in the wad of Kleenex that I carried in a navy-blue leather purse with a clipped opening and handles made of two thin straps. The blue matched my plaid Catholic-school uniform.

I didn't think of God as mean. Instead, I thought he probably felt bad for me, but that it wasn't my time to die, and "he," like everyone else, stood on the sidelines watching me get sick. Did I think that God could have intervened?

I thought that he could have at least interceded by letting me die one day from being terribly weak, but when he didn't do that, I thought he must have known something that I didn't and was keeping me around for whatever that "something" turned out to be.

Did I pray to God for help? I suppose when I stamped my foot and yelled, "Oh God," just before I was about to vomit into the white porcelain bowl, one could consider that outburst a plea of some form. Afterwards, I remember feeling wiped out and saying, "Oh, God, why does this keep happening to me?"

I never heard an answer. Nor did I expect one, really. If I want to think of those crying words of help as prayers, then I guess I did pray to God, the imaginary, hovering figure, an aloof kind of being, a man sitting back allowing his son to take the rap for earthly dealings, while he floated above all.

Betty and I stopped and talked in between thoughts. She commented about feeling sick in her soul when she heard about my years of sickness and asked me questions about that time in my life.

It began my freshman year at St. John the Evangelist High School, which I attended after graduating from the eighth grade at Blessed Sacrament, the Catholic grade school in my neighborhood. I told Betty this nausea started soon after my mother's younger sister, Aunt Josie, died at the age of thirty-three from complications of the autoimmune disease lupus a few weeks before I began high school.

Once the heaving began each morning, it became a pattern I couldn't stop. It had nothing to do with anorexia or bulimia. I was a nervous wreck, and whenever I was anxious or excited, including as a child on Christmas and Easter mornings, I would vomit.

I remember, when I was only a second-semester freshman, a senior girl at St. John's came into the nurse's office where I was lying down one day and asked me if I was having morning sickness. Having never heard the term before, I told her that must be it and thanked her for giving me a name I could attach to my illness. I was so naïve!

My parents waited, hoping I would get over whatever it was that was making me such a wreck most school mornings. Eventually they brought me to the doctor, who diagnosed me as having a nervous stomach. Of course, I was nervous, anxious, uneasy, worried, and, bottom line, reduced to rubble.

Much later in life, I realized that what was going on might have been a hidden worry that if my aunt died at such a young age, my mother could, too. I hated leaving Mom at home every day. If I stayed there, then I could be sure to keep an eye on her and never let her slip away like Aunt Josie did in the hospital.

The doctor prescribed medicine that made me fall asleep at my desk at school, until my mother split the pill in half. Even that was much too strong, and I was left feeling groggy. Instead of the vomit coming up and out, the bile tumbled around in my stomach making me feel nauseated but unable to throw it up.

Most of the nuns at St. John's saw me as a problem, except for Sister Inez, the art teacher. Sister Marion, the Mother Superior, called my mother in at the beginning of my sophomore year and told her that my parents should hold me back from participating in any social activities outside of school and force me not to be sick.

That was exactly what she and some of the other nuns planned on doing by not letting me try out for cheerleading. These were my early high school educators.

Sister Marion even asked my mother not to allow me to pledge for a sorority that I was invited to join. Later, I found out that my gentle, quiet mother told the Mother Superior not only was she going to let me pledge for sorority, but that she would also see to it that I would get through Hell Night even if she had to drag me through herself.

The summer before my junior year began, my parents pulled me out of St. John's and registered me at Bishop Ludden High School in the West End, clear on the other side of Syracuse from where we lived in Eastwood. Ludden was the first regional Catholic high school in the city.

A priest friend of my parents, who my mother went to high school with, was a counselor at Ludden and said he'd be available for me to talk with if I ever felt ill.

It was at this new regional Catholic high school where I hung out with kids who were much more assertive and willing to stand up to overbearing and critical nuns and priests. In a short time, with support from my parents' priest friend and most especially from my own friends at Ludden, I learned to be more confident and stand up for myself.

I suppose that after two years of grieving over my aunt and seeing that my mother was healthy and not going anywhere, I slowly moved into a more normal teenage life.

Sister Brigid or Sister Donna from Well of Mercy never fell into the category of those nuns from St. John's. In fact, I remember at lunch one day at Well a few years back pointing out to Brigid that she and I came up in the same Catholic tradition at around the same time, except Brigid's family was Irish, mine was Italian.

Even though Brigid was a sister in the church, she was not like the sisters I had in the parochial schools I attended. She was never a Mother Superior type or a teacher wielding power over me. Brigid and I were peers who chose different professions and life styles. I was never afraid of her, and she would have never wanted me to be.

Reading these memories aloud to Betty helped me to realize that the next time I saw Sister Brigid I was going to be honest, direct, and clear about how I felt before I left Well the last time. Just as I learned to do from my friends at Bishop Ludden, I was going to speak up and be more self-assured. It was my responsibility to let Brigid know what I needed from the Healing Touch process that we were moving through together.

I ended up sharing with Betty all of what I'd been feeling. As she listened, with no judgment, I felt her care and encouragement.

"As my grandmother always told me," Betty said, quoting Shakespeare's *Hamlet*, "This above all: to thine own self be true, And it must follow, as the night the day, Thou canst not then be false to any man."

As this month's meeting ended, Betty asked if she could keep the entire seventeen-page copy of my story that I had printed, *"Who Is God for You?"* It warmed my heart that my story mattered that much to her.

Chapter 10
Spring

At my next Healing Touch session and during our initial talk time, I told Brigid about the uncertainty and discomfort I felt during my last visit at Well of Mercy. She listened with no judgment or negative comments. I sensed her care and encouragement, saw warmth in her eyes.

It didn't take Brigid and me long to sort out what I'd been kicking around in my head for the past two weeks. Brigid seemed to know exactly what energy I picked up without my having to elaborate. She didn't tell me exactly what it was she'd been experiencing, but it didn't matter. I knew Brigid and I were fellow seekers on this spiritual journey through Healing Touch.

Brigid did share with me, though, that with my level of sensitivity, she was not surprised I was able to sense any uncomfortable feelings that were around me.

My former therapist used to always make comments about my ability to notice things beyond the norm. It wasn't that I didn't believe her. I just thought that it was her way of affirming me, as therapists often do.

Now, years later, Brigid was saying the exact same thing. Perhaps I do have a way of noticing details that others don't see. It's part of who I've been all of my life, including in my profession as a creative—writer, poet, artist, teacher.

Once Brigid assured me that her judging, which I'd picked up on the last time I was with her at Well, was an old issue of hers, I thought of the nuns who taught me in high school and how judgmental they had been. Many of the girls I knew who went into the convent after high school eventually left. I'd learned how stern and critical much of their education had been while they were in the convent.

Even though Brigid was nothing like those nuns, for some reason that whole scene from my high school years played out for me after the last time Brigid and I were together. What a coincidence, too, that right after my time with Brigid was when I read my story aloud to Betty, which included my experiences with the nuns in my early high school years.

Then I had another *ah-ha* moment. I was taking Brigid's judgment personally, even when I knew I was not doing what Brigid thought I was doing—not taking time for myself. Taking things personally has been an old pattern of mine, one I've wanted to stop replaying for years.

Wouldn't it be nice if Healing Touch could rid me of taking things personally once and for all?

"A therapist/client relationship is not what I'm looking for," I said to Brigid.

Not wanting Brigid as a therapist was not personal. I simply did not want to be in therapy with anyone right now. Therapy was something I spent almost a decade doing. It's not to say I would never go back. I'd learned a lot about myself that I hadn't really known. I was now on a mission to shift from old ways of thinking, that I'd hung onto for far too long.

A Spiritual Director, a Healing Touch facilitator, an acupuncturist, a naturopath were the kinds of healthcare professionals from whom I wanted support at this juncture of my life.

Brigid made it clear that therapy was not how she saw our time together. We figured it out. We were equals, peers, sisters. Sisters—a word Brigid used that I hadn't even thought of. I'd been thinking of myself as one of Brigid's case studies for Healing Touch.

Energy work was what interested me in the hopes that it would unleash any negativity trapped in my mind and body. I also wanted to write about my experiences on the Healing Touch table. The experience and *writing* the experience would give me a clearer and deeper understanding and purpose.

Brigid seemed just as enthusiastic about where we were going with all of this. In fact, she not only referred to me as "sister," but she also called me "friend." Since that was probably true, it was also true that we were each responsible for setting boundaries around the energy work we were doing together.

Brigid and I decided to limit our talking beforehand to no more than thirty minutes. Healing Touch would be around forty-five minutes. A quick ten-minute or so follow-up would end the session.

I was glad that Brigid and I were on the same wavelength. Healing Touch had already become important to me. Perhaps this experience with Brigid would be a new way of relating to people versus tiptoeing around situations trying not to hurt someone else's feelings.

Brigid was healthy, aware, and had worked on herself for years. I couldn't imagine always being that clear with certain people. I'd felt guilty over the years for not doing some things in ways that appealed more to others' sensibilities.

In one of our conversations, Brigid shared with me that she'd eliminated people from her life who were no longer healthy for her. We talked about me letting go of some people, too.

Since my initial conversation with Brigid back at the end of January, almost two-and-a- half months ago, I had cut ties with one friend. She was easy. We hadn't been friends that long, and one day she was pretty blatant about not wanting to hear what she considered liberal thoughts about the church.

But there were others in my life who were draining and more difficult to let go of. There were also some people I wasn't going to be able to totally let go of, such as family members. The only thing I could do was to set better boundaries. Whatever the case would be with other people in my life, I was relieved to have worked out my situation with Brigid.

After stepping into the Healing Touch room, I lay down on the massage table and covered up with a light-weight cotton blanket. Brigid entered quietly, started the meditation music, immediately placed her hands on the crown of my head. I was at ease.

I forgot to ask Brigid to help stop the busyness, the whirling in my head …

again. I remember the irritation … not in my head … in my sacral area.

Today, I'm more conscious. I want to let go. Brigid takes her hands off my

head, and I am aware of her walking around and down.

She's at my hips. She never asked to cover my eyes.

I open one eye to see what she's doing. She is holding her hands a foot above my

ovaries and uterus. Her palms face down. She's directed

energy there before.

An old feeling of fullness returns. My feet.

Brigid is now at the end of the table. She holds my ankles. The whole table

vibrates. Brigid's hands vibrate, shake. Small … rapid … movements.

How does she keep an even tempo.

Finally I feel calm, relaxed. I'm not sleeping, but I am clear, centered.

Acupuncture gives me this feeling.

And then, Silence.

Only Silence.

How long have I been in Silence, before I hear Brigid whisper something.

She must be done. The door is closing quietly.

I want to bring this centeredness out of this room

into my every day.

Back in Brigid's counseling room, I asked her about the small rapid-movement sensation. She told me that it's a technique called *spinning,* and that the whirling motion came from the energy of her spinning her own chakras and transferring that energy to me.

"My hands were not shaking at all," Brigid said, and seemed intrigued that I felt the movement.

She looked up "sacral" in one of her books. This second chakra rules the ovaries and uterus. Brigid also mentioned that it ruled *feelings.* I recognized my old resistance to feeling emotions that surface. Is that why my head would get busy?

When feelings have come up, I've sent them directly to the brain to analyze rather than feel the extent of the emotion. Back in therapy, when a particular feeling appeared, I would push it down and my therapist would point it out.

Emotions have seemed safer in my head than in my heart. But once a feeling would enter my mind, it would go over and around and never stop churning.

When Brigid told me that she spent time ridding my head of the busyness, I was excited. While driving up on the interstate earlier, I told myself that I must tell Brigid to work on that tiring babble.

I couldn't believe that I forgot to mention it to her beforehand. But both Brigid and I smiled and talked momentarily about the realization that telling someone isn't always necessary to get a message across.

Brigid told me about a drumming workshop that would take place before I returned to Well. Drumming had never really appealed to me, but I'd often listened to others talk about the experience. Brigid mentioned that it didn't appeal to her at first either. We laughed at the similarity of our interests and non-interests.

"I feel good energy from the guy who's coming to do the workshop," Brigid said, "and I'm sure it will make the energy of the land here even more powerful."

Unlikely I'd be driving back up for the drumming workshop, but anything that supported this land was important. I loved the ground this retreat center sat on, the way the wind blew or didn't. The way the birds chirped or remained quiet.

In the long run, it had not mattered how my experiences at Well of Mercy unfolded. What truly mattered was how I felt when I was there. Whatever existed at Well had been beyond calming.

Even when I stayed overnight and struggled over a problem or two or more, there had always been something centering about this place, this land. The answers I would receive to my internal questions became clear.

Chapter 11
Emotional Body

The Monday after I saw Sister Brigid, my local NPR station contacted me to tape and air the commentary I had told her about awhile back, "Pedophilia & The Red Sea," the one on the Catholic church's sexual abuse problem. It had been some time since I'd sent it to the station so I was surprised when I received their message.

Besides dealing with a bit of my own Catholic guilt for having written what I really felt, a man I had met years back at one of the Catholic churches in the area sent a message through a mutual acquaintance. It was a few days after the airing went out on our NPR station and this guy questioned why I had to do a commentary on the problem at all.

I spoke a short time with the person who called and who agreed with my stand, but she was only delivering the message. It ended there, probably because the next day I flew to Boston.

What I didn't realize was that I would soon be jumping from the frying pan into the fire once I arrived in New England and headed further north to attend a nephew's Communion/Confirmation sacrament in a Catholic church up in Maine.

As the plane landed at Logan Airport on Thursday night, May 2, a spring snowstorm whirled around the aircraft. I stayed overnight at my sister Nicki's in Concord, Massachusetts. On Friday, Nicki and I waited for my parents, one of our nieces and a nephew to drive in from Syracuse.

We celebrated Mom and Dad's fifty-fifth wedding anniversary with a delicious codfish dinner, cake, and ice cream. Early Saturday morning, we all drove up to Camden, Maine, to share in my nephew's special day.

The Catholic church in that northern area of Maine had been performing an ancient ritual that combined the two sacraments of Communion and Confirmation. The information I looked for on the ceremony was minimal at best. I found something on the Internet that seemed to be from 18th century France, but the information didn't offer much.

One of my younger sisters, who now lives in Maine, told me that the bishop up there had decided to return to practicing an old ritual. I made up my own story that maybe it was because they were so close to the French-Canadian border, but the narrative was simply conjecture on my part.

After crossing another border, from New Hampshire into southern Maine, we headed up the coast to the most northern New England state and drove right into my second spring snowstorm. May? Snow? Is this some kind of omen?

More family showed up in Camden. Although I had a great time being with them, I struggled with the far-right conservative priest who not only said my nephew's Mass but ended up sitting across from me at the luncheon that followed the service.

At one point, I heard the priest defending the priesthood and minimizing the number of men involved in the sexual abuse problem. The hair on my neck rose.

I couldn't believe this was happening now, when only a few days earlier I'd attacked that brotherhood on public radio. I wanted desperately to speak out, but I would not create a scene at my nephew's celebration.

I pushed my back against the chair. My chin tilted down the way it does when I begin to feel tense. My whole upper body tightened.

The priest, totally unaware of my struggle, focused on the others coddled around, supporting him and what he had to say about the priesthood. I stood up trying to remain inconspicuous.

At that very second, my sister Nicki, at the other end of the table, looked toward me, then motioned with her hand for me to come sit next to her. Maybe I wasn't as inconspicuous as I thought, or at least not to Nicki.

After all, Nicki was my sister who practiced Therapeutic Touch for over a decade and felt my reaction from more than ten feet away.

"You're like a moth to fire," she said, when I sat down next to her.

No way could she have heard what the priest was talking about from the other side of the room where she'd been sitting. It intrigued me that Nicki had picked up on the energy.

Energy! The work I'd been doing with Sister Brigid.

Nicki had performed her type of energy work on me when she and I went to Worcester, Massachusetts, for the Medjugorje conference back in the early 1990s. Just as *Nonno* Stagnitta, our maternal grandfather, had brought over a form of energy work from Sicily decades earlier, my sister had also discovered an ability to do another form of energy work.

That night in the hotel in Maine and then on the drive back to Concord, Nicki and I discussed at great length our anger over the Catholic Church's sexual abuse crisis. We had been raised in a strict Catholic environment, including attending parochial school from kindergarten through high school.

Nicki went on to a Catholic nursing school before landing at Boston College, run by the Jesuits. I went to the now-defunct two-year Catholic junior college, Maria Regina, in Syracuse, before finishing up at the State University College in Buffalo, New York.

Catholicism had permeated every bit of our foundation, although Nicki and I are also products of the 60s generation and we both made a turn toward a more feminist stance. I, perhaps, speak out a bit more than my sister. I felt I had every right to be infuriated with the priests and hierarchy as more and more sexual abuse cases started to become public.

After flying back home from Boston, there were lots of things to catch up on over the next few days, including calling friends who had left phone messages with various concerns. Then I ran into an acquaintance in the grocery store who spilled her heart out about her family.

I had little energy for myself and was now losing more. A few days later, I drove Stu to the hospital for a colonoscopy. Everything turned out fine, but the process, both on the day before and the day of the procedure, was stressful since Stu had experienced earlier bouts of melanoma, making any procedure related to cancer nerve-racking.

The morning before driving up to Well of Mercy, I had my own follow-up appointment with my gynecologist. She'd been keeping a watch on cysts in my ovaries for almost a year.

It had been only two weeks since I saw Brigid, but it felt like months. Needless to say, I was spent and spilled out my angst. To think that the last time I talked to Brigid I was adamant about not needing a therapist! Now I was grateful for her counseling background, and I wanted to hug her, her guardian angel, any divine force nearby.

Our talk went past the thirty minutes we'd agreed upon. I shared with Brigid my frustration at not being able to escape all the people who came to me with their problems after returning home.

"Phone messages had piled up from people I know who are struggling with health issues, family concerns, grief over loved ones dying," I told Brigid.

"You're a good listener," Brigid said.

"Everyone needs someone to talk to," I responded, "but I'm not a therapist. A good listener, yes. But maybe too good for my own sake," I said twisting and turning in my chair. "Being so sensitive, I take it in and wipe myself out."

Of course, I told her about having my commentary taped and aired, and about my entire experience in New England, including the incident with the priest in Maine.

After we entered the Healing Touch room, Brigid said that she was going to try a new technique on me this time, something that had been done on her by her own Healing Touch practitioner. First, she eliminated the pillow under my head. This gave her room to place her hands beneath my neck.

She told me she'd be touching my head lightly, which she did. Then, she shifted her hands away from my head. I opened my eyes slightly and watched as she floated her hands, palms down, above different parts of my body. She moved slowly from my head toward my feet. Then she walked over to the right side of the massage table.

"All your chakras are open," she said, and I was shocked after all I'd just been through.

"Even the ones over my ovaries?" I asked

"The sacral isn't as open as some other chakras," Brigid said, "but there's still energy moving through there."

I was relieved but a little confused as Brigid stood on the side of the massage table smiling. If my chakras were open, would I even need Healing Touch? I needed something, that was for sure. How could I go back out into the world without some clearing of the energy that had bombarded me?

By the time I sorted through my thoughts and questions with Brigid, she assured me she would still be doing Healing Touch. Then Brigid moved to the top of the table and, from behind my head, asked aloud for my highest and best good. Her words included God's use of energy in my creative pursuits, and I lost focus on whatever else Brigid was saying, closed my eyes, and relaxed.

After I could feel Brigid working on my head, I opened one eye and watched her hold her hands slightly above my ovaries and uterus. I felt a cold sensation, ice cold, in the space between Brigid's hands and my body before the feeling quickly moved to warmth. As Brigid moved her hands above my heart, my chest felt hot. Not warm. Hot.

Brigid walked to my left side and began a gentle massage on my arm. In the past, I always begged my massage therapist to rub deeper. Now the light swishing of energy over my skin felt as deep as any intense bodywork I'd ever had. I was so present in my body that I wondered if I had already fallen into that total place of silence I've gone to while on the Healing Touch table. It didn't matter, it was only a thought and before I knew it …

Uncle Flip appears, his profile in a doorway, and in my mind I ask,

> *"Why are you here? You died last year. I hardly think about you anymore.*
>
> *You're my childhood uncle dead from my life for forty years."*

Uncle Flip sits in a chair looking like he did when I was little.

Tall, light hair, a huge, huge smile. I loved him so much back then.

> *"Uncle Flip you disappeared from my life after Aunt Josie died,"*
>
> *and then, and then, he's gone.*

> *Brigid massages each finger on my hand.*

I love having my fingers massaged, maybe from drawing, from working out poems and stories on the computer.

Brigid sends energy to my left arm, my left leg, my left foot.

She moves over, works on my right side.

I am awake, but keep my eyes closed. Sometimes I feel myself

breathing, heavily, almost as if snoring.

I want to open my eyes and say, "I'm not asleep. I'm wide awake,

aware of my body."

I don't sleep, concentrate instead on each slight brush of energy.

And then, I slip into ... a void

The gift for staying present in my body, out of my usual busy,

busy head, and that's when IT appears ...

a heart, a headless heart wrapped with copper and gold, and I know

this session is over.

Brigid handed me the usual glass of water to drink after energy work. It seemed larger than normal, and she suggested that I take a second one along. She filled a paper cup and then encouraged me to stay in the place I was in and not let myself get pulled off center.

As I climbed into my car, I saw Sister Donna. We talked briefly.

"I hate to leave," I told her.

I've hated to leave this retreat center ever since I found it.

"Come up with a suitcase next time," she said.

I started to think about when I could do that again. With all the attention on having traveled to New England, I yearned to get back into my journal. I barely had time to read and research about more archetypes, at least to the extent I like to probe.

But I didn't want to think very long. Instead, I wanted to stay out of my head and flow back into my heart. My eyes felt full when I drove away from Well of Mercy. Those moments on the massage table, especially in the void, were such gifts.

I had entered Healing Touch with my emotional body, not my thinking head. The previous time I was at Well, I realized that by flipping my emotions into thoughts, I didn't have to deal with my feelings.

Just like in therapy, I never wanted to deal with emotions that surfaced. Feelings can come at me so intensely—the anger around the church and the priests, the patriarchy, the dogma of my education. The grief after Aunt Josie died at thirty-three—Uncle Flip's wife, my mother's only sister. Then the loss of Uncle Flip when he disappeared from our family's life.

When I found out last year that he had died, I cried like I'd never cried for him before. Then, out of nowhere, feelings about other concerns began popping up: anxiety that I'd felt over the years about never being good enough in art, in writing, in life. So much was surfacing, including old feelings around not having had children.

Did the cysts my gynecologist had been keeping an eye on remain because I had pushed away feelings around being childless? I had at one time analyzed the death out of my emotions before ever allowing myself to drop down into my deep, gut feelings.

Perhaps the cysts had been the remnants of what remained in my body before finally facing my loss head-on. I did that by writing poems that I would in time compile into a chapbook on childlessness.

I believe that our issues, whatever they are for each of us, cycle around and around at deeper levels until we deal with every aspect of them—front, back, center, middle, above, below, beyond. With the discovery of the cysts, I must still have some loose ends. And with Sister Brigid working on my energy, it appears that I still have feelings of inadequacies to resolve.

The next day, Friday, when Stu came home, he told me that he had to go to work the following morning. I've fussed over the years about him working extra, especially on weekends—our time. Early on in our marriage, when Stu still ran the kart-racing business, I spent years of weekends alone while he was off working at races.

Living away from family and life-long friends in a community of people who spent most of their weekends with their own next of kin, I lived some pretty lonely times. But when Stu told me that he needed to work the next day, I realized I also needed time alone to journal and address feelings that were attempting to surface.

Ever since returning from my Healing Touch session, I'd been dragging myself from one room to another: studio to kitchen to bedroom. I thought that this Healing Touch with Brigid would have been easy going like the one before. Maybe that was the Divine's way of catching me by surprise.

Once Stu left for work Saturday morning, I stayed in bed thinking about the various weekend possibilities: The Mind/Body Convention in town and Christina Baldwin's Sunday workshop on "How to Have an Inner Life that Supports Your Outer Life." Perhaps it was my state of mind or strictly semantics, but I thought one should be arranging their outer life around their inner life. It must have been saying the same thing, but I was too drained to get it.

The next morning, I did not get out of bed. I didn't go to the workshop or to The Mind/Body Convention. I didn't deliver my angel drawings to the gallery. I did not stop by an art opening I was invited to attend. And I didn't rush down to a "Taste of Charlotte," where restaurants, artists, and vendors exhibited their wares in the center of town for an annual festival. The rains helped me decide to stay put.

Soon after Stu left, I found myself crying. It must have had something to do with Healing Touch and the vision of the heart that appeared—the thick torso, half-heart, half-gray textured shawl hugging the form. Overlapping the whole image was a layer of copper.

Peeking out from behind the copper was gold. The gold and copper looked like the metal leafing I'd been using around the angels I'd been drawing for a number of years.

I knew what the image was saying. It was related to what Brigid and I had talked about before I settled onto the table for Healing Touch. I pulled out my journal and wrote. The message I took from the image had to do with protecting myself from the sheer numbers of people who came in and out of my life, my inner struggles about all that went on out there in the world, including things such as sexual abuse cases that I couldn't do anything about except, perhaps, to write my thoughts and feelings in commentary, poetry, prose.

I also had to start protecting myself from all the things that people called me about. It was time for me, no—past time—to not always be available to others so that I could be available to myself.

Then there were the emotions about my uncle appearing in my Healing Touch session. It was way past time for me to address the many deep, heavy feelings that I'd been holding onto. What a huge step that will be for me.

Chapter 12
Rehashing

Something didn't feel right but I couldn't pinpoint what it was. Or maybe I could and was afraid to admit it. I'd grown to appreciate Brigid as a friend, a fellow seeker, a facilitator of my energy, but I couldn't stop falling into a therapist/client pattern with her even though what I really wanted, or thought I wanted, was Healing Touch.

My session, after returning from Boston, had not helped me make the shift from therapist/client to strictly energy work.

I had Betty, my Spiritual Director, and Spiritual Direction seemed different than therapy. Our sessions together were not always just about me. We also focused on what transpired in my life, in all of life, including what happened in the outside world—the holy and not so holy.

Besides being supportive, Betty was also willing to call me on my stuff. She took me to task when there was something I needed to face, acknowledge, or act on, like the time she wouldn't relent on how available I was for my siblings. I didn't see myself being that accessible. It had been so second nature, even when it took me away from other longings.

Betty's expertise in the Myers-Briggs Personality test, from a spiritual perspective, helped me to see myself in a new light. Fortunately, Betty has many of my same characteristics. So instead of responding, "You are *so* sensitive," something I have heard a million times in my life, Betty would kindly say, "Being sensitive is just how you were made."

Back in January, after Betty returned my results of the Myers-Briggs, she was pretty sure that, after all my years of self-discovery, my results would show my true nature. I had been conscientious about having taken the test late at night, my favorite time of day, so my responses were clearly coming from the truest part of me. Siblings, old roommates, and now my husband have all claimed that I function better during the bewitching hours.

I remember Betty had told me at the time that only a little more than one percent of the population were INFPs, referring to my Introverted, Intuitive, Feeling, Perceptive personality.

She also told me that even less than one percent were INFJs—Introverted, Intuitive, Feeling, Judging types. That was Betty. It was no wonder she understood me. Our imaginative world of possibilities did not quite fit the rest of the world of Extroverts, Sensors, and Thinkers. There were a whole lot more of them.

Each time I met with Betty she encouraged me to know myself. This way I would not be rattled by how others responded to my different ways of looking at life—from an intuitive, creative perspective.

Betty had reminded me that an extrovert related to the world in quite a different way than an introvert. Since we live in an extroverted society, she said that introverts understood extroverts. But extroverts found it harder to understand introverts. I learned that most people in our American culture *think*, which I also do. After all I live in this culture and know the demands of it. So even though the T-Thinker is not my strongest function, I use it, knowing that I operate at capacity in the feeling function.

At our meeting, I talked with Betty about feeling uncomfortable with the therapy/client relationship that developed with Brigid. "Brigid is a caring and loving human being," I said, "But I just want to do Healing Touch. I've had enough talk therapy."

Betty prodded me to face my part in the sessions with Sister Brigid, until I was forced to ask myself, "Who keeps the talking going, anyway?"

On a Thursday morning, two weeks after I'd met with Betty for Spiritual Direction and three weeks since my last Healing Touch session, I fought the morning commute into Charlotte for my poetry group. Afterwards, I made a quick stop at home, touched base with Vickey, the woman who cleaned my house, then headed up I-77 to Harmony and Well of Mercy.

I couldn't believe that Brigid and I talked even more than we had in the past about everything rambling around in my head. We talked about too many things. Even though I told myself I wouldn't, we did anyway. There I was rehashing the same issues I'd spent over ten years in therapy working out. My own concerns had come to a point of annoyance, and I didn't want to speak about them anymore.

I needed something different. I thought that Healing Touch would be it—anything to shake me out of stuck ways, hoping that, if those old ways were trapped somewhere in my body, working with energy would release them for good.

I asked Brigid if she could work on my sore back. An old wound that hadn't hurt in over a year had resurfaced. It was what prompted Brigid to show me the *Chakra Tune-Up Chart* that she picked up at a Healing Touch conference.

In it we saw that the lower back is controlled by the solar plexus. Personal power, social identity, and self-esteem were some of the characteristics that controlled this third chakra.

Brigid offered to pick up a copy of the chart for me the following week at a conference she'd be attending near Albany in Upstate New York. I was going to be up in the Northeast, too—at a wedding, a graduation, and a visit with one of my sisters near New York City.

After reviewing her chakra chart, Brigid, out of nowhere, pointed out the root chakra—the source of family and tribal ways. The chart listed red foods that could strengthen the root chakra—tomatoes, beets, cherries, red cabbage, plums, strawberries.

Maybe Brigid's intuitive side was stronger than I'd given her credit for. After all, I was heading back up to see my family, my roots, my basic foundation.

After talking and rehashing my old issues for at least forty-five minutes, it gave us little time for Healing Touch. I lay face down so that Brigid could get to my back more easily. I never floated off for more than a few seconds. I hoped for a long dreamy-like session on the table, as I was used to experiencing. But only one major image came and stayed ...

A dinner table, "The Last Supper," not Leonardo da Vinci's

but the expressive Baroque artist – Tintoretto's painting. The table cuts

diagonally into the picture plane, not with Jesus and the apostles, but with my father at the far end, at the head, where he usually sits.

This time his body leans left pulling my mother toward him,
away from us.

All eight of us children are on one side. The visual weighs heavy
to the right, as my sisters, brothers, and I line up in birth order.

Nicki, Gilda, Anthony, Fran, Teresa, Gerard, Jo Anne, and Bridget.
I didn't see Mary, our sister who died at birth? Nor Ann Marie,
our cousin, like a sister, who lived with us?

The table is in Mom and Dad's dining room, where they still live,
and where I grew up from eleven years old until … until college.

Paralleling the table behind our back is a large
yellow-white wall.

That's it.

I wasn't on the massage table very long, maybe twenty-five minutes. I wasn't even sure if I'd been sleeping or meditating or what I'd been doing.

But when the time came to a close, I felt disappointed that I'd fallen right back into talking, going over old stuff and never doing what I told Betty I wanted to do—cut the excess therapeutic prattle. I needed to get past it, at least in this juncture of my healing life.

At the same time, that was a pretty strong image at a Baroque-like table.

I drove back down I-77 feeling centered but unsatisfied. I couldn't pinpoint my mixed emotions. Although I wished that I had the courage to have directed our time together more efficiently, I wasn't blaming Brigid.

I was fortunate to have had her ability to facilitate whatever energy she moved around. In fact, it was during our discussion I learned she was only the facilitator, that I was doing the work. Despite my concerns over talking too much, my back felt better. Now I was really confused.

Once home, I went for a long walk in Jetton Park. While pounding the pavement, I tried to work things out. The thought came to me that, in spite of Brigid's talent as a Healing Touch practitioner, maybe she was not the best person for me.

Maybe I was too sensitive after all, just as I'd been told most of my life. But I felt so sure back in January when I was on my retreat at Well that Brigid was going to be the best Healing Touch practitioner for me. Maybe my own intuition was wrong.

Chapter 13
Traveling North

After a weekend of pondering, I wasn't giving up on Brigid. Yet, there was something still out of kilter. I didn't know what, but I wanted to wait and see where Healing Touch would lead me. I decided to write Brigid a letter and mail it out so that she got it before she left for her conference in Albany.

In the letter, I wrote that I would like to shift our time together away from so much talking to focusing on the energy itself. I wanted to put the attention on what I experienced in my body and what Brigid picked up in my energy around my chakras when she did Healing Touch on me.

I suggested that we let my body dictate where the blocks were and allow the energy work to pull me back to center. I did let her know that my back was feeling much better and that I was eating tomatoes, beets, strawberries, and watermelon, all colors of food for the first chakra—the root. After all, I was returning soon to see my family up north.

I also suggested that, the next time we met, we start with a simple five to ten minutes of sharing how we each were doing. Perhaps we could make that connection in the Peace room, rather than in her counseling area, and then go right into the Healing Touch room.

We could still follow up with our few minutes of talking about what I experienced on the massage table, especially if she needed any information for her case study. I wished her safe travels on her trip to Upstate New York and hoped that this format would serve us both.

On Thursday afternoon, Stu and I left for Cape Cod and his cousin's son's wedding. It would be two weeks before I knew Brigid's response to my letter and if she would be willing to work with me differently.

Once we reached the Cape, my focus shifted. We rarely spend time with the few family members Stu has left, so it was a nice change to be eating, talking, and socializing with his brother, sister-in-law, cousins, and their children.

The day of the wedding was sunny and warm. We meandered around outside the restaurant where the reception would take place, on the shore of the enchanting seaside New England town of Chatham, Massachusetts.

I'd always loved that location, with its beautiful sandy beaches overlooking Nantucket Sound. The gentle roar of the slate-blue salt water was held back by a striking stone and rock rip-rap sea wall. Shimmers of white sliced through the clear-blue sky.

The mild temperature of the day made our time together relaxing. Before the reception, Stu and I took a short walk with his brother and sister-in-law. The sun glistened on this joyous occasion.

A gentle, light breeze moved around us. We each took our right foot, touched each other's toes with our shoes, and I snapped a picture of the circle we created. We enjoyed every moment of our time with Stu's family.

The Cape—once a pleasurable place for us to visit after we met in Boston—became more problematic when we moved back to New England after having been married and living away for over thirteen years. Our move from the Carolinas to Cape Cod in 1990 was the beginning of a change from an old, dependent reality that I'd functioned under most of my life toward a more independent way of being with my husband and others.

If there was any time our marriage ran up against bumps, it was during the two years we lived full time on the Cape, and the few years that followed as we tried to sell the dream house we had built there.

Years ago, when I was still single, whenever I crossed either the Sagamore or Bourne Bridge onto the Cape, I felt butterflies in my stomach fluttering with excitement. On this trip, after having crossed the Bourne Bridge, I sensed the need to be on guard, monitor myself, and be aware of each emotion that surfaced.

Now I know, although I didn't know then, my struggle, during those years of living full time on Cape Cod, was about being an introverted, intuitive, feeling, sensitive sort. I didn't quite fit into the boating and drinking lifestyle while we were there. After more than fifteen years of marriage, Stu and I were being pulled in different directions, which encouraged both of us to return to Charlotte.

Once we moved back, it took us some time to settle into our own flow again. But we did, and it was a relief when we rediscovered our niche. My life as an artist, writer, poet, and teacher, and Stu's numerous entrepreneurial ventures fit us individually and as a family.

During this trip to the Cape, Stu and I tootled around the island a few days alone. We biked on paths through quaint villages, by lighthouses, ponds, bays, and ocean beaches that offered breathtaking seascapes surrounding the island. We stopped in unique shops and bookstores, ate old-fashioned New England clam chowder, cod fish, and lobster in restaurants overlooking Cape Cod Bay.

On our last day, there was one quick lunch with my husband's friends joined by Stu's brother and sister-in-law. Then I dropped him off at the T.F. Green airport in Providence and drove away, ready for my next stop before heading to Upstate New York.

I was eager to see one of my sisters, who lives outside of New York City. A few months earlier we'd planned to take the train together into Manhattan. Since the Twin Towers had come down, my sister had already been there, but she was willing to go back with me so that I could pay my respects to those who lost their lives at Ground Zero.

September 11, 2001, and my phone starts ringing earlier than usual. A friend is calling, her voice a high and frightening pitch. "Hurry, hurry," she cries, "turn on the television."

"What station?" I ask.

"It doesn't matter," she says. "They're all showing it."

"Showing what?" I respond as I hurry across the room and turn on the TV.

There, while standing in my living room in North Carolina, the sun partially shining through the extra-large windows in the French doors, I watch as fire spews out of the first Twin Tower in New York City.

"What's going on?" I call out in distress. But my friend doesn't know any more than I do and is anxious to get off to call her sister who lives on the other side of the tunnel over the New York line in New Jersey.

Within minutes after turning on the TV, the second Tower breaks into flames. Soon the first skyscraper begins tumbling down, and I hold my hand over my mouth in shock. In horror. In fear. I begin rushing around the room not knowing what to do with myself. I grab the phone and call Stu at work describing the live scene I am watching on television.

Masses of people run down the streets away from the explosion, covering their faces from the smoke and ash engulfing everything around them. They are frantic, and I am anxious for them as I pray them away from the site and the destruction at their backs.

Now, nine months later, I was heading toward the location people had been running from on September 11, as my sister Fran and I walked toward the very site where the Twin Towers once stood. We periodically glanced at each other, shook our heads slightly side to side, as if acknowledging the anguish in the air. My eyes fixated on those narrow Manhattan streets that I've always loved.

Looking at the faces of those walking on the same path—going to and returning from the site of the once-standing Towers—was painful. Heads and eyes faced down. Lines on foreheads wrinkled in despair. Some moved with their mouths dropped open, as if still in shock.

My sister and I commented under our breaths to each other, as we moved closer and closer to the site of the tragedy.

"This is painful." "I can't believe what this area feels like." "The grief that hangs here." "I know." "I want to burst out in tears." "Me, too."

We couldn't stop noticing and commenting. We both acknowledged the energy we felt. So intense.

We were walking a journey of grief with complete strangers, who did not feel like strangers now. We had all shared an experience that would never be forgotten. This was a pilgrimage to holy ground honoring lost souls.

Much debris had been cleaned out of the thirteen square blocks where the Towers once stood. Still hanging on buildings, fences, and any place someone could find a space, were photographs of relatives and friends who had been missing in the early hours and days after the disaster when police, fire fighters, medics, emergency drivers, doctors, nurses, complete hospital staffs, and others had been waiting to take care of the wounded. But there were few survivors and even fewer bodies left to be buried.

My sister and I stood around the barriers with people overlooking the hole still full of remnants of the two structures that had crumbled to the ground. Staring into the depths, I was reminded of the ruins beneath the floor of the Colosseum in Rome, Italy, where gladiators and animals had been held in cages before fighting to their deaths.

During this solemn visit we moved around the outside of the open hole with many others who didn't seem to know what to do either, except stop and stare, whisper a thought.

Our hearts, heavy with sorrow, shortened our stay. We got back on the train and returned to my sister's home in what had been, on 9/11, a close and safe community.

The sadness of visiting Ground Zero was only the beginning of the emotional experiences I would have on this leg of my journey. I suppose I could have placed the blame elsewhere. But from one day to the next, I realized my belief that I was an easy visitor might not have been as true as I once thought.

I had always prided myself on being the second mother in my family, having been my mother's helper growing up. Often, I'd made it a point to get around and see each of my seven siblings in their own homes. I must have hung onto the second mother role far too long. It was easy for me to do, not having children of my own. I had always been grateful to Mom for having had the younger five for me to nurture.

While staying at my sister's outside of the city, I was alarmed when her two-year-old threw a toy that hit my right cheek. It felt like I'd been smacked across the face.

"Aren't you going to reprimand him?" I asked, but my sister told me that she was raising her youngest differently.

I had always felt close to her and had gone to help her numerous times before she remarried, raising her two oldest after a divorce. I began to wonder. Had I been too intrusive? I had yet to figure out that you don't tell parents how to handle their children.

Before I left, I bantered with her seventeen-year-old over politics and history. My opinions began to feel meddlesome even to me. I sat back deep into the love seat and tucked myself into the corner. Had my presence been interfering in my sister's life?

I was confused. All of these experiences, having started with Ground Zero, were throwing me off.

When I left, I drove up to Syracuse for another nephew's high school graduation. I was taken aback by the way he failed to acknowledge anything I had to say, not once but a few times, when I thought I was showing interest by asking about the end of high school and the beginning of college in the fall.

Communicating with an adult aunt was not necessarily what a graduating high school senior was interested in doing. I decided that I best walk lightly and be careful not to say anything to anybody about what I saw or didn't see, what I thought or didn't think.

Even silence backfired. On the last day, another sister pointed out that I had not responded enthusiastically enough to her son's video. Why hadn't I complimented him more on it? I thought it was quite creative, but by then I had decided not to talk too much about anything. I was learning the hard way to MYOB—mind my own business.

The best solution I came up with was focusing on getting home to my own life and making a graceful yet inconspicuous exit. Stepping out of the role of mother's helper, which I'd held onto for so long, was not going to be easy. But that was what I'd have to learn to do.

Instead of driving half-way back to North Carolina from Syracuse and staying in a hotel, as originally planned, I loaded myself up with unsweetened black tea. As I drove the next eleven hours home, I thought about all that had happened, including learning how I had not been aware of my own shortcomings before now.

Stu had been anxious and couldn't sleep while he waited for me to pull in at one in the morning. I climbed into our bed and stayed in it for the next two days.

During that time, I journaled, cried, and wrote, fell back to sleep, woke up, and journaled again. Before now, I hadn't realized that receiving Healing Touch was creating a huge internal shift and awakening me to face my own accountabilities. Nothing would be the same, including family.

Chapter 14
Home

Scheduling a massage and a Healing Touch session in the same week was not something I usually did. But I was depressed, and I wouldn't be going to Well of Mercy for energy work until Thursday. Luckily my massage therapist had a cancellation on Tuesday.

For years, I'd been living with the misconception that I knew what it was to be a parent because I'd helped Mom with her clan of children—my younger siblings. There were eight of us and I was the second oldest. I couldn't believe it had taken me decades to realize that I never really knew what it was like to raise a child, only what it was to be a mother's helper. I'd given myself way too much credit.

I never went through the angst of sending a child off to kindergarten, high school, college, nor had I experienced the trials and tribulations of doctor visits, emergency rooms, putting food on the table, clothing, shelter, and everything else that came with being a parent. I helped my mother, yes, but I was also busy going to and from school along with social activities and friends. Having lived under the delusion that my role was hugely significant, I was not at all prepared to have learned that my feedback was not as important as I had always imagined.

On Tuesday afternoon, I climbed out of bed and went for my massage. Each stroke released the tension built up over the weeks I was away, along with the anxiety of the long and emotional drive home. Being emotional has always been a part of me—good or bad. I was relieved that when any tears flowed, my massage therapist just rubbed my body gently.

Luckily, on Wednesday mornings, I had my other writers' group close to where I lived, GABS (Gilda, Ann, Brenda, and Suzanne). Those three women threw me right back into my creative world and my life near my own home outside of Charlotte. I needed firm ground to stand on now that I was feeling unsure of my place in the family. Since my group had not met for a while, we took our time catching up before easing back into critiquing our writings.

My colleagues were as driven with poetry and writing as I was. They were also sensitive to their lives and their environments. It never failed that, when one of us was going through some uncertainty, at least another was experiencing something similar or had already come through a piece of life that would give the one who was currently challenged a helpful response.

When I boo-hooed about being hurt and unsure of how to act with my family, they were there for me, knew what I had experienced, and what I'd been feeling. I learned a long time ago with this group that the deeper we went in our writing, the more we revealed to each other

Not only had I received a great critique of my story, but I also got words of advice to lift my gloomy spirits. I was reminded of a number of truths I'd heard before but had disappeared from my consciousness, until I realized I had never let go of being a mother's helper to my younger siblings, now adults and parents of their own children.

When I begin to be concerned about whether someone is appreciative of what I have done for them, then I'm giving too much .... Often very giving people can become stretched too thin, even if they do not recognize that in themselves .... The overly giving person usually Wants to help, but often gets into the habit of Shoulds .... All of this dilutes one's energy.

Well, it's not that I hadn't paid tons of money to learn that in past therapy sessions. But to have people in my life remind me of those pearls of wisdom was and still is a gift

Preoccupation with my comings and goings over the last three weeks helped me forget that I'd asked Sister Brigid in my letter for some response as to whether or not she was willing to work with me in a different way. As I drove north on Thursday up I-77 toward Well of Mercy, I started to get anxious. What if Brigid didn't want to do Healing Touch differently? After all, Brigid was a counselor by profession and she may have wanted to combine talk therapy and energy work, even though I wanted to work on talking less and letting the energy in and around my body dictate what needed to be healed.

When I walked into the Peace Room, all the staff members at Well were sitting in a large circle. A few were on the sofa, others were in big, comfy chairs. Sister Brigid jumped right up with a needed, welcoming smile. Sister Donna walked over, too, and hugged me. Julia, the administrative assistant, and Brenda, the massage therapist, both called out a hello. Brigid also made it a point to introduce a new person, Karin, who would now be doing the cooking.

"We're just finishing a staff meeting," Brigid said. "You're right on time."

She walked over toward her counseling room and I followed. It was awkward to do anything else; after all, there was a room full of people. Where else could we go until they left?

"Are you okay in here?" she asked. "I know you said in your letter you wanted to say a few words out in the Peace Room and then go immediately into the Healing Touch Room. But the others ...," Brigid said, and motioned out towards them with her hand.

I held my hand up slightly above my heart, only for her to see. "It's okay," I said.

Brigid handed me a chakra chart that she'd picked up for me in Albany.

I thanked her, of course, and said, "I hope your trip went well."

Brigid's face continued to be as kind as ever, and she thanked me for the letter I sent and said, "It's what we've been trying to do, so let's go right in."

I was relieved that Brigid had not given up on me after I had written and asked for our sessions to be different. As I sat on the massage table for a minute, feet dangling, I mentioned that my left ovary was still in question and that I would be seeing my doctor tomorrow.

My primary care doctor was also an oncologist. I found him years earlier and liked his bedside manner, his ability to diagnose problems, his willingness to work with my sensitive nature. Even though his focus was working with cancer patients, he told me a few years back that he wanted to keep a few primary-care patients so he could still work with a handful of healthy people. How ironic. Now here I was being watched for ovarian cancer.

Back in the fall, my gynecologist had taken blood work after detecting a cyst in my left ovary. By now she had done three vaginal ultrasounds. With the results of those procedures and blood tests, she was confident there were no signs of cancer. But she cautioned me to stay abreast of any unusual feelings or changes that I experienced.

I also could not have been luckier that my primary-care physician, an oncologist who wanted a few primary-care patients to even out his day, was there for a second opinion. Both physicians knew that I used alternative medicine—a naturopath and acupuncturist. I hadn't told either one about Healing Touch yet.

After I settled onto the Healing Touch table, Brigid put on meditative music and prayed over my head as she had done in the past. I kept my eyes closed, sensed her slowly moving her hands above each chakra in my body: crown (head), third eye (forehead), throat, heart, solar plexus (stomach), sacral (genital area), root (tail bone down to feet).

The heat from Brigid's hands was intense as she floated them above my ovaries. She walked around to my left side and rested one palm on top of my left ovary. Pain shot through.

She lifted her hand slightly then set it down again. Heat poured into my skin, and the pain that I felt on my ovary seemed to move down almost in a line to my vagina. I wanted to call out for her to stop, but my determination to heal whatever had settled into that part of my body took over.

A voice I've heard in the past comes to me —

You were never meant to have a child. Never. Children are not your purpose.

Out of nowhere tears and emotions well. I do not want to cry. Why had I been born into an Italian Catholic family where producing children is the ultimate purpose?

I had wanted children of my own. I breathe in and out a few times, hold back from crying.

"Stay with the process," Brigid encourages. "Stay with the process."

I don't want to cry in front of Brigid, in front of anybody. Not about

*this. It's too private, these feelings about not having children. I cried
plenty before, sometimes in front of people. But not like the sobbing I once
did alone, after Stu left for work.*

I sit in a bathtub immersed in water, grief ... release ...

*Why, of all six girls in my family, was it me who couldn't conceive?
I was prepped to be a mother. It would have been easy for me ...
So, I think.*

How do I know?

*My gynecologist says the growth in my ovary might be old
endometrial tissue. Perhaps it has been in my body for as long as I've had periods,
cramps, pain every month starting at thirteen.*

*If I can stick with the thoughts in my head, I can hold back
the tears, not cry aloud in front of another person, like my body is trying to do.*

*Then, thoughts of one of my sisters. We're sitting on the couch, Mom and
Dad's living room.*

*"I know you never talk about how you can't have children," she says.
"I know you too well. You love kids. If you can't have them, I'll carry
one for you."*

*Oh my God, she is offering her body, a vessel—making herself
available to Stu and me.*

"Why you can't conceive is not my concern," she says.

*As close as I felt with my sisters, I never talked about not being
able to have children.*

They have respected my privacy.

The memory of her offer floods back, as intense as the burn I feel in my left ovary.

I cannot hold back anymore. Tears pour, stream out.

My body throbbing. My heart pulsing. My sister's offer.
Unconditional love.

I put my right hand to my mouth, weep. I want to stop. How can
I stop this.

"I'm sorry, Sister Brigid. I'm sorry for crying."

"Stay with your process," Brigid says gently. "Stay with your process."
I don't move from the table, keep my eyes closed, lift my hand away
from my face, whimper longer.

Brigid places her left hand below my back, holds her right hand
on top of my left ovary. The pain from my ovary begins to subside.

She continues moving energy above the rest of the sacral area,
the right ovary, The uterus. She seems focused in that area.

Eventually, the feelings exhaust me, and I lose track of Brigid's hands, of the
room,

of everything ...

"Take your time," Brigid said, after pressing down on my legs
from knees to feet.

I know she is grounding me, and I need it. I lay still on the table.

When I walked back into Brigid's counseling room, I was too worn out
to be embarrassed. Her eyes, soft and melting, spoke warmth and
compassion. Talking might have been easier.

A part of me wondered what Brigid thought, another part knew
that my struggle to get to this point with Healing Touch did not have
to do with Brigid. In previous discussions, Brigid told me that Healing

Touch was not about the practitioner performing the energy work. It was about the energy of the person receiving the Healing Touch. It was the receiver's energy willing to be changed. It was my energy choosing to heal.

Brigid, or whoever moved the energy, was strictly a facilitator. A good facilitator stayed out of the person's way, does not judge. That's what I felt from Brigid. That's what she had been doing all along. Anything else I was experiencing came from my mind, not hers or anyone else's.

I also couldn't help but feel uncomfortable revealing so much pain to another human being. Even though in my letter I said I didn't want to talk, I was driven to tell Brigid about the memory of my sister's unconditional love. I had to get it out. Yet, once I did, I wished I hadn't because I'd promised myself no talking.

But Brigid was kind and listened. Her eyes remained warm and compassionate.

Then we opened the chart she'd picked up for me at the conference, and we looked up the sacral chakra. The words "I feel" are associated with this second power point. No wonder I felt so emotional.

Foods coupled with the sacral chakra were in the orange family. Funny, I had been experimenting with a macrobiotic diet and eliminated many kinds of fruit, including ones that were orange— peaches, oranges, apricots, tangerines. I realized that I would need to put those fruits back into my regimen, along with being sure I ate orange vegetables—carrots, squash, sweet potatoes, and the like.

As I got ready to walk out the door, Brigid said, "Take a look at this area in the chart. It's about feelings."

Once at home, I studied the chart further. The sacral chakra was not only about primal feelings but also about sexuality, openness to others, personal creativity, and relationships. I thought of my experience with my siblings last week, along with friends in my life with whom I wanted to improve relationships.

Perhaps if I could work on relationships, a lot would clear up in my life. I thought of Brigid, too, her generosity in letting me be a part of her case study. All these things I had been wanting to shift were aspects of the sacral chakra.

The next day, Friday, was my doctor's appointment. It had been six months since the earlier blood test and, even though the physician felt certain we were not looking at ovarian cancer, he took another CA-125 blood test to ease both his mind and mine. The results would take about seven days.

Over the weekend, I went shopping for orange foods for my sacral area—sweet potatoes, oranges, tangerines; I threw in a few red items for my root chakra (family and tribal issues) — tomatoes, radishes, watermelon.

At the metaphysical store, I picked up two gemstones that the chart recommended for healing the first two chakras. I placed the orange carnelian in my left pocket near my ovary and a bigger chunk of agate in my right pocket for my root chakra. Stones symbolizing acceptance of life on earth, primal trust, courage, grounding.

Chapter 15
Approaching the Wheel

This whole Healing Touch experience—uncovering internal struggles and having my chakras balanced—came at such a significant time, back in January when I arrived at Well of Mercy, soon after I'd met with my Spiritual Director for the first time. Now, here in mid-June, almost five months later, there was no way I could have created this scenario unfolding in my life.

One could call it synchronistic, but I hadn't yet heard that word. Of course, I'd always been aware of coincidences and knew there was more to them than serendipitous circumstances occurring around the same time. But now something in my consciousness was expanding beyond what I could have ever imagined.

There was no rushing through any of the books I was reading on spirituality, archetypes, chakras, and the like. I also continued to stay focused on journaling different archetypes. I wrote all kinds of thoughts and ideas that surfaced in dreams, meditations, and daily inspirations.

Since I had looked over the contents page in the *Sacred Contracts* book early on, I knew that something near and dear to my heart would be coming up soon. I couldn't wait to get to the chapter on astrology, which was entitled "Reinventing the Wheel."

The wheel was a round twelve-piece, pie-shaped chart I had learned about years ago when studying astrology. Having skimmed through the pages, I could see that the information on astrology was second nature to me, a subject I had spent decades studying.

At one point in high school, I became obsessed with reading the horoscope column every day in Syracuse's *Post Standard*. Here I was a K-12 Catholic schoolgirl drawn to that slight narrow column, usually on the same page with the comics, listing twelve different astrological signs and messages for the day.

None of my other friends seemed interested in such matters, but I read my Pisces sign every day. I would often read the other signs, too, and observe whether or not the people I knew who were born under another zodiac sign—Aries, Taurus, Gemini, and others— would experience what I had read about their sign that morning in the paper. I'd watch for people's actions and reactions, to see whether they aligned with the three or four short lines about their sign.

I was one of those annoying people who would ask, "So when is your birthday?" And then I'd immediately figure out in my head the person's astrological sign.

One day, around my senior year of high school, I told myself that I needed to do one of two things. Either stop reading my horoscope every day or throw myself into learning what astrology was all about.

I spent a number of months trying to avoid the horoscope column until I finally couldn't stand it anymore and caved in to my curiosity and started reading it again. I bought a few basic books and knew that, at some point in time, once I was through school and didn't have to focus on required reading, I was going to learn more about astrology.

After receiving a Bachelor of Science Degree in Art Education from the SUNY College at Buffalo, I moved to Boston and shared an apartment with my older sister, Nicki, and other friends, whose astrological signs I knew, of course. While trying to find a full-time teaching position, I taught art part-time in an elementary school and worked part-time as a secretary for a trucking company. As it turned out, there was a middle-aged guy in the sales department of the trucking company whose wife was quite interested in astrology.

Before I knew it, I was traveling from Boston to Weymouth on the South Shore every Wednesday night to attend an astrology class that a neighbor of my new friends was teaching. I continued to attend that class even after I landed a full-time teaching position in a high school and was no longer working at the trucking company.

All kinds of new books started to fill my shelves: *The Astrological Home Study Course, Astrology A Cosmic Science, Keywords, Planets in Transit, The American Ephemeris for the 20th Century*, and a slew of other books on related subjects. As time went on, I invested in more books, *A to Z Horoscope Maker and Delineator, Pluto in Libra, The American Ephemeris for the 21st Century*, among others.

My collection kept growing. I read many of the books thoroughly and others became helpful reference materials.

In my Weymouth class, I learned how to cast an astrology chart by hand, long before anyone accessed charts on computers. I was in my twenties and immersed myself in the study of the stars.

Now, many people found my interest in such matters strange and so I held back, reluctant to share my new knowledge with just anyone. But what I learned at the time was that astrology is more than just one's sun sign in the horoscope column in the daily newspaper.

For example, having a Pisces Sun sign, as I do, was only one aspect of my astrological chart. There are numerous other celestial bodies that rule each chart: the Moon, which reflects emotions, is in the sign of Aquarius for me—a life saver, since Aquarius being a mental sign in an emotional planet helps stabilize my sensitive nature.

The planet Mercury has to do with the mind and how one thinks. Venus, of course, is about love. Experiencing love in an emotional-type sign, e.g. Cancer, rather than in a practical-type sign, e.g. Capricorn, would not be the same. So, every planet affects each person differently.

The twelve astrological signs are pretty well known: Aries, Taurus, Gemini, Cancer, Leo, Virgo, Libra, Scorpio, Sagittarius, Capricorn, Aquarius, and Pisces. They have been considered by some as archetypes of the zodiac. They can also align with planetary archetypes—not only   the Sun and Moon, but also Mercury, Venus, Mars, Jupiter, Saturn, Uranus, Neptune, Pluto, and other minor planets that get less recognition.

The astrological system is much more layered and complicated than the horoscope column in a newspaper. For me, learning more about the zodiac was a way of touching into something beyond the ordinary. What I would learn is that astrology is one way of accessing the Spirit.

During those years in Boston, I would stay up late reading my astrology books. At times I would go in search of a question about life: a guy I was dating, the next step in my career, or a question about Neptune in Libra at the time my generation was born (creative idealism, seeking harmony and balance in all relationships—I'm not saying everyone achieved balance, but we certainly went in search of balance).

Most nights I would find something in the charts I'd drawn up that gave me a clear answer about a direction I could choose to follow, or not. I would always remember the answer. But sometimes, out of curiosity, I would test the process and go back another night looking for the same answer to the same question.

I couldn't always find that same answer again among my books, papers, and journaled thoughts. It was not because there was something wrong with the first answer I found. But I had a sense I needed to find the answer once and then trust myself with what I'd discovered.

Astrology was a practice I was learning more about, a practice I grew to understand and have more confidence in over time. It didn't give me definitive answers, but it helped me to believe in my own discernments during those young adult years I lived in Boston. It was a system that has continued to help me trust my awarenesses and discernments over time.

During those earlier years, I learned the meaning of the houses of the horoscope, those twelve pie-like segments of a circle. I studied and delved deep into the charts those years traveling to the South Shore of Boston. My youthful mind helped me in learning, understanding, and, most of all remembering all the details of what astrological sign ruled each house and each segment of the pie.

The 1st House was about Self; the 2nd House about everyday resources, including money and ordinary life. I saw a connection between the value of our day-to-day resources and that of money, since money has been our culture's primary means of exchange.

On it went from the 3rd House of communication, brothers and sisters, down around the circle, each house representing different aspects of our lives — 4th home and mother; 5th children and creativity; 6th health, work, pets; 7th spouse and partnerships; 8th long-term finances; 9th higher mind, higher education, spirituality, religion; 10th profession and father; 11th friends, hopes and wishes; and finally the 12th House of the unconscious, dreams, and secrets. That was the house that Pisces, my Sun sign, ruled.

Each house was a bit more complicated than a few words, but this was the general gist of the houses. Astrology was pure fun. I sat back and enjoyed rereading about the signs and planets as if I were visiting old friends.

In the meantime, I was still seeing Betty once a month and had shared with her what I'd been exploring through various archetypes, chakras, and my long-extended love, astrology. Betty had been forewarned at the beginning about my interest not only in astrology but also in other alternative fields: Animal Medicine Cards, Runes, Dreams, Intuitive Readings—you name it, I tried it. While a slice of my generation was experimenting with drugs, I was exploring metaphysics.

Right from the onset, Betty never flinched. After all, she had told me that these various modes were tools for accessing Spirit and, if it worked for me, that's what mattered. I was relieved that I could actually mention any one of my philosophical interests to Betty without ever rattling her.

By this time, I had been seeing Betty in Spiritual Direction for five months and had long past worked out my concerns over Brigid, thanks to Betty's help and insights. Fortunately, I'd had the courage to be honest with Sister Brigid. Even more fortunate for me, Brigid was willing and able to hear and accept me as I was. Betty and I also continued talking about aspects of the Myers-Briggs, my INFP nature, and where and how God was working in my life.

Chapter 16

Eagle's Wings: Entering the Mists

Two weeks had passed, and I was heading back to Well of Mercy. White cumulus clouds bubbled through the blue sky as I drove down Eagle Mills Road. I took the sharp right onto Troy Mill and looked out my left window. The expanse of an eagle's wings glided through blue, moving right to left and right again.

I remembered what the *Medicine Cards* book had to say about the eagle. Its presence encourages one to look higher, "to touch Grandfather Sun with our hearts and to love the shadow as well as the light."[5] Was this a message that I must learn to love both the positive and the shadow (vs. negative) parts of myself?

The bird soared, paralleling the road. I looked in the rearview mirror to be sure there was no other car behind me, then stopped and watched the eagle fly straight ahead. At first the large bird appeared to be caught in an air current, wings dipping side to side. Then it took off in flight.

By the time I turned left onto Hunting Creek Road, I lost sight of the creature behind the distant evergreens. Knowing the eagle was out there somewhere nearby brought me peace.

Dash Road then Mercy both came up quickly. Pink and purple pansies surrounded the stone wall around the Well of Mercy sign. I took a right and headed up the gravel-dirt path. I hadn't noticed a car ahead of me.

A local person must have entered from the opposite direction. The light brown SUV began to spin its wheels so deeply that I hung back trying to avoid getting my smaller, charcoal gray Honda Accord covered in dust.

---

[5] Sams, Jamie, & Carson, David, *Medicine Cards, The Discovery of Power Through the Ways of Animals,* Revised, Expanded Edition, New York: St. Martin's Press, 1999.

The haze from the dirt reminded me of one of my favorite books, *The Mists of Avalon.* In the story the priestesses share their teachings passed down from ancient wisdom. As I waited for the fog from the dust to settle, I wondered what I would receive from today's Healing Touch session. The mist floating above the road along with the appearance of the eagle made me wonder if I would be receiving more insight than I'd expected when first heading up here to Well.

Patches, Sister Brigid's dog, greeted me at the door leading into the Peace Room. I didn't see Brigid right away but eventually I noticed her sitting at a round table against the right wall.

A lot had transpired in my life since I had been here less than two weeks ago. I had an appointment with my primary-care physician/oncologist for my ovary and had gone to the acupuncturist for an alternative treatment.

I'd made a decision to take a two-month sabbatical from life—no writers' groups, spiritual circles, workshops, classes, or any other outside commitments, except for Healing Touch and Spiritual Direction, of course. Instead, I began the process of digging through and cleaning out old files, papers, drawings, and anything that no longer served me.

I was excited to see Brigid and had no intention of talking her ear off. Now that I realized I was the one responsible for keeping the conversation going, it was up to me to not talk so much. It's hard because sharing experiences with people who are on a spiritual path has always resulted in deeper understanding for me.

During our planned fifteen minutes of talking before entering the Healing Touch room, I told Brigid about my test results from the doctor's office. Everything was normal with both the CA-125 blood work and the CT scan. When the nurse called yesterday, she made a point to say, "You are in good health."

It's not that I didn't believe her, but I still felt a sensation in my ovary and wanted to continue receiving healing energy until every remnant—physical, emotional, and mental—disappeared.

I also told Brigid that my bladder, which we had worked on a few months earlier, was still sensitive at times, especially during my pelvic exam. I had this niggling feeling that the whole sacral area still needed more healing.

Brigid pulled out her anatomy book and Louise Hay's small blue book, *Heal Your Body*.

I sat quietly while she tried to figure out what I was sensing in my body. Then she read from Louise Hay, "Bladder Problems: Anxiety. Holding on to old ideas. Fear of letting go. Being 'pissed off'." [6]

I was going to have to think more about those words, along with the chart that Brigid had given me. "Like that book you're reading from, Brigid, the chart you gave me has also been helpful," I said. "I had given up eating many of the orange foods from the second chakra, and need to add them back into my diet."

From my pocket I pulled out the two stones I'd been carrying. Brigid's eyes lit up as she told me she had some stones that she used. As we moved over into the Healing Touch room, Brigid encouraged me to put the stones in my pocket during the session. I placed the orange carnelian into my left pocket for the left ovary, second chakra, sacral, and the deep-red agate went into my right pocket for the first chakra, the root.

"Please don't forget my head," I said to Brigid as I rested it on the pillow, "my busy, busy mind." Then I closed my eyes.

Heat from Brigid's hands instantly hot, burning hot.

She moves her hands inches above my body. Is she scanning my seven chakras?

I peek.

One hand suspends slightly above and over my heart

then moves over my stomach, then the solar plexus.

Warmth from her hands increases. With each movement hovering over

a different part of my body the heat gets stronger and stronger and, I wonder,

"Can those hands get as hot as an iron, too hot to touch?"

Thoughts of my trip north over the last two weeks, all the people coming in

---

[6] Hay, Louise L. *Heal Your Body*, Carson California: Hay House Incorporated, 1988.

and out. And, I stop thinking, am aware of Brigid on my left.

Her palm floats above my ovary.

A sharp excruciating pain slashes over my ovary and down.
My brow tightens, thoughts scatter, and then the voice again,

"You were never meant to have children this lifetime."
My uterus cramps like it did so many years during my menstrual cycle.

A memory: Rolling from my parents' bed onto the floor, lie in a fetal
position. I hold my legs to my stomach—pain, cramps, hot, summer, no air
conditioning, 1960s Upstate New York, rarely this hot.

The floor. It's cooler. I gasp for air, moan over and over, never ceasing cramps.

Mom at the store, young sisters outside the door. I'm thirteen. Startled
when a large, buxom woman stands over me. Our next-door neighbor,

"What's the problem?" she booms.

"Cramps," I mumble.

"GET UP. Get back in the bed. You're scaring your younger sisters."

Cramps continue that day, forward. The cause never traced — all
the doctors, all the years, never finding a source. The cramps went on indefinitely.

Sister Brigid places her left hand beneath my waist, rests it
onto my back, her right hand lightly touches my stomach. The heat radiates
from back and stomach. The pain, once there, subsides.

The memory of a mantra years ago rises from that area of my body:

"I want a baby," the words repeat.

Then the voice, again, "You were never meant to have biological
children during this lifetime, no matter what."

A thought surfaces: I'm okay with it now, perfectly okay.

Maybe my body held onto the memory of not having always been okay.

Two messages:

"I want a baby" - "I'm okay now" go back and forth, back and forth like my mind does until Brigid leaves that spot and the voice stops.

Do I want her to leave or hope the energy she sends completes what has to be healed? Brigid moves around to the other side of my body. She stands over my bladder.

Within seconds, I am agitated, impatient, try to connect this emotion to something, anything.

I open my eyes, see Brigid holding her hands above the middle of my body, above my bladder, and I know, somehow Brigid is working on that very area, again.

I close my eyes.

I'm irritated with someone walking away. In between the anger, the thought keeps returning. I could jump off this table and out of my skin, feel my feet and hands moving, unable to hold still.

A flash: me in a white summer dress years earlier, my hair short. I'm in the Weaving Room at the community college where I taught eleven … twelve … who knows the number of years. I'm irritated with the system.

Numbers of students, one class, all levels of weaving. I don't remember being mad. Me jumping from one group to another and another. No time to think, to feel.

The dress I wear, like a canvas with bold red and yellow splashed across white fabric. Why that design?

I cried so deeply, the last time here.

Brigid had warned when first starting Healing Touch, "expect different emotions to surface."

Thank God for the warning. I want to get up … run away. Healing Touch no longer pleasant, not like in the beginning.

I'm mad at the world, no at myself, my own weaknesses.

By the time I sense Brigid walking around toward my head, I am relieved, can't imagine how Brigid rid me of the intense agitation I'd been feeling. After a few passes over my face, around my head, she slips away the pillow, cradles my neck comfortably in her hands.

The irritation gone. Calm.

The word "grounded" flashes by.

Brigid at my feet, cups them in her hands, holds the right and left ankles, presses the ball of each foot gently but firmly. I am relieved.

"I'll meet you next door." Brigid whispers in my ear.

I lie still, open my eyes, and as if she is called back, Brigid makes large, circles above my head with her hand a gleaming whiteness, then

she is gone.

I did not feel like jumping up and running out like I did a short time ago. I needed to be alone with myself, quiet, and still. Finally, I placed my hands behind my head and stared out, not really knowing what had happened. I waited awhile before pulling myself up.

I was surprised to feel a stone on the edge of the table and a beautiful Ikat cloth draped over my sacral and root chakras. Striking in all of its oranges and yellows, red and blue hues blended together.

The stunning fabric draped over me reminded me of those years teaching fiber and fabric design at the community college, and the students who did elegant Ikat weavings in the same classroom where I taught and came to me during this Healing Touch session.

I draped the cloth around my shoulders, remembered the white dress splashed with red and blue that I loved and wore often during one of those spring terms. Synchronicity!

All of the irritation was now gone, and the memory of the students and their beautiful work was around me, represented by an elegant dyed-ikat piece of cloth. And the stone, I was surprised to discover, was my own agate that had fallen out of my pocket and not another stone that I thought Brigid may have placed on the table.

I walked next door into Brigid's counseling room. "That was so powerful," I said.

And as if our words were occurring simultaneously, as if in another dimension, she was saying, "I know."

"Do you know what area was the most resistant at first?" Brigid asked.

It turned out to be my root chakra—family and ancestors—even more than my sacral chakra—the ovaries.

"Brigid, the agate stone for the root fell out of my pocket."

Her mouth dropped open. She was just as surprised as I had been. She came up with two possibilities. With the stone no longer in my pocket, I didn't need any assistance in that area or that the stone fell out after all of the deep energy work.

"I'm sure it's a sign, a message that the energy was received in the root chakra," I said.

Brigid told me about a physicist who worked with energy. She had gone to one of his workshops and heard a first-hand account of a pen falling out of the sky once when he put out the thought that he needed a pen.

I told Brigid about all of the sensations throughout the session. We talked about how my primary-care physician/oncologist's certainty that all would eventually be fine. My gynecologist also felt the same way, although she also mentioned that it's close to impossible to diagnose ovarian cancer before it appears, sometimes even in the early stages.

I don't think of myself as a risk taker, but both Brigid and I agreed that I had covered all of my bases. The medical doctors had wanted to wait and be assured that the tests were okay before performing any surgery.

I had agreed. I wanted to give both acupuncture and Healing Touch a chance to get to the core of anything that could possibly still be lingering in my energetic body outside of the physical.

As we ended our time together, I told Brigid I was comfortable waiting to see how my medical situation unfolded. There was nothing needling or gnawing at me. I could wait.

Chapter 17
Vickey's Story

One of the ongoing frustrations in my life that I hadn't talked about at all in Healing Touch was my struggle with clutter and organization. Two days after having returned from my northern trek, I called a place that I had read about, the company Get Organized, in *Today's Charlotte Woman's Magazine*. The owner was on vacation, but her assistant was available and we spent almost thirty minutes talking about dealing with clutter.

She provided a great Therapy 101 session, asking me what was going on in my life that made me fall back into clutter. She also asked if my whole identity was tied up in my work. At first, I was responsive, saying that I had a great deal of drive for my creative life. Then I found my energy pulling back, not wanting to reveal my foibles to a complete stranger.

Even still, my conversation was a great impetus to start thinking about why I clutter. What was I afraid to get rid of? What in my life was I unwilling to let go of? What part of my work didn't sustain my creative spirit any longer? I set up an appointment two weeks later for the owner of Get Organized to come out and work with me in the studio.

The day after that conversation, our financial advisor called. Walter was young enough to be my son but had the wisdom of a guru in a business suit and tie. Initially I'd had a hard time handing over the investments to Walter. But after I made him go through every detail on our statements more than once, it became clear that I could let him handle the business of which he was clearly capable of doing.

Although he had a conservative perspective that often bumped up against my more progressive thinking, we respected each other's differences and honored each other's strengths.

Walter was actually calling to ask my opinion about an instructor with whom he wanted to take a painting class. He confided that he had a yearning to look at himself in a more well-rounded way, not just as a financial business person.

Since the owner from Get Organized wouldn't be available for two weeks, I decided to ask Walter if he knew of any companies that offered organizational services. We had talked before about organization, getting rid of unnecessary papers, even trying to establish a paperless office.

It was unlikely that would ever happen for me as a writer and artist coming up through the late 20th century, but any kind of organization was something I craved. I admired that both Walter and his office reflected a tidiness that put my mind at ease.

"The house is extremely clean and orderly," I said. "Stu has helped me in that regard. But my studio is constantly falling into disarray."

"People who clutter sometimes are afraid to face some things head on," Walter said, "afraid to admit what they no longer want in their life, afraid to get rid of the old and make room for the new."

I thought of all the changes that had been taking place since 9/11, since finding a Spiritual Director, since stepping into Healing Touch. Walter recommended I cut through all the paperwork, throw out what no longer fed me, pack away things I was unsure of, including projects that I had left spread out over the room.

"They'll only make you feel guilty," he said.

"Oh my gosh," I gasped, "I have a project I'm staring at right now."

A drawing of an angel lay on my table, so close to being finished. I kept choosing to spend my time writing instead of drawing.

"You don't have to throw it away. Finish it if you can or put it out of sight, neatly and organized, into a box in a corner of the attic. You'll know where it is when you need it." Walter said. "The only person you need to make an appointment with is yourself."

I'd been avoiding digging deep into files for a long time. Even though we'd just moved to this new house three years ago, and I had rid myself of multiple things, I never dug deep into the old files from graduate school, letters from teaching at the community college, old invoices from angels that I'd sold, or even further back twenty-five years when teaching high school art in Mansfield, Massachusetts.

Since I'd already made the decision to take the summer off from participating in any groups or professional activities, I decided this was as good a time as any to start the big dig.

What I initially thought would take a few days turned into a week by the time Vickey arrived. It was obvious that I had a number of weeks still ahead of me. After all, how could I possibly expect years of accumulation to disappear in a short time? Since I had been spending hours flushing out files each day and feeling guilty for not having finished the angel drawing, I decided to take three nights to complete the piece of art.

During the past week, I had gone to Well of Mercy on Tuesday, two days early, because Brigid was going to be traveling on our usual day, Thursday. Vickey, who cleans my house, comes every other Thursday. I always say *cleans my house*, versus calling Vickey a *cleaning lady*, because my relationship with her has been much deeper than that of an employee.

I had not been in the house for the last number of months while Vickey cleaned because of my Healing Touch sessions at Well of Mercy. Sometimes Vickey would arrive soon before I would leave. We would have only a few minutes to chat and catch up on any news about our families or our lives.

This particular Thursday, I was in the studio when Vickey arrived. No drawing or writing was going on. Cleaning out files and throwing away and recycling piles of old papers that I'd hung onto were the tasks of the day.

After letting herself in, Vickey ran upstairs to see me and we talked briefly. She was excited to show me a picture of her new grandson. After our conversation, I continued throwing away files and organizing papers that I'd decided to keep.

That's what I was still doing when Vickey came into the studio and told me she was leaving. It was twenty minutes after four, and she'd been there for only two hours and twenty minutes. Somewhere in my head I believed she needed at least three hours every other week to clean the house.

Vickey and I had talked about the time issue probably fifteen or more years earlier when she cleaned our house on Rocky Knoll in Charlotte. In between then and now, we'd moved back up to Massachusetts for a few years. When we returned to Charlotte, we moved out to Lake Norman, about twenty minutes north of the city, because the people who'd bought Stu's company and asked him to return had relocated the business near the lake.

At first, I cleaned my own house. But when Stu decided he wanted to build a larger house than I wanted to keep up with, I told him I would only agree on the move if I had someone to help me.

Vickey agreed to drive forty-five minutes every other week out to where we now lived. I knew there were other house cleaners in the area but Vickey was someone I trusted to enter my living space, someone I always believed had the values and wisdom of Job.

Vickey was more than a worker. She was part of our family.

When she came back to us after nine years, she still remembered Stu liked his top sheet on the bed a tad shorter than most people. She knew my obsession with clean floors, the shower, cobwebs in corners. It didn't take her long to note my fixation with a particular area by the door leading to the garage, the light fixtures in both the dining room and the kitchen nook, the dust that built up on the plant in the master bathroom.

Vickey's professionalism had always been reflected even in the way she communicated with me. Out of respect, she went back to calling me Ms. Syverson rather than Gilda when she returned to clean our home.

I don't know what possessed me to question the amount of time Vickey was staying except that the issue of *time* has been a bone of contention for me, living with the fear that there will never be enough of it.

When Vickey agreed to come back, she even pointed out that she would get the house the way it needed to be and then would maintain it. There was no talk of how much time it would take. Some Thursdays it took over three hours to clean the house while other weeks it took less time. This particular day it seemed much less.

"Vickey," I said, "can you get the house done in two hours and twenty minutes?"

"I just did," she answered.

That's when our two-hour conversation began. It wasn't an easy conversation. Truth be told, it was difficult. I told Vickey things I'd been thinking but never said before, for example, that my sister's and cousin's cleaning people would stay for five and six hours at a time.

She shared with me that she had been so souped-up from scrubbing the shower that she was on a roll.

"Some days I'm sluggish, other days I can work faster than even I realize," she said.

Vickey even asked if I ever sat down and wrote an article that took an hour and then another day write another piece that took five or more hours. That stopped me in my tracks, since that had indeed happened. The odd thing was I never even looked to see how well the house had been cleaned. I was caught up in time—quantity.

In my mind, it seemed impossible to notice everything if someone moved through the space too quickly. It was my perception of cleaning, not Vickey's. Eventually, through many tears and much duress, Vickey told me that she did things for me no one else ever asked her to do, and that she wanted more than anything to please me.

"I don't think I'll ever be able to do that," she said. "Maybe I shouldn't come back anymore."

Wow. That was a slap in the face, as if someone were saying, "wake up and look at what you're creating here."

"I don't want you to leave," I said, while still thinking that maybe I could find someone else who would do better.

Better than what, I don't know. Someone who would stay in the house for three hours no matter what they did or didn't do. I didn't want to let Vickey go. We talked round and round. Eventually we agreed to think it over, even pray about it, and get back to each other over the weekend.

When Stu came home, his rational mind helped me to see my perception of hourly work versus Vickey's salaried work. He understood the pros and pitfalls of both, having managed people in business for years. Stu and I talked throughout the evening. Needless to say, it was a restless night of trying to figure out what in the world I'd done.

At 11 p.m. I said to Stu, "You know I have a huge critical part of me that can be tough. I've been that way with you. Is that what's going on here?"

My husband refused to put me down, insisting that both of our theories about cleaning were valuable. He suggested that perhaps there was a whole different way of seeing cleaning than I had ever thought of before.

I remember Vickey's words when she said, "Why didn't you say, 'How wonderful that you finished your work already,' rather than question me in a critical tone about doing my work in such a short time?"

Vickey was right. My whole orientation as a teacher, an artist, a person had been one of quantity. Now quality has always been important, too. But I'd felt that in order for something to have been done right, it needed lots and lots of time. That was what I'd been doing to myself—and my students—for years.

At one o'clock in the morning, I wrote in my journal, "Now I've gone and done it. I may have lost the most trustworthy and best cleaner I will ever have."

I prayed that night for guidance for both Vickey and for myself, and hoped that she would find a place in her heart for forgiveness. At 7:30 a.m. I woke up feeling happy before I remembered what I'd done the day before.

Then it came to me like a bolt of lightning: my father's obsession with my sisters and me having to clean things over and over again, and yet it was never good enough no matter what we did. I also remembered on Tuesday Sister Brigid had worked on my root chakra which had to do with family and tribal issues.

Is that what was coming up here? If so, perhaps Vickey had been put in my life to help me heal my pain around house cleaning.

Neither of these, house cleaning and being good enough, has been a "Morina" forte—at least the Morina part of my family. My father's mother and sisters were obsessive about keeping a super clean and organized house. But the Morina/Stagnitta clan, all ten of us including my parents, have had problems keeping a house organized.

While growing up, my sister Nicki and I would clean all day on Saturdays. Then my father would come home and pull out a white glove to check the very tops of doorframes, places my 5'2" self didn't even know existed.

Was I metaphorically checking Vickey's doorframe, too? I waited until three minutes before eight and then picked up the phone. Even after all the pain I'd put her through, Vickey's immediate response was uplifting, loving, and caring. She greeted me on the other end with warmth and compassion in her voice.

"Good morning, Ms. Syverson," she said. "Thank you so much for calling."

As we talked, I shared with Vickey about the hourly versus salary model that Stu helped me to see. I also told her about my childhood with my father and his critical nature around cleaning the house. Then I finally shared with her about my Thursday appointments, where I received energy work through Healing Touch, and that I believed my old issues on cleaning and organizing from my father had been dug up earlier in the week to be healed.

"I'm sorry you had to be the soul stuck with providing me with that message," I said.

Vickey told me that she'd already decided she wasn't going to leave. I was so grateful! She also shared with me about, when growing up, no matter what she did or how she did it, it was never right. How brave of Vickey to have stood up for herself. That was exactly what she had been referring to the day before when she said, "I'm not going to let anyone put me down for the hard work I've done."

Our phone conversation went on for about a half hour, and I was thankful, truly thankful, that Vickey was able to go with me into the realm of Spirit. Her language and her traditions are a tad different from mine, but it's all the same. I spoke of God as energy.

She knew what I was talking about. Vickey said something that I'd believed for years: "These relationships we have in life have nothing to do with whether someone is cleaning house, writing an article, or teaching a class."

How wonderful that Vickey had the willingness to go the extra mile as I began healing my anxiety, frustration, and feelings of inadequacy around cleaning and organizing. I couldn't wait for her to come into my home again, so that I could see cleaning in a healthier, happier way. What an awakening!

I thought about last night and how I'd prayed that Vickey would forgive me and give me another chance. Just before turning off the family room lights for the evening, I finally got around to opening my mail. There, in a beautiful cream-colored envelope, neatly typed, was an announcement from Vickey's son and daughter-in-law. It was a notice of their first baby's birth—a little boy. I remembered that Vickey had shown me photos of her grandson when she first arrived.

Inside the envelope was a picture of the bottom of two baby feet printed on clear vellum overlaying a sheet of blue-gray paper. The words announced the newborn's parents, his name, and the date he was born. A blue-satin bow was neatly tied in the center between the two tiny feet of a new birth.

Top: Nonna Egidia, Nonno Francesco Stagnitta, and Mom
Bottom: Aunt Josie and Uncle Alex

St. Egidio Abate Church in Linguaglossa, Sicily

**With Sister Brigid McCarthy at Healing Touch Conference
in Boulder, Colorado**

Well of Mercy

**Sister Brigid McCarthy and Sister Donna Vaillancourt
Foundresses of Well of Mercy**

SACRED CIRCLE at Well of Mercy

Hunting Creek at Well of Mercy

**Jackye, Gilda, Nicki, Hillary Rodham Clinton, and Rosemary
The National Women's Hall of Fame**

Chapter 18
In My Heart of Hearts

Driving out of Charlotte, my heart was ahead of my body. It felt like a child was calling out from inside of me, "Are we there yet? When will we be there?" I had to laugh when I recognized that small, sensitive voice yearning to be back at Well of Mercy. Not only was I excited about my Healing Touch session, but this time I'd also made arrangements to stay overnight and finish a part of the *Sacred Contracts* book that would help me discover my own sacred contracts.

I still had to stop home, eat lunch, pack, and drive up I-77 north past Statesville toward Harmony. I'd gone into town for a breakfast with my Thursday writers' group. Even though I had not planned on meeting with any of my groups over the summer, Mary Wilmer's daughter Emily was visiting Charlotte. She and her siblings had spent the Fourth of July holiday at Emerald Isle on the North Carolina coast, and I wanted to see her.

We arranged ourselves in the same circle as we always did, except it was Emily sitting in her mother's chair. We talked about Mary's funeral service at St. Peter's Catholic and all of the writers from the community who came to honor her life. Emily shared that she and her siblings had brought Mary's ashes to the coast to release them into the ocean.

The family had their own intimate farewell ritual on the beach, and Emily described her brother carrying the urn while walking out into the sea until the water was up to his waist. Then he dove down, disappeared into the deep blue, and released Mary's remains.

Emily and the rest of the family watched until their brother resurfaced. Their mother, our friend, fellow poet, and writer, had been returned to the greater cosmos from which she came. Having Emily with us was like having Mary present.

It was hard to say goodbye to Emily, although she assured us that she'd be coming back to Charlotte to visit her younger sister, who still lived there. I'd lingered longer than planned at our breakfast meeting, so I had to stay on track from here on out and not get distracted.

My appointment with Brigid was at three o'clock. Since I would be having my own two-day retreat at Well, I stopped home to pick up my suitcase, books, and satchels to bring along. I spoke to Stu on my cell on the drive up I-77, fretting about the stock market plummeting even further than it had in years.

"Bristol Myers stock is being questioned," I told him.

Just two nights earlier, I'd opened our statement from Merrill Lynch and noticed that our financial advisor had bought into Bristol Myers. Of course, I would notice that one, since one of Bristol's locations was not more than a mile from my childhood home in Syracuse.

"Well," Stu said, in his usual nonchalant manner, "if we lost money, so did your father."

I'm sure he was trying to quell my fears or at least point out that we were in the same boat with the rest of humankind, including Dad who had always been great with money. I hadn't looked at our financial statements for some time, instead handing them over to Stu when they arrived, because I couldn't stay calm during the post 9/11 roller-coaster economy.

Over the weekend, I'd decided that ignoring our finances was not the responsible thing to do, and I needed to start looking at our accounts again—as if I had any clue what to do. I wasn't alone, the rest of middle-class America didn't know what to do either.

I drove the fifty minutes to Well worrying about money, a relationship with a friend, one with a sister, too, before I realized I was struggling with second chakra issues, *again*. That and the first chakra—my foundation—seemed to be the two always crying out for energy.

When I took a left onto Eagle Mills, I looked quickly out over the open field. The sky seemed more vast than usual, and the white billowing clouds extended in the distance. For a brief moment, I felt an ever-consuming presence assuring me that all would be well.

Then I thought of Stu, his faith. Where did it come from? He went to church as a child, yes, but he did not have the ultra-religious upbringing I did. He was the one making a good percentage of the income in the family so that I could pursue my art and writing. Yet, he wasn't worried.

So much for my faith-driven Catholicism.

There was no way a divine source would lead me down a path of writing, of art, and now of Healing Touch, and then pull the rug out. That was not the God I'd grown to know, nor is it the Divine I'd learned to talk about with Betty in Spiritual Direction.

In my heart of hearts, I knew that I'd been conscientious about listening to my intuition, to that inner voice inside, to my desires and urges. Would a loving God dangle such intrigue in my path only to pull it away?

When I looked up, the road was full of green almost to the point of covering my car. There were bushes lining the roadside and tall cornstalks—rows and rows of abundance. All of a sudden, distracted by my own meanderings, I started to wonder if I had turned off Eagle Mills Road?

I kept driving on the pavement, as if following my own nose, until I saw the Stop sign ahead. I took a right onto Hunting Creek Road, finally recognizing the route I always took. I chuckled to myself.

This is just like life, isn't it? When you think all is clear, there's a turn in the road, distractions camouflaging the view, more obstructions, then clarity—hopefully. It's amazing that a short three-mile ride off the Interstate can become a metaphor for living.

My heart leaped and the busy voice quieted as I took the right turn onto Mercy Road. The flowers at the foot of the sign were still in bloom, and I wondered if the sisters or the staff carried water to the plants in that location.

After driving the pebble-filled dusty road, I pulled my car in front of the main house. Since I would be staying overnight, instead of going directly to the Healing Touch room in the bottom of Sunrise House, I went into the front door of the main entrance to let Julia know I was there.

She was walking down from the second floor. I always loved seeing Julia, talking to her, sharing thoughts and ideas about books we'd both read. I remember a conversation we had about *The Dance of the Dissident Daughter*, a book by Sue Monk Kidd that set off an earlier change in my life toward the divine feminine. From the moment we'd met, Julia felt like a kindred spirit.

I had about eight minutes before my 3:00 p.m. meeting with Brigid, enough time for Julia to show me my room. When we entered

Sunrise, I was attracted to the first-floor room on the left with a double bed and peach coverlet. But Julia walked me across the hall to the room on the right, still on the first floor, above the Peace room below.

As much as I usually prefer to be up in a corner room and away from the communal kitchenette area, after having loaded my luggage, laptop, and bag of books into the trunk of the car at home, I had secretly hoped not to have to drag everything up a set of stairs to the top floor.

Because I was relieved to be in a first-floor room, I didn't say anything to Julia. But the energy of the room she gave me didn't feel right.

Now, finally six months after I began Spiritual Direction, Healing Touch, exploring archetypes, revisiting Carl Jung, and reading the *Sacred Contracts* book, tonight I was going to undertake a step of discovering my purpose in life through my own sacred contracts. It was important that the energy be just right.

There was nothing physically wrong with the space that was assigned to me. It was fine, but I have this sense sometimes when something doesn't feel quite right. It wasn't because the room had twin beds. The last time here, I slept in a twin bed. Maybe the issue was that there wasn't a low enough bureau to put my laptop on.

I couldn't say, just as I couldn't initially speak up and admit to Julia that the energy of my room wasn't going to work. That might have been an indication that it was time for another Healing Touch session, especially before working on my personal sacred contracts.

There I was ignoring the energy again, even after having told myself that I was going to pay attention. Now this whole thing about the room not feeling right, along with my fretting on the drive up about money, friendships, and family, made me say aloud to myself, "Get me to The Peace Room. Please."

As it turned out, Julia had let me know that Brigid was running half an hour late, which was no problem since I was staying overnight anyway. It gave me time to bring my luggage in and all of the other paraphernalia I'd packed. I drove the car up to the long-term parking area, then walked back down and around Sunrise House to the bottom level and the Healing Touch Room.

I arrived at 3:20 p.m. knowing I had ten minutes before Brigid would get there. I sat on the comfortable white couch, calm and peaceful, and began to doze and fall into a relaxed serene space between reality and rest.

Startled, I jumped when the door opened and Brigid was walking in. After we greeted each other with a hug, she noticed and mentioned that my hair had been cut and styled close to my head. I'd had it done just the day before. My hair hadn't been short for years, at least fifteen, maybe longer.

Last week, after telling a writer friend that I was cleaning out my files from years of writing, she remarked about how telling that was.

"But it's not half as telling as when a woman gets her hair drastically cut," she had said.

"Oh, God, I'm doing that next week."

Now, Brigid remarked that she loved my short hair, and she loved it long too. That was what I'd been feeling. If I didn't like it short, I'd just start growing it out again, although I had actually been considering having it trimmed even closer to my head.

At the end of the summer, after my self-imposed sabbatical, maybe I would figure out more specifically what it all meant—the cleaning of files, the cutting of hair, a hiatus from meetings, classes, workshops, life.

For now, I didn't want to think. I just wanted to *be*, to feel free, light—at least two pounds lighter without the large, bushy head of hair that I'd been carrying around. I did feel a freedom, although I was unaware of how different I must have looked to Brigid until I passed a mirror near the Healing Touch room.

We started chatting more than I had told myself I would. But I enjoyed hearing Brigid talk about her uncle, a priest down in Florida.

"I was talking to my uncle," Brigid said, "and he was the reason for my delay."

"Not a problem," I said, "I love older people. Besides it gave me a chance to rest for even ten minutes."

Our conversation meandered from working with elderly family members, to relationships with other family and friends, to investments, and to how to handle money now that we were both in our fifties.

Funny how it works. I had no earthly idea how I would ever start the subject of money, especially since I'd decided a few times ago that I would just talk about the parts of my body that were acting up.

"Brigid," I said, "it's so odd that we're talking about money and investments. That's what's been on my mind, finances and all the other second chakra concerns—relationships, my female organs, and my bladder, still."

Brigid had shared with me before that she was reading very little news these days. I filled her in on why the media thought the market was tumbling. One study that came out two days earlier said Hormone Replacement Therapy was not doing what the medical community had thought it would and the drug could be unsafe for many women.

Just like what had happened with Bristol Myers, more drug company stocks had started to take a downturn. On top of that, Americans had lost confidence in President George W. Bush here in 2002, almost a year after 9/11. Many felt that he had not gone far enough in his speech on reprimanding corporate America. My conversation with Sister Brigid flipped among money, investments, hormone replacement therapy, energy.

As we headed toward the Healing Touch room, I said to Brigid, "If I really have been following the Spirit, then how do I stop worrying about money? How do I stop taking some things personally? How do I stop the whirlwind of chatter in my head?"

Brigid explained how stress, illness, or any other disruption could immediately flip us back into old patterns of thinking. Perfect timing for an energy tune-up.

When I first lay down, I closed my eyes like I usually do. Brigid hadn't placed a pillow over my eyes. Sometimes she did, sometimes she didn't. I didn't say a word. Something told me to go ahead and open them again. Brigid was holding her hands above my sacral chakra. I'd missed seeing what she'd done over the root chakra.

But she was clearly lingering above my sacral, my navel, and genitals. Her hands seemed to be moving back and forth, right to left, until Brigid finally moved and positioned her hands over my third chakra, solar plexus, stomach. That's where her hands relaxed in space, appeared calm, even made some round clockwise circles.

I had learned from Brigid that clockwise circles, whether small, large, or in between, meant the body centers, chakras, were open. As Brigid continued floating her hands above the solar plexus to the crown, the more her hands moved in a circular formation—above my heart, my throat, the center of my forehead (the third eye), the crown of my head.

We both opened our mouths in astonishment. "Did you see that?" Brigid asked.

"Most of it," I replied.

"Your root chakra was a little open. Your sacral was totally closed, and the rest ..."

"I saw the rest," I said.

I thought of when Brigid once told me that she was only the facilitator, emphasizing that I was doing the healing on myself. She was there to feel and move the energy around for me. I was beginning to get it, realizing that healing takes place within our own consciousness, at the same time she shifted the energy, moved it out of its stuck place, released it from any congestion.

It had been a number of sessions since I'd fallen into that place of my mind being completely clear and still. I closed my eyes and let Brigid go to work. It was no wonder that I went deeply into my psyche almost to a point of forgetfulness to heal the one area that continued to torment my life — second chakra, sacral.

It was not only about money, but about relationships, too. I always thought that if someone had a problem, I would take it on for them, even though the problem did not belong to me. I stepped out of my reverie and was aware that Brigid was performing Healing Touch in the space above my sacral area, and ...

I fall immediately into the void.

How long have I been in this state of not knowing, not thinking.

Brigid is still working. I sense around the navel. I squint. My eyes open slightly and her hands make large, sweeping, almost raking motions. She's above my head.

*I close my eyes, again, sense tingling energy in my bladder. My hands
and feet move. That sense of irritation, anger rises out from me, again
but not as bad.*

This time, I don't feel like getting up, ending the session.

Instead a flash, and my older sister comes to mind. It's time to let go.

*Her life is her life, she has a right to live it the way she wants. I can too.
I don't have to feel responsible for others. I was raised to … take care of others —
a challenge to let go.*

*I calm down, accept the anxiety, the irritation. If I let go I know my
irritation will release. With that awareness the angst is gone.*

*My eyes stay closed I want to say "don't stop working on my left side,
my left ovary." I don't talk, but open my eyes.*

*How does Brigid know without me telling her? There she is holding
her hands way above my body, raking over my left side. She places her hand
behind my back and ever so gently touches the side where my left ovary resides.*

*It doesn't pain like it pained the first time and the time
before when she focused on that area
Time — irrelevant now. I open my eyes. The clock on the wall is above my feet
            Forty minutes have passed.
Time — where has it gone? I close my eyes again
Time.   Suddenly, I feel centered, and if I move my head to the right,
            even a fraction, I feel perfectly in the middle.
Brigid's hands on the side of my head, over my forehead large wings appear, cover
            my face — a mask, then white — white light.
My fingers stretch out in a blessing, pointing straight down*

Then a white, white circle and light appear in between wings

and I hear a strong, firm voice,

"Let go of judgment of any person, of any sister, trust they are following

their own path."

The circle of light shifts. It is no longer as white.

But, a presence is here, and my fingers stretch farther, as if in another blessing.

The voice, assures me: "There is nothing to worry about with money.

The world will do what the world will do, and you, you, you will be fine.

God has not put you with a man so grounded, so able to work in the

work world for no reason. God has other work for you.

You have organized your life well, you and your husband.

It is now time for you to do the core work you are here to do — your purpose.

Writing   Art   Healing Touch."

I'm startled!

Healing Touch? What does that mean?

My purpose feels so clear except – how does Healing Touch fit in?

Just as clear if not clearer the message, "NOT to worry about

the money, all will be well. You have your work to do."

In my heart, I feel confident and sure I will follow the voice.

I opened my eyes. Brigid was holding her hands above my naval and sacral area. Her hands were moving in a strong, wide circle, as she continued moving all the way up and above my body. The circles took a wider and wider swing.

She stepped away into the open space of the room around me. Her hands continued moving around indicating my chakras were clearly open and willing to accept messages coming through. I looked at Brigid. She looked at me. I wanted to cry with excitement. And I did shed a few tears.

"Wow," Brigid said, and it was exactly how I was feeling.

We spoke softly to each other, describing what had just occurred. Brigid told me she focused on the closed sacral chakra, going slowly and refusing to rush. We kept our words to a minimum. Our voices only whispers.

"Take your time getting up," she said, as she walked out the door. I thought I'd like to stay in the room for a while and rest quietly.

"Brigid," I said, at the same instant she turned around and walked back toward me.

Simultaneously we said, "Why don't you lie here." "Can I stay in here?"

We were thinking exactly the same thing.

"Stay with this energy," Brigid said, "you might even want to bring your dinner to your room tonight."

I slipped off the table to grab the pink throw on the corner chair, lay back down with the cover over me, lingered in the Healing Touch room for about twenty more minutes. I felt quiet, alone inside the chrysalis of a cocoon, comfortable with myself.

Images of hearts filled the space. Heart-shaped stones rested on a shelf to my left, and a beautiful wreath of dry greenery shaped in a heart lay above it. To my right hung a handmade quilt by an artist I happened to know. Fabric of black and white surrounded nine rainbow-colored hearts in three rows; small bits of color spotted the background.

An angel holding a heart sat on a table in the corner near the door. The hearts must have always been there, but I had never noticed them quite like this before.

On the wall to the right was a contemporary cross and an arched holy water font. The door beyond my feet was closed. The entire room felt like a womb of warm energy, a place of total love, total acceptance.

Chapter 19
My Sacred Contracts

When I returned to the room where I had put my luggage, I was absolutely sure the energy was not right for discovering my purpose in life, which I would be uncovering tonight. I stepped out the front door of Sunrise House in search of Julia. She happened to be walking in my direction.

"How can I help you?" she asked.

"Is there any chance I can change my room to the one across the hall?"

"No problem," Julia said, "take whichever room you're most comfortable in."

I moved my belongings to the room with the peach coverlet that I'd noticed when I first arrived. There was an extra rocking chair with a lap pillow for reading and writing, and the low enough bureau that, in my case, served a dual purpose—one was a spot to place my laptop before and after the altar I'd create for the ritual I'd be performing this evening.

Later, I did what Brigid had suggested and ate dinner in my room. Sitting in silence in the big stuffed chair, I stayed centered while savoring every morsel of baked chicken, wild rice, green beans, and salad. I returned my empty plate before heading to chapel.

Since I'd stopped going to Mass regularly, I missed ritual in my life. The thought of participating in any institutional religion did not appeal to me. But a service led by Sister Donna or by Julia always felt right.

Sister Donna was away, so Julia guided us and invited each person to put on one of the woven stoles stored beneath the seats. She turned on inspirational music before telling everyone about the unusual troubles Well of Mercy had experienced throughout the day—a leak in one of the air conditioner units, a flooded room, a broken oven that delayed dinner for about thirty minutes, along with other facility mishaps.

We learned that the staff at one point had stopped what they were doing, gathered quietly, and settled into Centering Prayer. Then they walked the land together.

Julia asked us to think about where we had seen God in our day. I waited for a few people to speak before I talked about the vast opening and white billowing clouds in the sky I'd seen after turning onto Eagle Mills Road on my way to Well.

"It felt like something supernatural was peeking through," I said.

After people shared their different God experiences, we gathered in a circle and held hands. Julia prayed for Spirit's presence through the night for all of us and for Well of Mercy.

Feeling calm and centered from Healing Touch and having attended the chapel service, I settled in my room and wrote in my journal about the day. My plan for later in the evening had been in the works since I'd scheduled my stay two weeks earlier. Night would be the best time for me to finally cast my sacred contracts.

After having read dozens of archetypes, and journaled about many of them in relationship to my life, I decided to follow the *Sacred Contracts* book and put these characters I most identify with into perspective. I wanted to be honest with myself and show how I present to the world, as well as to reveal, if only to myself, the shadow side of me that many do not see. Since earlier on I had decided to include what the book referred to as "The Four Archetypes of Survival: Child, Victim, Prostitute, Saboteur,"[7] I would only be picking eight other archetypes.

Darn! I was going to have to face my fears and vulnerabilities through these four survival characters.

The next seven companions in my life that I personally chose were: Artist, Angel, Writer, Heroine, Networker, Mother, and Teacher/Mentor. That came to eleven archetypes. I had one more to

---

[7] Myss, Caroline, *Sacred Contracts, Awakening Your Divine Potential.* New York: Harmony Books, 2001.

pick, twelve altogether, just like the twelve houses in an astrological chart. That twelfth archetype I'd been considering was The Seeker. But I've never been *just* a Seeker.

Throughout my life, I have been interested in all aspects of mysticism—those I was raised on in my Italian Catholic heritage and others I discovered on my own over the years: spirituality, supernatural phenomena, metaphysical and magical experiences, along with being intrigued by various other cultural rites, including Buddhism, Sufism, Judaism.

The list continued to deviate in different directions like the writings of Joseph Campbell and my attraction with anything related to Carl Jung—dreams, astrology, the Myers-Briggs Type Indicator, and more.

Two days earlier, before heading up here to Well of Mercy, I started getting clearer about my twelfth and final archetype choice. After much soul searching, I accepted the challenge of claiming my Seeker as a Mystical Seeker. Step one, choosing my archetypes, was finally completed.

The second step in the process outlined in the *Sacred Contracts* book was to place each archetype into one of the twelve astrological houses through a particular process that Myss described. Since I am inherently comfortable with astrology, the minute I selected the archetype for one of the twelve houses, I knew I would understand how the house and the placement of the archetype in that house would affect my world.

The third piece of the contract would come through the chakra system. My time in Healing Touch had deepened my understanding of what each chakra meant. I also knew how each chakra would correspond to its astrological house.

Next, I took twenty-four 2x3-inch pieces of paper that I'd brought from home and divided them into two piles. In the first stack, I'd written one of my twelve archetypes on each piece of paper. In the second stack, I'd written a number one to twelve on the remaining twelve pieces, representing the twelve houses in the astrological wheel. Then I waited until around ten o'clock to begin, when there were no sounds from other guests in Sunrise House. After unfolding the chakra chart that Sister Brigid had given me, I placed the triptych-like altarpiece in the back center of the low bureau.

CHAKRA	LOCATION	COLOR	REPRESENTS
First	Root of Spine	**Red**	Family, Primal Trust
Second	Sacral Between the Navel and Genitals	**Orange**	Sexuality, Money, Creativity, Relationships
Third	Solar Plexus The Stomach	**Yellow**	Personal Power
Fourth	Heart	**Green**	Divine Love
Fifth	Throat	**Blue**	Self-Expression, Speaking, Choices
Sixth	Third Eye Center of Forehead	**Indigo**	Intuition, Intellect, Wisdom
Seventh	Crown Top of Head	**Violet**	Higher Mind, Relationship to The Divine

Altars had been a prominent part of my landscape growing up. I thought back to those years at *Nonno* and *Nonna's* house in the front room where my grandfather did his healing work on his *paesani* who came to him for help. I remembered the altar I'd created in front of the fireplace and I knew, even as I pretended to say Mass at the age of five or maybe even younger, that only a male priest could perform this service. But now all these years later I was creating my own altar for my own spiritual ritual.

From my suitcase, I pulled a pewter candle holder with angel wings sculpted around an opening in the center. I placed a small tealight in the opening, struck a match, and lit the wick merging from the votive candle. I placed the stack of papers with the twelve archetypes on the left side of the candle, and the stack with the twelve numbers to the right.

In front of my simple altar, I followed what the *Sacred Contracts* book had said about clearing all of my chakras.

How fitting! Brigid had done that for me hours earlier. My chakras were as clear as they would ever be. To be absolutely sure, I moved through chakras one through seven and stared at each color on the triptych-like altarpiece in the back of the bureau.

After six months of research and reading, journaling and exploring, this was the moment of unveiling that I'd been seeking: my personal sacred contracts that supported my purpose in life. The position of an archetype in an astrological house, with related chakras that had been included in *Sacred Contracts*, was not being left up to chance. No! For me it was being left up to the energy, to the Divine source, to whatever Spirit existed.

I shuffled each stack one more time, placed them back down on either side of the candle, said a small prayer, and chose my first archetype from the top of the stack on the left. I turned it over: "Teacher/Mentor."

Then I picked the top paper from the stack on the right for the astrological House #3—the home of writing, communications, brothers, and sisters. How fitting! Not only was I a writer, I'd also communicated as a teacher in some capacity for over thirty years: speaking, lecturing, showing, telling. Even if I was now trying to back off from the profession by not working full time in an educational system, teaching was too much a part of my life to have omitted it as one of my archetypes.

Since I was the second child, second-oldest female in the family, I spent a lot of time helping to care for the five youngest. I loved being around them, and my mother needed the help. (They are now lovingly, but with humor, called the second family). I felt like a mentor of sorts to each of them at one time or another.

The chakras for House #3 were telling as well: third chakra—the solar plexus, ruler of my own personal power. Teaching and mentoring were places where I felt assured, especially in the subjects that I've taught—fine arts and memoir writing.

And the fifth chakra—the throat—I definitely used my voice to teach and talk. I've learned the hard way about keeping my mouth shut: sometimes with students, sometimes with siblings, sometimes with others.

I was relieved. Because of recent experiences with some siblings and their offspring, I'd feared that House #3 would be that of the Saboteur.

But Saboteur showed up soon enough in my second pick from my stack of archetypes.

I was taken aback. There was the Saboteur in House #4—Home, Mother, Family History.

I didn't know what to make of this selection, so I opened Myss's book. She calls the Saboteur "The Guardian of Choice," and then says, "The core issue for the Saboteur is fear of inviting change into your life, change that requires responding in a positive way to opportunities to shape and deepen your spirit … it is impossible to stop the process of change."[8]

Oh my! Life was full of changes, and I didn't move through change easily. Dad actually pointed that out to me one day when I was in my late teens. My father was sitting at the head of the kitchen table. I must have said something that I was struggling over. Dad stopped whatever he was doing, and as if a light bulb appeared over his head, he told me that he just realized how difficult change was for me and then in a calm and kind manner gave me some wise advice.

"Change is inevitable, Gilda," he said. "It's part of life. If you start to accept change as it comes, it will make your life easier."

---

[8] Myss, Caroline, *Sacred Contracts, Awakening Your Divine Potential.* New York: Harmony Books, 2001.

Dad had been right, life was full of changes, all kinds of different changes including the homes I've moved through. And this segment of the pie is the house about one's home—where they live now or have lived over their lives. I have changed homes way too much for my sensitive INFP (Introverted, Intuitive, Feeling, Perceptive) nature. I've never been comfortable with the constant change of residences. Over the years I'd moved more times than I could count without tallying each one on my fingers and toes.

The corresponding chakras for House #4 were the first and fourth chakras. The first chakra deals with roots and family foundation. The fourth chakra is the heart.

House #4 is also about *mother*. Not being a mother in an Italian American family was not always easy. Having children was elevated in the culture I grew up in. Life was about family and having a family.

Being childless, while not by choice, had at times made me feel less than. No one did that consciously. Heavens no! It's similar to living in any environment that reflects the values of a culture. After much soul searching, it was *my* choice to stop various medical procedures, let things be, move on into a life different from the way I'd been raised.

Now the sabotaging I had to face wasn't just about not being a mother nor was it just about my own mother, who ended up living the way a woman was expected to live in the years after World War II in our large, extended Italian Catholic family.

There was more to it: I had been rooted in my own family's traditions—brought over from the "mother country," from where my relatives had emigrated, Sicily. Instead of following the women in my family, I would inevitably change, veer off in another direction.

In the end, by making the choice to stop trying to have children and put my focus on my work as an artist, writer, teacher, and pursuer of all things creative, I was stepping away from my culture's expectations.

Even though I ended up living in a whole new way, I still loved my family deeply. (Fourth chakra—heart) And despite my uncomfortable feelings when I had recently been up to visit them, I knew they loved me.

I took a deep breath, pulled another card. This time I decided to start on the right and flipped over the 10th astrological House. I gasped in surprise, when its archetypal match in the left-hand stack turned out to be the Artist.

Artist! Of course. Why in the world was I surprised? Artist was in the 10th House, that of profession, of one's status in the world. For heaven's sake, I went to college for art education, ended up getting a Master of Fine Arts in studio arts. I'd been out in the world teaching art for over thirty years and also doing my own artwork.

Over the decades I prayed and meditated, asked God what my purpose was in this world. If I'd only looked in the mirror of my life, it was right there in front of me. Why did I have to pull a series of two small cards to recognize my purpose? I've always been involved in some kind of creative pursuit. It was and is who I am.

Plus, House #10 also rules the father and his influences. My father was both a creative barber and entrepreneur, coming up with all kinds of out-of-the box ideas and building quite a successful business in more than one location in Syracuse. Dad also won many awards for creating new hair styles for men.

Sitting right on the top of my natal astrological 10th House is the sign of Pisces, my actual sun sign and Dad's, too. The fish is about the unconscious and the spiritual seeker.

I have been drawing angels for years, reading metaphysical book after metaphysical book. And Dad, well he was a bit on the religious side. My siblings and even Mom would open their eyes wide and say, "A bit?"

I closed my eyes, shook my head in disbelief. Then I considered the corresponding chakras. Fifth chakra—the throat. I've used my voice to give programs, talks, workshops, and lectures related to my own exhibitions, including the angels, and eventually participated in poetry readings along with numerous other readings, talks on memoir, and other significant speeches.

And since the seventh chakra, the crown, represented the connection to the Divine, I began to become aware of how God worked through me. Was I being told that the way I united with Spirit—or expressed who the Divine was through me—was as a creative being?

How obvious.

Whew! I needed a break but was too excited to see where my other archetypes would land. A flip of the next card on each stack revealed the Writer and House #1. Surprise! Here I am writing away and the 1st House is about self.

Why am I surprised? How can I be so naïve?

Me. I am a writer, poet, memoirist. I'd even written articles on art and artists. When I was getting my MFA in fine arts, my thesis and writtens (questions from my thesis committee compiling my years of study that I was required to respond to in essay form) were not nearly as big a challenge for me as they were for many of the other visual art students in the program.

All those years ago when I studied astrology, I learned that the 1st House is the house of *I am*. I am Writer according to the archetype that I picked. Writing had become such a part of me, I knew it was something that would weave through the rest of my life.

Even though I didn't come into creative writing until midlife, I'd spent years in my artist sketchbooks inscribing words around and in between the images I drew. Often there were more words than images, but it all felt like art to me.

The chakras for the 1st House: first chakra—my roots and basic foundation; third chakra—the sacral, all about self-esteem. When I sit down with either a journal or at my computer and begin to write, I am lost in time and space. Whether it be journaling, poetry, or prose, writing invigorates and centers me.

Plus, so much of my poetry and memoir writing has been about family and family roots—first chakra. And the sacral, third chakra in my 1st House, is about self-assurance. Writing has certainly given me lots of awareness, understanding, confidence, compassion, and support for who I am.

As I continued through each of the two sets of stacks on the altar, there were some combinations of archetypes and houses I suspected might match. Others were a revelation and some I was confused about.

The archetype Networker showed up in House #12, home of the unconscious. It seemed almost opposite from the way I had understood networking, when I'd written about the Networker in my journal months earlier. From my father I'd learned how to make connections: professional, friends, family members—immediate and extended—doctors, lawyers, and others.

Now, my Networker suggested that my sacred contract was about interacting with and through my own unconscious, my soul, the realm that can be so easily avoided in this busy world. Having incorporated meditation into my life over the last decade and writing down my dreams most mornings, making many into poems, indicated that the need to network with my own unconscious was not really that far-fetched.

It turned out to be supported by the sixth chakra, the third eye—through my intuition, and the seventh chakra, the crown—through my connection to the Divine.

When I finished matching all twelve archetypes with their astrological houses and the corresponding chakras, I breathed a huge sigh and quietly opened my door. I stepped out of the room and out of Sunrise's main door. The celestial night sky was beaming with stars.

What had unfolded in there?

Just as it took months to read and journal and write some more, it would take time to sort out some of this new, yet not so new, information that had always been in my life.

Like Glinda, the good witch in the *Wizard of Oz*, when she said to Dorothy, "You've always had the power …," I realized I'd been living my individual sacred contracts right along even without recognizing them as my purpose.

In all good time, I would have a better understanding of my family of archetypes just as I would learn to absorb all of who I am in a new way. I felt grounded, ready, and willing to let all these new awarenesses unfold.

Once in bed, I wrote in my journal thoughts and fragments of thoughts. My favorite line: *I saw myself.* By midnight, I reached over and clicked off the lamp on the bed stand. I slept well, peacefully, and through the night.

Chapter 20
The Morning After

Six a.m. was too early for me, but I was wide awake. Although hungry, I didn't want to go out to the kitchenette since I was sharing it with others staying in the guest house. Instead, I drew a circle in my journal, and followed an idea I saw in the *Sacred Contracts* book. I divided the sphere into twelve segments, representing the twelve houses of the zodiac.

In the center, where they all met, I numbered the astrological houses, starting center left with number 1. Then I circled counterclockwise to the next piece of the pie, where I wrote in the number 2. I continued down and around and up again writing each number in the middle, until finishing with House #12.

In each section of the pie, I filled in the names of my archetypes, placed the chakra number or numbers, on the outside of the circle. I reviewed in my head what each house meant, something I've clearly remembered since the days of traveling to the South Shore of Boston to study astrology.

Now to add to this knowingness were my individual archetypes and their relationship to each of my houses. I began to write about those two relationships—the meaning of each house and its relationship to the archetype now sitting there.

I wrote a great deal about the Artist strategically positioned in the 10th House, at the very top of my chart, the placement of one's highest potential, the house of profession, the house of father. That's where I began reminiscing in my journal about what my father had hoped for me.

There's no question Dad was the one who pushed about working in the world and also about religion and spirituality. But when it came to making an income, he wanted me to be a hairdresser and open up a place right next door to Eastwood Barbershop in the building that he owned. He would not have chosen the arts for me. In fact, he feared I would not make enough money to survive when I told him that I wanted to be an artist.

I have never forgotten one sunny spring Sunday in my parents' living room when Dad was sitting in a hard, wooden chair, his back positioned in front of the piano. He wasn't in his comfortable recliner, but he seemed to be in a jovial mood. We were all casually chatting, laughing, and talking—Mom, Dad, and a few of my seven siblings scattered about. I was sitting to the left of my father on the wall-to-wall, padded olive-green carpet. Having graduated from high school two years earlier, I finally realized what I wanted to do with my life and blurted it up toward Dad who'd been looking down at me. His jowls dropped. His mouth fell open.

"An artist?" he bellowed. "What in the world will you do with art?"

I was clearly taken aback by his response and didn't know what direction to look in—up at Dad or down into the deep-green carpet. In my head, I repeated over and over again, *think fast, think fast, think fast!*

"Teach. I'll teach art," I said quickly, hoping to ease Dad's concern.

"Teach?" he cried out, pushing his back against the wooden chair. "You're going to go to four years of college and then teach? I make more money cutting hair than teachers I know who've had years of education."

I didn't know what to say to Dad, feeling disappointed that I had just spilled out a burning desire for my life. I hadn't thought about money in the same way my father did, a man who had eight children to raise. It was me at nineteen years old trying to find myself.

Maybe that's why the Victim showed up in my 8th House of long-term finances and other people's money. It had been my husband who made the sizable amount of our income. In my 7th House was where my partner had been positioned and where the survival archetype of the Child sat. There is no question that my husband has taken good care of me and supported my desire to put so much of my life's energy into the arts. On and on I wrote about how I felt with the pairing of each archetype and what it meant in relationship to the house that they each landed in.

It was 11:30 a.m. before I looked up and realized that lunch would be served in thirty minutes. I took a quick shower, made my bed, and arrived in the main house's dining room just as Sister Brigid was gathering everyone in a circle for a blessing. Since I never made it to the kitchenette in Sunrise for breakfast, I counted on lunch grounding me, bringing me back to earth. Then I promised myself that I would get out of my head, come down from whatever star I'd been sitting on, and walk by the creek before jumping back into writing and learning more about my sacred contracts.

After lunch, I did just that, snaking along the bank of Hunting Creek, as I stepped farther away from the retreat houses and deeper into the woods following the gentle, flowing brook.

Eventually I sat down on one of the many benches that the sisters had over time put out along this favorite walk of mine. There was only the chirping of a bird now and again, and the sound of the murmuring water, as the stream slipped across and rolled over rocks and broken tree trunks, around curves and rough terrain.

I thought about my Spiritual Director and that I also happened upon Healing Touch around the same time I began working with Betty, almost six months earlier. I had only a few friends and colleagues who even knew about Healing Touch. I was certainly at the beginning of learning about energy work.

In one of my previous sessions with Sister Brigid, I mentioned how curious I felt about the Healing Touch process and how I found myself periodically wanting to reach out and rest my hand on someone's shoulder when they talked about a rotator cuff tear, a broken heart, or confusion over one decision or another. Brigid thought I was a perfect candidate to learn some basic Healing Touch techniques. She suggested I consider taking a Level 1 class simply to try it out.

I had looked up Healing Touch online over the past few weeks and discovered that there was going to be a course offered in Charlotte later in the summer, less than two months from now. Maybe I should sign up for it? After all, the Mystical Seeker archetype showed up in my 9th House of Higher Learning, Spirituality, Philosophy, Religion. What would it hurt to try one class?

Healing Touch Level 1 was now floating in and out of my head while I sat by the creek. It was such a peaceful time that I stayed there much longer than I ever expected.

I returned to my room and took a long nap. I never take naps. When I awakened, I explored my chart and wrote until close to dinner.

I ate with the rest of the guests that night in the main house, positioned myself in a chair at the large oval table overlooking the expansive windows that displayed the rich, green-forested scene beyond the main retreat house. After dinner, I attended chapel.

Then I decided to join Julia and some other folks for a long walk. I wondered if it was a good idea to take that walk with others for fear I'd get myself into some conversation I did not need to be involved in.

I wasn't concerned about Julia, she was always a joy to talk with, but I didn't know the other five people on the walk. Despite my reluctance, I went along so that I could get out of my head and ground myself. Plus, Julia was taking us on a different path than I'd ever followed before. I was curious and wanted to see what it was like.

I almost asked Julia if the walk was going to be silent but, instead, I kept quiet. Once on this new path, we were all walking on a paved road cutting through open farm fields of green on either side of us.

Before I knew it, a mother and her adult daughter moved up and positioned themselves one on each side of me. The mother mentioned that they were at the retreat center because of a family crisis.

Oh Lord, I thought, this was my time away. I didn't want to be in the middle of someone else's problems. Was this my 11th House of others and the outside world barging in? Was my habit, of always trying to help others, being tested?

Now there is nothing wrong with helping people. I believe in it. But I've never been good at balancing the doing for others and the taking care of myself.

I learned a long time ago that once you start opening the door to the spiritual world, you better be ready to receive the lessons that stepped through. I don't know how it happened that I ended up in the middle between the mother and daughter. Why was I unaware of the movements around me that had been made as we hiked down the road?

There I was with the mother on one side and the daughter on the other talking about their crisis to me, over me, around me, sometimes looking straight in my eyes. One of them even asked my opinion about their problem, which I can't even remember.

But what I do remember was the feeling of being in between them, a place I've often been in my own family— between a parent and a sibling, worse yet between a sibling and another sib. Sometimes it's been between two friends. I've attributed this to starting off as a middle child of three in what we have affectionately called the "first family." (Nicki, Anthony and myself.)

That was my position until the age of eight, when my mother and father started a second family and had five more children—Francine, Teresa, Gerard, Jo Anne, and Bridget. (Actually, Mom had lost a child between the first and second family—Mary.) I suspect it was then that I developed the characteristics of both a middle child from the first family and an older child for my younger siblings. It's no wonder I've facetiously said that I've felt schizophrenic at times.

What I thought would be a quiet walk with others turned into another lesson, which, of course, gave me plenty of writing material for the night. How do I keep finding myself taking care of others? Because of my experience with the mother and daughter, I looked into the Prostitute archetype in the 11th House, which answered many questions I'd been asking myself for a good long time.

I knew that the 11th House, where my Prostitute had landed, rules relationships, the outside world, friends, hopes and wishes. When I give myself away to anyone or anything in the outside world, I can be lost to what my soul is asking of me. My challenge has always been to balance my needs or, better yet, put my needs first before giving myself away to others or to what others want from me. It was always a natural thing for me to do having come from a large family where I felt like a second mother. Then, without realizing it, I automatically took that way of being out into the world beyond my family.

That night of writing was a wild one. After I finally fell asleep, a good wake-up call rattled me around 4:00 a.m. It was probably my Networker archetype, from the 12th House of dreams and the unconscious, asking me to look at one scene or another in my life.

As an avid dreamer, I had always gotten some of my best messages from my dream world. I also believe the unconscious wakes me up when it needs to so I will pay closer attention to something I'm either ignoring or struggling over during waking hours.

I write my dreams in my journal, even in the middle of the night, so they don't wisp away like visions often do. I use one of those glow-in-the-dark pens to jot down even a few lines to remind me of that dream in the morning. Many of those writings have ended up as poems over the years.

By the time lunch was over the next day and I was driving away from Well of Mercy, I felt I had unlocked a huge treasure chest of information. The key had now been handed over to me. It all felt familiar, like a distant memory from some past knowledge that now seemed available.

I was thrilled that my sacred contracts had finally been made clear. First, it was a gift to discover my own personal archetypes and how they had been affecting my life, especially the Artist and the Writer, and I could tell the Mystical Seeker had a lot more to say. I knew that some archetypes would have more influence than others and that they would shift at different times in my life.

The thought of facing the houses where the Victim, Prostitute, and Saboteur had landed was not as appealing as learning more about the archetypes I chose for myself. Little did I know when I drove away from Well that day that those three characters would be my partners until my return a short, but what would seem like a long, two weeks away.

Chapter 21
Syracuse: Old Survival Issues

On top of the world—that's how I was feeling after leaving Well on Saturday. Finally, my purpose in life presented itself in black and white: to be a Writer—1st House of who I am, and an Artist—10th House of profession. I'd been doing art and writing all along, and unearthing my sacred contracts was like giving myself permission to be me.

This next level of self-discovery would make my life easier to accept. Having excavated my own eight archetypes, I was willing to handle the survival ones: The Prostitute—Guardian of Faith; The Saboteur—Guardian of Choice; The Victim—ah, my Guardian of Self-Esteem booster or destroyer; The Child—Guardian of Innocence.[9]

I was elated and affirmed. At least that's how I felt until I woke up Monday morning and couldn't decide whether or not to go meet a friend for lunch. Obviously, I still had more figuring out to do with what I had learned about me.

Even though I promised myself back in June not to schedule any writing meetings or artists' talks or, for that matter, any work-related gatherings for two months, I'd made a luncheon appointment for Tuesday with Henry, a poet and a Jungian analyst.

I spent all day Monday trying to sort out whether to cancel or to go. *When in doubt, don't* is what I've tried to follow, but … the two hooks were poetry and Jung. Third and equally as important was that we were getting together to talk about starting a mythology group, after my own prompting of the idea earlier in the year.

It's not that I didn't want to do a group on mythology. After all, it fit right into my Heroine archetype—5th House of love, play, adventure, and creativity, as well as the Mystical Seeker's 9th House of the higher mind, philosophy, spirituality and religion. But I'd made a

---

[9] Myss, Caroline, *Sacred Contracts, Awakening Your Divine Potential.* New York: Harmony Books, 2001

strategic commitment to myself to put joining or participating in any group or organization on the back burner.

My summer priorities were still about cleaning out my studio of old papers, and I mean *old*. Books were being stacked in boxes, some stored, others carted off to the library, the community college, and numerous other locations. There were supplies I no longer needed, bills and tax reports, medical and insurance forms that I was determined to organize in either active or inactive files.

I'd already been in my organizational mode for a month. In between I was still working on my memoir of the trip to Italy with my parents and husband, as well as some angel drawings that I had been commissioned to do earlier in the year.

In spite of my full itinerary and the promise I had made about not going to any meetings or gatherings, I didn't have the heart to cancel my lunch meeting. What if I wanted to keep the option of a mythology group open for the fall? (My Spiritual Director would have told me that it was definitely part of my INFP nature — living in the world of possibilities.)

With my Heroine in the 5th House of creativity and play, what could be more fun than delving deeper into lore? The only problem is that the 5th House lay opposite the 11th, that darn house of the Prostitute, the very place where I'm always giving myself away to others, to groups, to the outside world.

At 11:30 a.m., I showed up right on time at 300 East, one of my favorite lunch haunts. I love talking to writers and therapists; they come from the same mold, always searching deeper. I'd become friends or acquaintances with many of both over the years, and belonging to Charlotte Friends of Jung put me in the company of more and more seekers.

It turned out that I was saved by the person I was having lunch with, someone who could hear me and honor my choices.

"Do you really want to do this?" Henry asked. "You don't sound that committed."

"It's not that I'm not interested in mythology," I said, "I had made a commitment to myself to not join or start any more groups until I got some other parts of my life in order, which is what I am presently working towards."

"Then you have to honor the promise you made to yourself," he said.

In the end, it was easier for me to admit that I wasn't ready to commit to another group. Wow! If I could be that clear with everyone, I would end up actually living my sacred contracts without interruptions for the remainder of what I hoped would be at least forty more years of life.

Of course, I had to take into account that my Jungian, therapist friend, Henry, was able to pick up on my reluctance to enter into anything new right now. I appreciated his help in getting me to be honest with him and with myself. I left the meeting knowing there was still a lot to learn after my recent ventures into Spiritual Direction, Healing Touch, and discovery of my purpose in life through my sacred contracts.

Four days later, my husband and I left for a quick weekend to be with my family in Syracuse. We were driving up to attend my Aunt Mary and Uncle Peter Colosi's fiftieth wedding anniversary party. Here would be a true test. After my week's stay up north in June, and now, after my new awareness about myself, I felt emotionally armed for whatever might happen.

What could go awry in the twenty-two-hour round trip car ride with my husband and the short twenty-eight hours in Syracuse? I was sure that I could work with whatever archetypes surfaced.

One summer seventeen years ago, I'd lived with my father's older sister, my Aunt Mary, and her husband, Uncle Peter, in the village of Gualtieri Sicaminò in Sicily, where my father, his parents, sisters, and Uncle Peter were born. Aunt Mary was my godmother, a significant role in my Italian Catholic upbringing.

After not having been back to Sicily in years, Aunt Mary and Uncle Peter had returned to visit their village for the month of August. I had been so excited when they invited me to come and stay with them. I had wanted to live in that village and experience what it was like for my father and his sisters. My aunt and uncle knew that, and I'd jumped at the chance.

Just before finding out about my aunt and uncle's anniversary party, I'd been reminiscing over my trip with them seventeen years earlier and wishing that I could do something in gratitude for everything they had done for me, not only in Sicily that summer but over the years.

Recently my aunt had begun showing signs of dementia, and I knew I had little time left with her and her conscious mind. When I heard about the party, there was no question that I was going to Syracuse for their celebration. Stu wanted to honor them, too.

On Friday afternoon around four, we headed north on I-77 toward Upstate New York. Despite an eleven-hour drive with one hotel stop this time, Stu and I relished the time alone together in the car without a slew of distractions.

Having felt on top of the world after discovering my sacred contracts, there was no way of knowing that life was about to test me further. I naively decided to tell Stu about the Victim archetype in my 8th House of investments and other people's resources.

In fact, I told him that if I could be provided with three things, I would be okay. First, I wanted to be kept informed about what was going on—not just with the money, since I stay pretty attentive to the bookkeeping part of our finances, but also with how the business he was involved in was handling our part of the investment.

Second, I told Stu I'd feel less victimized if I had some kind of say in the business part of the investments. Third, I wanted to be kept informed of changes that his company might be making that would ultimately impact us.

During much of 2002, the stock market was plummeting, losing hundreds of points in a session, falling faster than it took a piece of paper to slip from my desk on to the floor. None of us knew at the time that it would be the beginning of an up and down market.

Being in the middle of it with the rest of the world, I posed one of those *what if* scenarios that writers love and that my practical, down-to-earth husband avoids.

"What would happen," I asked, "if all of our finances dropped so drastically that we weren't able to cover our mortgage anymore?"

Being the positive thinker he's always been, Stu first made a point to say, "I don't believe that would ever happen, but I am willing to humor you here."

Humor me, I thought, before he started rattling off places where we could cut the budget. Since I did the detailed day-to-day accounting, I sat in the navigator seat playing secretary and writing down every place where we spent money. Traveling at seventy miles an hour, we went over specifics: mortgage, utilities, groceries, auto loan, fuel, maintenance, home upkeep—on and on we continued.

Contained in an enclosed space together, neither of us could walk away or dash to the bathroom. Stu rattled and I wrote quickly, throwing in my own input here and there. Soon my husband was in business mode, looking at the bigger picture and cutting through what he expressed were just *details* that I had managed, with great pride, to handle over the years.

My husband is appreciative that someone else takes care of details—but not at a time like this, when he was expounding on the big picture. I was beginning to feel he was minimizing my ability to handle the necessary minutiae. Someone had to.

By the time we reached the juncture of I-77 and I-81, one hour and forty minutes north of our North Carolina home, we were barely speaking. My Child, residing smack dab in the house of marriage and partnerships, was furious with Stu.

We were both comfortably—but irritably—back in our old paradigms. We stopped talking. Stu hates to talk finances or at least talk about them by digging deep, where I naturally go. I felt offended because it didn't feel I had a say, or at least the particular say I wanted to have, around the details of spending.

A heavy silence hung over us until somewhere down the road well after dinner. We attempted to acknowledge that each of us wanted the same thing but approached our way of getting there from a different perspective.

I listened to Stu's wider world outlook, and he tolerated my down-to-the-pennies-of-what-I-paid-for-ice-cream view. By the time we stopped in the hotel, we were back on comfortable speaking terms again.

Be careful, a voice whispered in my ear as I hit the pillow. *You knock on the door of awareness and you're going to get what you asked for.*

Although short, my stay in Syracuse brought up some more survival issues. How nice of the powers that be to accommodate my new-found knowledge. Any longer than twenty-four hours may have done me in. The Saboteur appeared in my mother's kitchen. Mom told me that one of my sibling's dogs could stay there despite my allergies.

"Take a pill," she said.

"You'd rather I take drugs than put that dog in the back yard?"

It was challenging growing up Italian where women kowtowed to others, just as I'd done, in my huge extended family. I guess I learned it from Mom. If I'd known that the dog was coming, I could have made other arrangements.

I know why she didn't tell me. Mom wanted us to stay there with her and Dad, and she wanted to accommodate my sister and her family, too, including the dog.

Choices, I thought. If she'd only told me, then I could have made my own decision about whether to stay at the house or get a hotel room. It's maddening to still be uncovering old wounds well into midlife.

The anniversary celebration was lovely—lots of cousins, my younger aunt and uncle, and lifelong family friends to catch up with. My Aunt Mary was dressed in a beautiful, gold-sequined dress, my uncle in a dapper black and gray tweed suit with a matching blue and gray tie.

Uncle Peter was not leaving my aunt's side: not when they renewed their vows at church, not when they sat together at the restaurant to eat, not when they got up for pictures with each other and with the different people who came to honor them.

At one point, after dessert and coffee, I went and sat at the table with Aunt Mary. I encouraged Uncle Peter to go off and talk to some friends and assured him that I would stay there with her.

I held her hand, while people stopped to say something to my dear aunt. In between, she would look at me and smile her big beautiful loving smile, and squeeze my hand tight as if she never wanted to let go. I continued to talk about one thing or another just to keep the conversation going as I noticed her eyes glazing over and her mind slipping away.

Luckily, a few days after I returned home to Charlotte, I had my monthly appointment with my Spiritual Director. I told Betty about my stay at Well of Mercy, my sacred contracts, and a test around some of my four survival archetypes since my time at Well.

I focused on the Saboteur and my struggle with my mother about the dog situation and my allergies. At the same time, how could I condemn a woman who was already vulnerable, who couldn't say "no" even if she had a mouth full of *N*'s and *O*'s.

Maybe it was me she was comfortable saying "no" to, and I'm glad I could open that door for Mom. But it was also painful to recognize that the Saboteur had always been in my fourth astrological house of home and mother. Sometimes understandings, especially new ones, don't always settle well with my sensitive feelings.

I had choices now. I always had choices, even if I had recently begun to realize it. Not only did I have Betty to help me recognize a more spiritual way of looking at my life and my interactions with others, I also had Sister Brigid for Healing Touch to help clear out any congested energy, and I also had my newly discovered and still forming sacred contracts.

The day after laying all of my new awarenesses and lessons out on the table with Betty, I would be heading back to Well of Mercy for a Healing Touch session with Brigid, where she would shift and clear out old energy that would help me go forward.

Chapter 22
The Energy Continues

Since the retreat center itself was closed for a Sisters of Mercy conference, Brigid and I met at ten in the morning instead of at our usual three in the afternoon. The Peace Room was full of large round tables covered with white cloths, and multi-colored candle holders, yet to be placed, were grouped in the middle of each table. In front of a podium draped with a woven shawl was a small stand with a picture of a woman dressed in a habit.

When I asked who the nun was, Brigid said, "That's our foundress, Catherine McAuley."

Brigid told me a bit about her, including the fact that Catherine was an Irish nun who never really intended on founding a community of religious women. I made a note in my head to look up more information about her.

I didn't think there would be much talking, since Brigid needed to continue preparing for her upcoming conference, and I'd just been with Betty the day before. But over the last few sessions, Brigid and I slipped out of therapy/client mode and into sharing our life experiences as women on a similar path—spiritual seekers and participants of Healing Touch. Brigid the giver, me the receiver.

I sat down in the counseling room and we started chatting about the Sisters of Mercy who would start arriving later that afternoon.

"I'll be a gopher," Brigid said, smiling and scrunching up her nose. "That's the way I like it."

She told me she'd given up being on committees and leading groups and activities as she once did. I understood, since I'd also backed off being on writers' and artists' boards so that I could focus on my own writing and art. I had gone through pangs of guilt for not saying "yes".

But my desire to do creative work was so much greater that sometimes I felt driven, as if backing off had been taken over by a greater spirit screaming for me to be what I came to this earth to be— Writer, Artist, Mystical Seeker, and more. Now, I know my own sacred contracts affirmed that very feeling, along with the results of my Myers-Briggs personality test that Betty had introduced me to.

After Brigid and I chatted about the Sisters of Mercy coming for their conference, she wanted to know about my stay the last time I was at Well. That's when I told her about the chart that I'd casted, and that I'd discovered where I sabotaged myself and where I gave myself away too much.

"Each time I take a right onto Mercy Lane, crest the hill, and overlook this retreat center," I said, "I feel I'm coming home, not only to this place but to myself.

"It's not that I don't run into some of my same issues," I continued. "But I feel more of who I am, who my spirit cries out for me to be."

I continued telling Brigid about a woman I'd met at lunch who was adamant about talking to me the last time I was here.

"It's how my life always goes. I give myself away."

Then I thought of the outside world of friends and associates, of my own hopes and wishes. Stu is forever telling me I'm a great listener, as if it were a compliment, and it is in many ways. But that trait has also pulled me away from myself too often, when I've reached out instead to rescue others.

I wasn't telling Brigid anything she hadn't already heard. In the earlier months of Healing Touch, it was Brigid who encouraged me not to feel obligated to sit at the table during meals, suggesting I take food back to my room.

Her arm went up like that of a cheerleader when I told her that when another Well guest had mentioned she wanted to talk to me during lunch, I took my food outside instead and sat quietly alone by the creek.

"The same woman was standing by the front door, waiting for me when I stepped out of the office after having checked out with Julia," I said.

I talked to the woman briefly, then excused myself, saying that I was late meeting my husband back home. It was no excuse, it was the truth, and Brigid strongly suggested that I practice what it was I needed to learn each time I came up to Well of Mercy.

"If someone is struggling with an issue, Donna and I are here to speak to them. Refer them to one of us."

My responsibility was to take care of myself first, one of my challenges as a woman, second born in a large family, someone who loves people almost to a fault. Oddly enough, we never even talked about whether I had any particular health problem.

Instead, we just seemed to flow from the counseling room into the Healing Touch room, as if Spirit directed our time, or maybe it was a subtle cue by Brigid. Whatever happened, I moved gently from one room to the next, stopping at the door to remove my red sandals.

"I'm entering holy ground," I said.

After taking off my ring, watch, earrings, and necklace and placing them in the replica of the ancient mother goddess symbol, the Venus of Willendorf sculpture, I reached in my pockets and felt my stones.

"I'll keep each right here," I said, and patted my hips.

I told Brigid that I kept the orange-like carnelian in my left pocket, the stone for the sacral area—relationships, sex organs, money. And in my right pocket sat the deep-red agate for my root chakra—family, foundation, genetics.

"I changed both stones two nights ago," I said, "after a friend of mine told me that the right side was for receiving, and, since the market was tumbling, I needed to switch the two."

"When did that happen?" Brigid asked.

"You won't believe it," I said, and Brigid started smiling before I even told her.

I had changed the stone and put the carnelian (for the sacral chakra—related to money) in my right pocket, instead of left, the night before the stock market, which had been tumbling, recovered 500 points.

Brigid smiled at me as if my switch of pockets could have made a difference, and I waved my hand, as if brushing the idea away. It was fun to be playful and not take myself so seriously.

"You never know," she said, and I could see a twinkle emanating from her sparkling Irish eyes, as if affirming something she saw in me. But I didn't know what.

I wish I did have some kind of power so that I could create imaginings that would work in books and art, while the world of stocks and bonds was clearly out of my realm. As I walked into the Healing Touch room, I turned towards Brigid standing there holding a green silk eye pillow.

"What do you think about putting this on?" she asked. "It will block out everything. You know how your mind can whirl around and take in so much."

I had opened my eyes periodically during our previous sessions, even looked at the clock once or twice. But I was willing to go along and wear the eye pillow to distract the busyness of my mind.

I lay down and Brigid placed the small pillow over my eyes. I heard her settle Patches, Well of Mercy's dog, near the door. I thought about my frustration with the dog back at Mom's house in Syracuse.

I told myself Patches was always at a distance, never on top of couches or in the guest rooms. Maybe if I were totally honest, I would admit that what I wanted was for my mother to stand up for me over the dog.

Then everything got quiet, including what was going on in my head. I started to breathe and release whatever I was hanging onto. Brigid must have finished checking my chakras when she spoke quietly.

"You won't believe how wide open all of your chakras are," she said.

Great, I thought, and yet wondered what was next. I surprised myself when I said, "We aren't done though, are we?"

"No," she said, "I'm going to do a Chakra Spread on you."

I had no idea what that meant, and it didn't matter as long as I received some kind of energy work.

I lay still breathing while Brigid moved to the top of my head, placed her hands on my shoulders. It felt like white angel wings covering my face, my brain, my thoughts.

She prayed aloud asking for my "highest and best good." Her words felt warm and comforting. She moved around to the right side, rested her hand on my stomach.

My stomach, solar plexus. Mom. I love my mother want her

to love herself or is it I want to love myself?

Brigid switches her hands to my heart, rests them in the middle

of my breastbone.

My heart, wide open. I am safe on this holy ground.

Unaware of Brigid's actions, I try not to think.

Although thoughts creep in: my drive to Well; conversations with others;

Betty my Spiritual Director; my brother's words: "You do know you cause tension

when you're around;" A younger sister: "We didn't spend enough time together."

Words I wanted to share with Sister Brigid but forgot.

I forgot what they were. New thoughts come to mind. Leave, Leave, Leave

thoughts. Leave me alone. Let me be.

"All that is God, my heart is open to you, come live in my heart."

Even this mantra has too many words.

"God

> *God*

>> *God"*

No Words.

Silence.

Someone, is it Brigid fumbling at the door just beyond my feet.

Sense her returning.

Air brushes above me. I must have dozed. Blanked out.

I'm in the Healing Touch room.

The door opens, but Brigid is still by my side. Patches shuffles in.

How did the dog open the door? I smile.

No thoughts.

Fear. I am alone, totally.

No one is here.

Fear. I've been totally alone before. I don't know how long it lasts.

I try not to get anxious, too anxious.

Then I hear, "You are never alone, really"

Is that an angel whispering? God energy? A test?

I feel Brigid's presence again. She had never left

What part of my body has she been working on?

Like a slide presentation, quick thoughts skip through my head:

The basement of a church in Norwich, New York. The town
we visited when I was a child. A bridal shower with my mother, my aunts,
the other Nonna—

Dad's mother, his sisters: Aunt Mary, Aunt Sarah
and Italian paesani: the women we visited from Dad's Sicilian village
fly in and out quickly.

Other brief moments: Dad looks at me. Mom sits at the edge
of her kitchen table

Thoughts flash by and Brigid takes my right hand in hers, gently shakes it.
I feel energy moving through, and when she takes my hand like that, I know
the session is coming to a close.

I hate that it's ending.

I like the energy that flows through her hand into mine and back again.
Before she walks quietly over to my left side,

Brigid repeats the action, rests her hands another time
on my ovaries, then uterus. I am grateful.

She walks down toward my feet, brushes the bottom of my legs from knees to feet. I am grounded, in place, called into the body where I reside.

"Take your time," Brigid whispered in my ear, as she always did when the session was over. Then she left.

I could have stayed in the room as long as I wanted, but I had to use the bathroom, although I didn't realize that human need the whole time I'd been lying on the massage table. I waited a few minutes, took the green silk pillow off my eyes, pushed my body up, swung my legs over the side of the table.

I was staring directly into the heart quilt. I counted the nine colorful hearts inside the grid designed for that number. I stood up, placed the silk eye pillow on top of the regular pillow on which my head had been resting for close to an hour, put my jewelry back on.

Brigid was waiting for me in her counseling room. I walked in, and even though she didn't say a word, I could see light in her eyes and in her face. She waited for a response.

"It felt so holy in there," I said.

"Yes," she responded, without acting at all surprised. But within seconds she asked, "Were you able to see what I was doing?"

"You know I had the pillow over my eyes. I couldn't see a thing."

Then she began to motion with her arms, explaining to me that it was a technique she'd used with me today as she moved her arms in, out, and around like a butterfly in motion.

"You just walked in here making those same movements with your arms," Brigid said, demonstrating once again how I'd moved my body. "It was the technique I'd been using on you."

I hadn't been aware of making any motion. I'd just come off the trance of being in wonderful healing energy, and I felt I was flying on top of the world. I suppose anything was possible. Brigid and I both chuckled a bit, or were they nervous laughs?

"There was no way I could see through that pillow," I said.

"I was performing what I had mentioned, a Chakra Spread. It's a holy technique, a holy gift."

I felt honored, blest really with the gift, and with now knowing the special spiritual quality of this Healing Touch session. Brigid went on to explain and demonstrate how she'd proceeded.

"Starting with your head, I positioned my hands above your crown chakra and then stretched out slowly until my hands and arms were wide open past your body on either side and then moved out into your energy field. I continued through all seven chakras from your head to your feet. Once I got through one set, I repeated the entire process two more times, having swept over each chakra three times altogether."

I told Brigid the little I could remember from being on the table. I described the sense of old memories, some seemingly insignificant, that had come and then swept away: attending a bridal shower in the basement church in Norwich with my aunts, grandmother, and mother; Mom sitting at the edge of her kitchen table; a quick glimpse of Dad looking at me.

Brigid listened to my memories and continued about my hand motions when I'd entered her counseling room. "You used the exact technique I was using," she said again, "a sweeping motion."

I wondered how that could happen, repeating her same motions. I was just as amazed as Brigid seemed to be. There were multiple things that I'd felt when I was on the table today.

"I went through a sense of being totally alone at one point," I said,

I could tell she felt bad when she said, "I never left you."

"I eventually knew you were there," I said. "It's one of my issues."

That feeling had always been there—a fear I've had over the years that I'd be left alone, totally alone one day. Sometimes I've wondered if that came through my mother's genetic line from my maternal grandmother, whose mother died when she was five years old. Since my grandmother, *Nonna* Egidia, had such a big influence on my life, that feeling she may have had made sense to me.

Nonna, the one I was named after, was the one I also took after at times when I was growing up, including her fear of being left. *Nonna* hung tightly onto anyone she loved always afraid we'd put someone else before her, although no female in the family would ever take her place.

Brigid questioned whether it was the time Patches came back in the room, but I knew it was some time after that. Eventually I assured her it was something I had gone through often.

"But you got yourself out of it in there, didn't you?" Brigid assured. And I had.

She mentioned that Donna had come by and opened the door slightly to let Patches back in the room.

"I wondered how Patches was able to open the door," I said, and we both chuckled.

Brigid handed me the customary tall glass of water to drink and ground me. We chatted a little longer about our Myers-Briggs types. I asked her what she thought INFPs did for a living.

I was surprised when she said, "What you do!"

"Artist and writer?" I said, as I continued to think about it all.

Then we chatted some more about our own spiritual advisors. I mentioned to Brigid that Betty reminded me all the time, and had just done so the day before, what her grandmother always told her. It was the Shakespeare quote from *Hamlet*, "This above all: to thine own self be true, And it must follow, as the night the day, Thou canst not then be false to any man."

Between Spiritual Direction, Healing Touch, and uncovering my own sacred contracts, I was now on a different path.

"You could do this work," Brigid said. "You could do Healing Touch."

I was taken by surprise, because I loved Healing Touch so much and had been drawn to receiving it here at Well of Mercy every two weeks or whenever Brigid and I arranged a session.

"I can't help but think of my grandfather, *Nonno* Stagnitta, and that he did his own form of energy work on me when I was growing up," I said. "Then there is my sister Nicki's ability with Therapeutic Touch."

"You can heal, too," Brigid repeated. "You were doing the techniques when you got off the table, even if you didn't do them consciously."

This all came on me suddenly, but not so suddenly, over these last number of months. After all, Brigid and I talked about the Level 1 class that I knew I wanted to take.

"I've wondered how I could take a class since I'm not a nurse," I said.

"I'm not either," Brigid said. "You don't have to be a nurse to do Healing Touch."

"One class won't hurt," Brigid said. "If nothing else, it will give you some basics of what I've been doing these past number of months with you."

And in my head, I'd already been thinking, *what could it hurt*.

Before leaving, I mentioned my upcoming trip to the beach with my family. I asked for her prayers. I love my family, and I also know that I can fall into old stuff when I'm with them.

It would be three weeks instead of two before I would return to Well of Mercy for Healing Touch again. Brigid assured me my chakras were open and balanced, and that she had seen I'd made a huge transition in my spiritual growth. I felt it inside and was pleased that Brigid, a person on her own spiritual journey, could see it too.

Truth be told, I had already decided to look further into the Level 1 Healing Touch class. Before leaving for the Jersey Shore, I had decided to register for it. What did I have to lose?

For now, I was well prepared to go back out into the world again.

Chapter 23

Feast of the Assumption: August 15, 2002

Everyone in my family except my older sister, Nicki, her husband, and one of their daughters was able to make it to the Jersey Shore, which put the number of us gathering at around thirty-three—not including boyfriends, girlfriends, and any other friends that popped in.

Nicki's husband had recently been diagnosed with non-Hodgkin's Lymphoma and started chemotherapy the Monday we were at the beach. Nicki's teenage son Tom drove to the beach with my sister Fran to be with us, and Nicki's eldest daughter, Andrea, stopped by with her boyfriend at the end of the week.

I was determined this time to mind my own business and stand outside myself if any comments were made that would hurt my feelings. I wanted the time with my family to be both a vacation and an opportunity to live out my sacred contracts, which I'd been diligently working on.

Having learned that my Teacher/Mentor Archetype dwelled in the 3rd astrological House of writing, communication, brothers and sisters, I had learned that students may not always been receptive to what I had to say. And being a mentor of sorts to my siblings, put us in the same position sometimes.

Besides, my siblings were adults now. I no longer had to teach them anything. They were on their own paths. If something I said while being myself inadvertently became a lesson for them, it was a mirror for me, too, because I learned a long time ago that whatever I teach, I also learn.

Before leaving for my week-long trip at the Jersey Shore, I jokingly said to a friend that I was going up for an end of year exam, and if I could get a B+ I'd be happy. The week turned out well. I may have even come back with an A-. Not a straight A or an A+. It's not that everything was perfect.

There were a few glitches—someone made a snide comment about one of my metaphysical interests, and I was hurt by some of my father's abrupt remarks about Stu having to put up with me. But I worked through them by walking them out, writing in my journal, even eliciting Stu's sympathy, which he willingly provided.

I have always been sensitive. It was a given. I'd been this way all my life, and my family has always known it, especially my parents. The story about me dropping my doll and crying because I was sure she was hurt had been repeated over and over again throughout my life to remind everyone of my feeling nature.

At the same time, there were tales about each of my seven siblings, too, pointing out their own particular characteristics—positive and … not so positive.

When all was said and done, I found myself plunking down a $100 deposit to join my tribe again next year. Over the course of the week, we'd had many more good times than bad. In addition to enjoying the beach, the boardwalk, and an afternoon drive into Atlantic City with my parents and two of my nephews, Stu and I took the extended family out to celebrate our twenty-fifth wedding anniversary.

That night there were thirty-two of us—my mother, father, six of my seven siblings and their spouses, plus sixteen of my eighteen nieces and nephews—who joined us at a restaurant with a private room that Stu and I had found.

The owners had been more than willing to set up one long table. We sat positioned as we did growing up in my parent's home—Dad at the head, Mom at his left. Since I was second in line, and my older sister wasn't able to be there, I moved up and sat to the right of Dad. Stu sat next to me. The rest of my large extended family positioned themselves along the table across from one another according to age.

They lavished us with unexpected flowers and presents, and their own presence brought tears as we read their cards full of love and affection and lots of humor for both Stu and me.

Even though I enjoyed the time with family, and it was quite rewarding, I was happy to get back to my own home. I was also looking forward to the Level I Healing Touch class being offered the following weekend. While I knew I would enjoy receiving energy work, I felt no sense of urgency.

Well, that was true until our mail, being held at the post office, showed up late in the afternoon the day after we arrived home, and I opened our previous month's financial report. The statement was for July 2002, the month the market took its final downward plunge during the tense financial times of post 9/11. Our investments, up until that point, had been faring well through the economic crisis of the year.

It's not that we'd lost everything or even fifty percent of everything like a number of people I knew did. But fifteen percent of our worth was now gone. My Victim archetype in the house of long-term financing was surfacing.

Fifteen percent was a lot for someone like me who had always believed more strongly in my ancestors' tradition of stashing cash away in a coffee can in the back of a closet or buried in the backyard, than in trusting a financial system. Of course, that had never happened in my house, living, as I do, with an adventurous, risk-taking mate, born and bred as a true American patriot.

Not even an abundance of beets, cherries, tomatoes, oranges, carrots, or even the gemstones that I carried in my pockets to protect my first and second chakras, were holding my fear at bay. First chakra, the root—survival, material security, and other primal affairs. The second chakra included financial concerns.

Darn! I'd done so well at the Jersey shore with my family, and now I was falling apart right here in my own home, for that matter in my own root and sacral chakras. Now I was more than ready for a Healing Touch session with Brigid this upcoming Thursday, the day before the Level I class began.

Fortunately for me, and maybe Brigid—and certainly for Stu—I spoke to Walter, our financial advisor, for over an hour on Wednesday, the day before I drove to Well of Mercy. He attempted to allay my fears as he helped soothe my terror, not just with words, but also with facts that indicated it was close to impossible for any one person in the market to not have been affected somehow or other.

We found common ground, and instead of going off to find a job in the corporate world or planning to head back full-time into the classroom, I went back to my studio and worked on an angel drawing that I was commissioned to do. I also spent time working on that memoir I'd started back in late fall—about my trip to Italy and Sicily with Stu and my parents.

By the time Thursday came, I was so happy that I'd be seeing Brigid I called her while driving up I-77 to let her know I was on my way. I arrived right at three. Hearing Brigid's voice on the phone had already put me in Healing Touch mode. Seeing her also subdued my uncertainties from the preceding days.

It felt like forever since I'd seen Brigid, but it had only been three weeks. And Brigid herself said, as I entered, how much time seemed to have passed and how much had gone on. In spite of my earlier anxiety about talking too much before Healing Touch, something had shifted, and I was comfortable spending time chatting. I told her about my concern with the economy and that maybe I should go back to work full time.

"Don't you remember what I said last time?" Brigid asked. "We need people like you out there in the world."

I'd half remembered her comments from last time, but it didn't stick until this moment. Brigid had been talking about my creative work and way of being through art and writing, about my love for energy when receiving Healing Touch, about how I operate in the world in a different way, a more introverted, intuitive way. It was so easy to forget when the world around me is about extroversion, sensing, thinking, judging—the same Myers-Briggs characteristics I'd learned in Spiritual Direction from Betty.

After having spent all those months on reading about archetypes that led to my sacred contracts, of course I knew my purpose in life. I just forgot—Artist, Writer, Teacher—and now what about this Mystical Seeker? But will this purpose I've discovered put food on the table or investments in the bank for our old age?

"Don't do anything drastic," Brigid said, "until you get through this weekend in the Healing Touch Level 1 class. You know what this is about, don't you?"

I believed I did. It was about faith in myself and in my husband, who functions well in the outside business world. But most of all it was about faith in something greater than myself, a higher power, a Divine source no matter what that source is called.

"Brigid," I said, "I was so mad at God the other day, I screamed at him."

Her round Irish face lit up, as did her eyes, which looked rather inquisitive. "You did?"

"Yes, I did, and I'm not one bit sorry. How dare he send me down this path and then pull the rug out from beneath me. At least that's how I felt the other day when I received our financial statement."

Brigid couldn't help but smile, and it made me smirk, too. "Gilda," she said, "It was yourself you were talking to, you know."

I suppose I did by now—or should have. With Brigid's response, my rational thinking returned. I told Brigid that God had broad shoulders and could handle it anyway.

"That's true," Brigid said, in a quiet and serious tone. "It's important that you follow your path and not get pulled in by the outside world."

Brigid had a sober look on her face, her eyes wide and attentive, her mouth in a solemn horizontal line that made me pay close attention. In fact, her words were the same another friend of mine had used two days earlier when I told her I thought I should go back to work in a regular job.

My friend, Susan, a therapist by profession, as well as a coach and a writer, insisted I look back at my sacred contracts and follow that plan instead. The fact that the same message came out of both of them was not that unusual given they were in the same line of work. Sometimes it's not knowing or even remembering the exact words someone says, as much as the feeling that comes through, an intuitive sense that radiates from the person.

I swore that Brigid and Susan had used the *exact* same words. The words were so particular that I wondered how two people who didn't know each other could say the same thing to me. Or was it even Brigid and Susan talking?

Whatever energy forces were there, I heard loud and clear where I needed to be in my life, and I hoped beyond hope that I was strong enough for this creative, but not so common, path I was choosing.

Brigid and I started talking about a lot of things, including the government's threat of going into Iraq--both of us strongly against war. We talked about the state of the economy, the underprivileged here in the United States and worldwide.

We even chatted a bit about Catherine McCauley, the foundress of the Sisters of Mercy. I had actually done a bit of research on her after that day Brigid was preparing to host a conference for her fellow Sisters who lived at the Mother House an hour and a half away. Brigid and I agreed on how important it was to hold fast to one of Catherine McCauley's quotes, "Let us take one day only in hands at a time. Resolve to do good today and better tomorrow."

Life experiences would come and go and come and go. To hear what Catherine McCauley encouraged her sisters to do with their good work, despite the world's outside forces, reinvigorated my way of seeing.

The first anniversary of 9/11 was soon approaching, and Brigid told me that there would be a morning of prayer, meditation, and reflection that day at Well of Mercy. I'd planned on staying home and being quiet. It was nice to know that I had the option to be with like-minded people. Also knowing there were others operating in the spiritual realm, whether I was there or quietly at home, gave me a sense of peace.

How grateful I felt to have worked through whatever mental meanderings went around my head about Brigid early on in the Healing Touch process. They were my own internal struggles, and she had the compassion and caring to support and help me through my wrangling.

That is what's so wonderful about working with and knowing people like Brigid and Betty, my friend Susan, and many others of like minds. We travel the same roads, recognize the same language, remind each other of different ways of being in the world.

Perhaps that was why I would learn, during my session, that my chakras were all open, despite my recent financial worries. I was somewhat surprised when Brigid would lean over and whisper her evaluation. I'd come back from the shore with a few aches and pains from my trip, mostly around my groin on the left side. I had assumed they were simply pulled muscles from playing *Capture the Flag* with family at the beach. But I also hoped it was not in any way related to the ovary that I had on watch until my next Ob/Gyn appointment in October.

Brigid had begun my session the way she always did with the words, "Mother, Father, God, I call in all angels and guides, Gilda's and mine, as I ask for Gilda's highest and best good."

I don't know what I'd expected during this particular healing session, but what happened had not happened in a long time. First my head was busy, the way it gets about all kinds of things when a thought refuses to let go. Then I went into a place of nothingness.

No thinking at all

I knew Brigid was busy working. Other than that, I was in a total place of

Silence.

A few minutes before Brigid asked me to turn over so she could work on my back, I did come out of that *no thinking* place and was present in the room. Then when I flipped back over and lay on my back again, Brigid put her hands on my left ovary and under that part of my back. She asked if I felt anything, and, at first, I only felt a slight airiness around that spot. Then something changed.

a feeling

Although I rarely talked during my sessions, today I said, "There is a release of some kind of tension."

that was it

I was in the void ….

Afterwards, Brigid told me that seconds before I mentioned that sense of release, she felt something pulling up and out of her hand. We smiled. We've become accustomed to and accepting of the process and each other. Brigid told me that she started with the Chakra Spread, a holy technique she had used on me before. After floating both hands above the crown chakra, she spread them out slowly three times into open space before repeating the movement over each chakra.

"You'll learn it this weekend," she said, referring to my upcoming Level 1 Healing Touch class.

Brigid was also excited about having gone through two sessions where my chakras were wide open even before she'd started doing any Healing Touch on me. It surprised me, given I'd come in churning about my hang-ups on money. I'd expected that the second chakra, and even the first, would be closed down. But Brigid said that, even with chakras open, old issues can still surface.

"You can self-heal around these beliefs," she said. "Self-heal around these concerns. You can do it."

"I can do that," I said, so emphatically even I was surprised at the words flowing from my mouth.

"I would be honored for you to bring this pink heart with you this weekend," Brigid said, as she held her hands out to me.

Brigid handed me her pink crystal heart for the Healing Touch class. She was excited about me attending Level 1, and I was excited to be taking Brigid's pink stone heart along. It would be a wonderful experience to learn more about what Brigid had been doing over many months.

There was a lot to learn about energy and how it works—information that Brigid had already been using on me. As we walked outside together, dark rich clouds started swelling with rain clouds finally arriving in this dry mid-August. We were both happy to see the dark billows building. The land needed water desperately. Mid-August, time of harvest, yielding of crops.

The next day, I realized the day before had been August 15, the Feast Day of the Assumption of Mary into heaven. It had come and gone, and I hadn't even thought of it until talking with my friend, Elizabeth, a fellow writer and spiritual seeker with whom I would be taking the Healing Touch Level 1 class.

How did I ever let such a meaningful day slip my mind? Mary is the Mother archetype I continued to hang onto from my family's Catholic tradition, the same Mary I had always wanted to visit first when my grandmother brought my sister Nicki, my brother Anthony, and me when we were children over to the church and walk us around to all of the statues housed in their own niche.

Part of me was shocked to realize that I had been in the middle of a Healing Touch session on one of Mary's feast days. Chills ran up and down my spine. Another part of me was disappointed that I would have forgotten such a Holy Day—for me.

My most memorable celebration of the Feast of the Assumption of Mary into heaven was when I was in Italy with Aunt Mary and Uncle Peter, August 15, 1985. I'd journaled about the Assumption church, *Assumpto*, in my father's Sicilian village of Gualtieri Sicaminò, and eventually included my experience in my first memoir.

> The building, which was closed for renovation, was reopened on that day for a short time after the traditional midday meal.
>
> A group of women from one of the church societies invited Aunt Mary and me to join them and pray the rosary. Inside, the church was unkempt. Cobwebs hung between posts, around the altar and from the pitched roof. Most pews were dusty, except for a few, where a handful of people knelt around the statue of the Blessed Virgin Mary.[10]

I didn't care that the church or the pews or any of it was dusty and old. I was thrilled to be kneeling there with my aunt, honoring an archetypal female that had and *always* had great significance for me.

I could never have imagined that one day I would be experiencing something mystical with a woman of the church, Sister Brigid, on the same feast day that I had celebrated the feminine with Aunt Mary, my dear godmother, seventeen years earlier.

---

[10] Syverson, Gilda Morina, *My Father's Daughter, From Rome to Sicily.* New York: Divine Phoenix and Pegasus Books,2014

Chapter 24
Level 1

Cicadas' high-pitch hum in Jetton Park sounded louder than I ever remembered this early Monday morning. In fact, I didn't recall them buzzing at all before now. Just the week earlier I had been walking around thinking about more than my brain ever wanted to hold.

This particular August morning was different. The pulsating cicadas and chirping birds hidden between and amongst the trees made themselves known, and I was aware of the Divine's living, breathing beings around me.

After having taken the Healing Touch class this past weekend, I was glad I'd listened to Brigid when she recommended that I try it. Before taking Level 1, I had actually spoken to the instructor, Joanne, a medical nurse, and was surprised to learn that she had been born and raised in Upstate New York, in Utica.

My hometown of Syracuse was less than a forty-five-minute drive from Utica on the Thruway. We hugged when I first walked through the doors of the classroom, as if we had a connection in addition to our foundational geography.

There were eight other women in the class and one of them was Joanne's assistant. It was established early on that what we shared and talked about with each other for two days—eighteen hours altogether—was confidential.

The material itself was published and available in the Healing Touch textbook. What was personal were the stories and lives that each person brought to the experience.

Our initial gathering began in a circle—round, female, no beginning, no end. That setting felt comfortable. It just so happened that only women registered for this particular session. Joanne was a gentle, kind, calm instructor for our small intimate group.

She was so knowledgeable about the body's energy system with its fields, auras, and chakras and how they worked through and around our bodies, between and among each other. The more Joanne talked, the more intrigued I became with the whole process.

When we actually began practicing the first technique, Therapeutic Touch, I couldn't help but think of my sister Nicki, only thirteen months older than me. She's the nurse, the one who took Therapeutic Touch courses more than fourteen years earlier.

I would come to discover that Nicki had actually taken a workshop with one of the pioneers, Dolores Krieger, who wrote the leading book, *The Therapeutic Touch: How to Use Your Hands to Help or to Heal*, published back in 1979.

The first time I experienced Therapeutic Touch was when Nicki and I went to the Medjugorje Conference in Worcester, Massachusetts in the early 1990s. It was when I had pulled into the parking lot and inadvertently twisted my head and ended up with a painful stiff neck. That's when Nicki laid her hands on the injured spot, and I felt heat pouring into my neck. Within minutes the ache had disappeared.

There were times, when I was with my sister, that I would be aware of her gently quieting herself and begin to move her hands, brushing energy around a hurt child's knee, an adult's headache, a cut, a sore, an open wound.

Most notably for me, Nicki performed Therapeutic Touch on our father soon after he arrived home to begin recovery from his 1998 heart operation. Dad's healing had taken place with little pain medication. He often asked Nicki for Therapeutic Touch instead.

Eventually, Nicki needed to leave Syracuse before I did and return to her husband and three children at their home outside of Boston. A few nights after she left, when I told her on the phone that Dad was showing signs of discomfort, Nicki encouraged me to continue Therapeutic Touch on him.

"You can do this," she said, and even though I had no idea of how at the time, a part of me knew she was right.

But when I asked my father if he would like me to give him Therapeutic Touch, he was not as comfortable with me giving him energy. "Only your sister knows what to do."

I understood his reluctance to accept a procedure from his daughter who was an artist, writer, and educator versus the one who was a medical nurse. Plus, my father came from a school of thought he had learned from his own father—everyone had his or her place in the family.

For Dad, Nicki was the medical person that he felt comfortable talking with about health concerns. And although my sister was the one who had encouraged me to do energy work on our father, challenging Dad's way of thinking during recovery was not the right time. So, I stepped back.

Having learned early on in Level 1 that someone had to give their permission for another person to work on them, I was glad that I had not pushed myself on Dad while he was recovering. My time had not yet come.

But the minute I started practicing one of the techniques during my first Healing Touch class, I felt energy in my hands and it continued—hot, cold, static, even pulsating vibrations—when laying my hands above someone's head, temple, heart, solar plexus (stomach), and other parts of the body. Just as my sister had assured me, my ability had always been there.

The more techniques and tools we tried over the weekend, the more I felt drawn to the process. I even recognized some of the procedures that Brigid had been performing on me over the last six months.

While in the class, I saw glimpses of swirling colors, like an azure blue to the left of a person's head, then to the right. I'd seen colors trying to break through space before, mostly when caught off guard, not thinking or focusing on anything in particular. I'd heard this phenomenon referred to as the "lifting of the veil." It even happened over the last ten years when I'd been drawing angels and their auras.

The discussion of the process and the explanation of the energy fields that my Level 1 instructor, Joanne, had talked about made more and more sense, especially in relation to what Brigid and I had been working on over many months.

Besides learning and using the technique of hands on or over the body, among other practices, I had been taught some of the same material about energy years before when studying with a metaphysical astrologer in the North Carolina mountains. It was captivating to see information about energy, which I had experienced from the astrologer, now being presented in the Level 1 class in a scientific way. As the weekend continued, my enthusiasm increased.

Of course, I could not help but think of my grandfather, *Nonno* Stagnitta, and the various movements he made when trying to heal me or one of my siblings, cousins, or others who came to see him for healing. How I wish *Nonno* were still alive so I could ask him how he learned the art of healing without having gone to classes or workshops or school.

The Level 1 weekend moved us into the Energy Centers—the Chakra System, where we would learn and practice two different chakra connections and a headache technique, Mind Clearing (something that Brigid had done on me often), along with a few other Healing Touch sequences.

When our instructor taught us how to assess the chakras, I thought of Sister Brigid and all the times she assessed my chakras. I felt in my pocket for the beautiful, glass pink heart that Brigid had sent with me to my first ever Healing Touch class. It brought her peaceful and loving energy into the room.

One of the last procedures that Joanne wanted us to perform on each other in class was the final clincher for me. I recognized the technique as one that Brigid had used on me at least twice that I knew of, and that she had told me was a sacred technique.

It was the Chakra Spread, where the practitioner would place his or her hands above the crown of the head, the seventh chakra, then slowly stretch hands and arms over the head and out into the open space of the energy field. I would repeat the entire process from head to toe. When I finished the entire body, I would return to the head and repeat the process again two more times until three full sets were completed.

My friend in the class, Elizabeth, performed the Chakra Spread on me. After finishing, we were all directed to go into a quiet space together and share what we had both experienced—first with me as the receiver, then with Elizabeth as the giver.

I talked about being in an altered state as I often was in Healing Touch—calm, relaxed, a feeling of warmth surrounding me. Elizabeth told me she couldn't help but think of T.S. Eliot's poem "The Four Quartets." *At the still point of the turning world … there the dance is.*

My friend shared that in performing this particular Healing Touch technique, it felt like a dance to her—a dance where she envisioned herself throwing white gardenias and rose petals across my body.

"What a beautiful image," I said, and felt such loving kindness in the description of her experience.

Then it was my turn to perform the Chakra Spread on Elizabeth. She got onto the massage table, and I covered her eyes with a piece of tissue and then laid a small, red satin eye pillow that I'd brought—a gift given to me by my sister Nicki.

When I held my hands over Elizabeth's head and stretched them out, I felt her energy extending way beyond where my arms and hands could reach. The more I stretched out to the perimeters of Elizabeth's energy, the more I felt my arms and legs trying to expand beyond the edges of her energy field.

I don't believe I ever reached her edge. It was truly the dance Elizabeth described when she had done the Chakra Spread on me.

At the end, when everyone regrouped in a circle, one of the women looked over at me and said, "You looked like a ballerina performing the Chakra Spread."

My heart leaped. "Thank you," I said, "I always wanted to be a ballerina growing up," and in that spiritual experience of giving, I became the dancer I had once wanted to be.

Everyone was smiling, and then we laughed together. I was delighted to have received the support for the part of my soul that had yearned for years to be expressed through my body.

Before we all departed, I asked our instructor about how it is that others, like artists and writers, have come to work with Healing Touch. After all, Healing Touch came through the nursing tradition.

Joanne's response was encouraging. "All kinds of people are being drawn to energy work now," she said. "Not just nurses. We have had every profession represented in these classes." Then Joanne said something that felt significant. "Don't brush away the colors that appear to you."

I'm not sure how she knew, but by this point of the class, anything seemed possible. "I was always afraid they were the beginnings of a migraine," I said. "Migraines that I used to have years ago."

"Did the colors ever turn into a migraine?" Joanne asked.

I thought about it for a few seconds. "No," I answered, rather surprised, and Joanne reaffirmed that it was important that I keep my mind open to new possibilities.

That same mind started whirling with thoughts and colors and forms. I thought of the angel images I'd drawn and wondered how they would develop from here.

That night at home, I fell into a deep sleep. My husband said I was so sound asleep that nothing could have jarred me.

The next morning, Monday, my walk in the park brought new awareness that had probably always existed. But I had been too caught up in my busy mind to notice. Birds, cicadas, and all of nature sang as I walked.

To my delight, my sister Nicki called that evening. We talked for over an hour about Therapeutic Touch, Healing Touch, and energy healing.

Tuesday was a full day packed with hours of studio work, a trip to the photographer and the gallery where my angels were sold, appointments, and then a writers' meeting that would not get me home until close to 10 p.m.

Yet I knew that before I started all this, I had to walk the park. I had to listen and hear if those cicadas and birds that I heard the day before were really there or a part of my imagination.

I arrived at Jetton Park on Tuesday at almost the same time as I had arrived on Monday morning. When I stepped out of the car, I saw a rapid flash of blue light and noted it briefly, as Joanne had encouraged me to do over the weekend. Then I walked around the park, taking the path off to the left instead of my normal right direction.

I heard an array of birds chirping, saw a few people I didn't know personally, but with whom I'd shared the walking path many other times. Some smiled, some nodded. Some walkers—including myself— were quiet. It felt contemplative, and I kept my eyes on the ground this particular day, honoring my own time and space.

After getting through the first section of the woods, I crossed the road and headed to an area of tall pines and into what looked like its own small forest of deep verdant greens beneath the trees. The scene reminded me of *The Wizard of Oz* terrain, where Dorothy discovered the cowardly lion.

I loved walking past that area and being in a natural setting different than the busyness of the world of malls, grocery stores, crowded parking lots. I was alone on that section that turned slightly like an elbowed path. This time there were no other walkers around.

Birds still chirped and finally, from the distant left, calls of cicadas started coming closer and closer toward me. A few yards down, interspersed with the singing of the birds, the cicadas' buzzing sound clicked from the right.

I must have lost track of time walking down the path for a while without running into anyone. That's when a thought about Jesus came. I was surprised my head went to Jesus, of all beings, knowing that my mind is usually directed toward female archetypes such as Mary or one of the female mystics—Catherine of Siena, Hildegard of Bingen, Teresa of Avila.

Is that what people had seen when they saw Jesus walking around? A light energy radiating from his body?

I felt I was walking on air, wondering if our auras could be seen by other people, like those who must have seen Christ's energy field. I remember being taught years ago that he'd said, "You too could do this." Whew! That came out of the past.

Other walkers now started coming my way, and I felt my whole being returning to Earth. Again, there were smiles and nods. Three-quarters of the way around, in between the buzzing of the cicadas, I heard in the distance a crow cawing from the right. I would definitely look up Crow in my animal medicine book when I got home.

I turned a corner and walked up the final hill. A red flicker, like a piece of glass, flashed in front of my eyes. I wished I had one of the books that Joanne had showed us over the weekend. It had pictures of colored auras laid out in the energy field.

Just before reaching the end of the path, I was startled when something rock-like fell from a tree above me that missed hitting my head by inches. I jumped back, then stopped and picked up what had fallen. The outer covering of a nut, chewed open, the meat gone. I looked up for the squirrel that let it go.

The critter was nowhere to be seen, but the nut startled me back into reality and grounded me before I stepped into my car to return home and get on with my busy day. But not before pulling out my medicine card book. There were a number of creatures I could have looked up: squirrels, birds, cicadas. But the one I was most intrigued with now was the crow.

If Crow medicine appears ... you must pause and reflect on how you see the laws of the Great Spirit in relation to the laws of humanity. Crow medicine signifies a firsthand knowledge of a higher order of right and wrong than that indicated by the laws created in human culture.[11]

---

[11] Sams, Jamie, & Carson, David, *Medicine Cards, The Discovery of Power Through the Ways of Animals*, Revised, Expanded Edition, New York: St. Martin's Press, 1999.

Chapter 25
The Week After

I couldn't wait to see Brigid and tell her how excited I was about Healing Touch and that I loved giving energy as much as receiving it. Even though I knew Well of Mercy was closed and Brigid would be away on vacation for a few weeks, I left a message on the answering machine.

"Brigid, I was thrilled about Level 1, and I look forward to telling you more."

Brigid must have picked up her messages because she sent me a quick email saying how happy she was for me. I wanted to communicate in any way I could with her or anyone who understood how I was feeling about the Healing Touch process.

The Wednesday after my Level 1 class, I met with my Spiritual Director. I could not stop talking to Betty about my experience giving energy. I told her all about the Chakra Spread I'd shared with my friend Elizabeth, and how it felt that working with energy had been a part of me all along.

"I don't think I'd ever be a practitioner," I said. "It feels instead like something I could incorporate in my art and writing."

How that would happen was yet to be seen, but I had the rest of my life to discover it. The material presented didn't seem all that foreign. In fact, I have always sensed there were other subtle forces around that I could not reach out and physically touch.

Since I could not produce material proof, I'd been accused most of my life of being a dreamer. Now that felt like a compliment, since dreams have given me clear and conscious messages most of my life.

In a graduate painting course I'd taken one summer thirty years ago while living in Boston and teaching high school art, I was corrected by the instructor for painting swirls of light around the figure I'd drawn on the canvas. A live model had been positioned on a wide platform for students to draw from. I'd laid out the drawing of the figure on the canvas as I'd learned to do years earlier in my undergraduate painting classes.

Then I began brushing light-turpentine washes of the model's beige-tone skin color in the drawing and swirls of color around the form. It appeared almost Chagall-like in mood—floating, dream-like, imaginary, unreal. I loved the feel of wistful shapes I created in the background. No longer being in a bachelor's degree program in which I had to produce for "credit," I was ready to blaze my own trail and paint what I sensed or felt. After all, isn't that what creativity is about?

Then the instructor walked by my easel. "No, no," he said in a fatherly manner, "you don't want to paint that way." He took the brush out of my hand. "These swirls of color don't exist around a person. Can you see them?" he asked, not really waiting for an answer. "Try this."

He started to lay in patterns of color that didn't exist around the model in front of us either. Well, they were similar to the patterns on the cloth the model was laying on, but he exaggerated the circles and triangles until the background in my painting looked more like the patterned background in his paintings.

My swirls of colors were squelched, as if they'd never existed. Being an unsure and not overly confident twenty-something-year-old, I surrendered to the instructor's style that summer in Boston and other styles that he and art critics had said were more appropriate for what must have obviously been their own sensibilities

Before I knew it, I was on someone else's path, highly educated in the art of creating according to what was expected. But that never really took off either. How could it? I was attempting to see something from another person's perspective and not my own.

In Healing Touch there were books, such as Barbara Brennan's *Hands of Light*, that showed, through scientific research, colors and lights taken by cameras that captured auras around people. There were also books by medical doctors and nurses who'd been working with energy for over thirty years. There were more books and resources that I never saw when I was studying art in an institutional setting.

Those resources affirmed the swirls of colors I had painted that summer back in Boston before the instructor brushed them all away with sweeps of his vision and eliminated my creative imagination. Finally, in Healing Touch I found myself in the world I'd been lost to for decades.

My Level 1 instructor, Joanne, had initiated practice sessions so that her students, and anyone else in the Charlotte area who had attended the different Levels of Healing Touch, had a place to meet with each other. I went to my first Healing Touch practice session the week after my Level 1 weekend.

It was wonderful having the opportunity to do a Full Body Connection on someone. I'd gotten used to receiving energy from Sister Brigid, so I had a harder time relaxing with a person I didn't know and trust as I did Brigid and my friend Elizabeth.

While I lay with a small pillow covering my eyes during that first practice session, I became aware of the parts of my body that the student practitioner had forgotten to do energy work on. She was no more advanced than I was, so I figured my day would come, when I would forget a part of the body or two. There was even this sensation throughout the entire session that something like a heavy warm hand was lying on my stomach—the solar plexus. But I would learn afterward, there wasn't anything there.

I couldn't turn off the sounds of others who were already finished practicing as they chatted, whispered, and meandered about. The person who was administering Healing Touch later told me she had experienced the same distractions while we were trying to complete our sessions on each other.

I hated not being as comfortable as I'd felt with Brigid in the sacred setting of Well of Mercy. Even still, I was in love with the process.

In the past, I'd been warned by a therapist that, being as sensitive as I am, I would need to be careful with whom I chose to do any kind of body work—Massage Therapist, Acupuncturist, Reiki Master, now Healing Touch Practitioner and the like. It was something I continued to keep in mind.

For the next few weeks, I corralled anyone who was willing so that I could practice the techniques I had learned. Mostly friends, and even my husband, let me practice Healing Touch on them in the study in my house now designated as my Healing Touch room. I didn't care if anyone returned the favor, I didn't want to forget what I'd learned. In a few weeks, I'd be seeing Sister Brigid for Healing Touch again.

A few days before my appointment with Brigid, I went to a jewelry store close by. I needed to have the prongs secured on Stu's grandmother's diamond that he'd given me for our tenth wedding anniversary. As the jeweler worked on the ring, I looked around the store and was especially pulled in by the gemstones that I had read about on the *Chakra Tune-Up Chart*.

One of the young saleswomen asked if I wanted to try on a particular necklace I was admiring—a yellow-citrine gemstone embedded in the center of an elegantly designed silver arrangement. When she asked if I was interested in a particular stone, I told her that I'd been attracted to the citrine more than the emerald, amethyst, quartz, or ruby.

"I've just gotten interested in gemstones," I said. "I'm looking at ones in relationship to the chakra system. Do you know what that is?"

"Is it a particular designer from one of the magazines?" she asked.

I backed off. It would be too difficult to explain, especially in the open area of a rather classy jewelry store.

But before my ring was ready, she and two other saleswomen gathered around, and I found myself telling them a little something about what chakras were and what gemstones to wear when working on a particular health problem.

"You can even eat food with the same color, and it would help. For example, eat an orange for your sacral chakra if you're having cramps or PMS," I said.

All three of them, in their early to mid-twenties, fit stunningly in a chic jewelry store. It was not a place I often frequented.

I was there in running shorts and no makeup, having just finished my three-mile walk in Jetton Park. The girls were dressed in fashionable summer dresses that accented their slender figures. Their hair, nails, and makeup matched their stylish tastes.

One of the gals, slim with long-gorgeous blonde hair, asked me what gemstone to wear to lose weight. I stopped talking and smiled.

"You're quite beautiful the way you are," I said, and she blushed. Then I jokingly added, "Maybe one of the stones for the head."

She chuckled and said, "What stone is that?"

"It's one of the violet stones, like amethyst," I said, "but you don't need to lose weight. Let me give you another example. See that blue you've chosen to wear today? That's the color of the throat chakra."

She stopped positioning one of the necklaces she was fiddling with in the case and looked up at me with eyes wide, her mouth dropped open. "I have a sore throat today," she said.

"Aren't you wise!" I replied. "You unconsciously picked out a color to help heal your throat."

All three young women were now intrigued. But I wondered what I'd started. I was excited about having learned more about the energy system. Like I do when I get eager, I spurt out information in the darnedest places. At least when I was teaching, I had a forum to talk about some of my unusual discoveries.

But here in a fancy jewelry store that I'd probably never enter except to keep my husband's grandmother's heirloom in good shape, I found myself talking about what I'd been obsessing over for days— my love of metaphysics.

"What do some of the other stones or colors mean?" one of the ladies asked.

"Look at the red dress she's wearing," I said, pointing to the young lady who'd initially waited on me and thought that the chakra system was a designer from a classy magazine.

"That's the color for the root chakra, and you're probably pretty grounded today."

She came running out from around the counter with no shoes on, and I smiled and pointed at her feet. She stopped in her tracks, seemingly embarrassed that a customer caught her wearing no shoes. But that was not my intention.

"See," I said, "you're letting your feet touch the ground."

A sense of relief spread across her face. As we talked about what each chakra meant, more questions poured out: *What does the diamond mean? What stone should I wear for my heart? Can I just wear the color in my clothes? It sounds like I can eat the foods of the same color, too, right?*

When it was time for me to leave, I told them that I'd color-copy a chart and bring it in.

"Will you let us know about the diamond?" one asked, and I called when I got home to let them know that, like the amethyst, the diamond was for the head—the crown chakra.

I eventually ran a copy of the chart by the store, not knowing if what I'd done was the sanest way of introducing energy to mere acquaintances. It was all so new to me, and what I gave them was rudimentary bits and pieces of something bigger than what I knew at the time.

Maybe I needed to be more careful spurting out my enthusiasm over my latest newfound passion or maybe, unbeknownst to me, one of the three young women was meant to begin her own understanding of how energy and the chakra system worked.

When I walked into Well of Mercy the following week, I was still on top of the world. I told Brigid all about my Level 1 experience, and that I had already found a Level 2 class in Charlotte to be offered in another month and half.

Brigid and I agreed that, even if it did come with some distractions, the practice sessions were a good opportunity for me. I went to the practice groups often, while still going up to Well of Mercy for Healing Touch.

As Brigid's apprenticeship was coming to a close, I continued taking various Level classes. The more I went the more intrigued I was with the Healing Touch process. At each weekend event, I met a new instructor who specialized in teaching a specific Level.

In Level 2, I was taught more techniques, including a full-hour sequence on connecting the body's energy. I also learned a heart-centered technique, and back and neck techniques, along with additional mind-clearing processes.

Level 3 was probably my favorite of all. We worked not only on the body but in the fields that surround our bodies. Each Level drew me into the Healing Touch process more and more.

Then came Level 4, an overnight program held at Well of Mercy with Janet Mentgen as the instructor. Janet was the founder of Healing Touch. How lucky was I to have sat at the feet of the person who created this healing program!

There was even a time when all of the participants, including me, followed Janet, Deborah, who had been assisting Janet, Sister Brigid, and Sister Donna to an open field on Well of Mercy's property. It was a spiritual experience for me. Although I never quite knew what it was about, it didn't matter.

We all quietly followed the directions to write what we each felt rising from the land we were sitting on. When we were done, we handed in our papers and peacefully walked back to the main house together.

After my Level 4 experience I realized that my Mystical Seeker archetype had boldly surfaced. Like Sister Brigid had been doing, I made a decision to continue on and become an apprentice in the Healing Touch program.

Chapter 26
Apprenticeship

My next step in my Healing Touch training was to choose a mentor for my apprenticeship program. Initially it was a difficult decision because I thought the utmost of Joanne, my Level 1 Instructor, who was also a mentor to apprentices.

But in Level 4 at Well of Mercy, I bonded deeply with others who were ready to start the same journey I was about to pursue in Healing Touch. Most of the people lived in and around Winston-Salem, about sixty-five minutes north of my home.

Deborah Larrimore, the instructor who had assisted Janet Mentgen during Level 4, was going to start the first-ever Mentor Group in Winston-Salem where she lived, practiced, and taught Healing Touch. I was eager to continue with the people I had spent the long, intense Level 4 weekend with—giving each other energy exchanges, sharing conversations, and getting to know and learn about another way of living a deeper life with fellow Healing Touch travelers.

So, I made the decision to drive up I-77 toward Well of Mercy before turning off onto I-40 East to Winston-Salem, North Carolina, a few times a month or more for the next year.

My fellow mentees and I shared and practiced the various Healing Touch techniques on each other. Deborah encouraged us to grow and develop in a way that was more expansive than it would have ever been working with only one person.

It happened so naturally after we had all been together at Well of Mercy. Besides having Deborah, we were mentors for each other. Fortunately, there was still Sister Brigid, who was very present in the Healing Touch community, and who in reality had been my first mentor through all those months of having given me so many Healing Touch sessions.

Deborah was also generous with time and connections, bringing in additional healers who knew even more advanced techniques and processes. Some of those healers specialized in Healing Touch. Others who came were acclaimed international healers, such as Rosalyn Bruyere and Dr. Christine Page.

To meet some of the requirements of the program, I made appointments with different types of energy practitioners and wrote up my experiences— the good ones, along with the not so good ones. Discernment was certainly what was being asked of me. I also wrote about the books and authors I read related to various forms of energy healing topics, which covered categories that had been especially present in my life, including archetypes, dreams, and astrology.

Like Sister Brigid had done for me and others, I practiced Healing Touch on many people during my apprenticeship program. When I was with my mentee colleagues experimenting beyond what we were expected to learn, I never forgot what I had also learned from Brigid. She had been the perfect model for me as I continued through my own apprenticeship year.

I would open many of my sessions with similar words that Brigid had spoken, as she called in all of my angels and guides, hers too, asking that they work together for my highest and best good. When appropriate for the person on my Healing Touch table, I would start, "Mother, Father, God ..." with the same loving and kind tone that I had learned from Brigid long before I knew I would be doing for another what she had done for me.

A year after having traveled frequently to Winston-Salem and working intently back home as a Healing Touch apprentice, I, along with most of my fellow mentees, completed the requirements necessary to attend the Level V resident program, again to be held at Well of Mercy.

How great it was that these higher-level learning opportunities, where we stayed overnight for a four-day intensive program, were so close by and at a place where I felt at home.

The last night of Level V, I learned that I had passed and was awarded a Certificate as a Healing Touch Practitioner. Right then I made another decision. I would now continue on and apply to the program's Board of Nurses to become a Certified Healing Touch Practitioner. That included more trips to Winston Salem for meetings with my mentee-colleagues and Deborah, my mentor.

During my year of preparing for certification, I worked on a case study, wrote and revised descriptions of required work: books read related to energy, visits to alternative practitioners, and community projects where I would give Healing Touch to volunteer clients, along with my own 100 client sessions required to complete the program.

In the fall of October 2004, after having had submitted an application for certification, I was indeed approved as a Certified Healing Touch Practitioner.

My grandfather, *Nonno* Stagnitta, never needed certification to perform healing on various people and animals. Perhaps if there were other ways in this so-called modern-day age, I would have learned healing energy techniques through grandparents or parents, medicine healers or shamans.

Some cultures still do. But at the turn of the 21st century, I had followed my internal voice into Spiritual Direction, then listened to the prodding I felt within to get on that Healing Touch table of Sister Brigid's, all the while searching for my true purpose, which I found through my sacred contracts.

I don't think it mattered how I got to my Mystical Seeker. The fact is that some grander source—call it what one may—led me from one step to another, to another, as I followed the path and answered the call.

It wasn't an easy route. There were many questions haunting me, not only about myself, but also about other people in my life. I made some unnecessary judgments in the process and learned to recognize erroneous conclusions.

Nevertheless, it was a journey driven by desire and passion. With every step, I had devoted healers: a Spiritual Director, Healing Touch practitioners, instructors, mentors, fellow mentees, and other forms of helpers who assisted me in seeing over and over again that my sacred contracts, which I had discovered and brought to light, had always been a part of my life.

Along the way, I also learned that healing energy had always been a part of me. It hasn't necessarily made life easier, but it certainly has made my life clearer knowing where I've needed to be.

I don't believe the ability is mine alone. Therapeutic Touch came easily to my older sister, Nicki, and now my sister in line behind me, Fran, has found herself drawn to Reiki. I suspect, in some cases know, there is another younger sibling or more who've had some mystical experiences, and a niece who periodically writes me about her interest in such matters. My cousin Frank—now a veterinarian deep in the mountains of North Carolina—has his own healing powers, through a medical perspective. Frank was named after our grandfather, *Nonno* Francesco Stagnitta.

Back when I was reading those horoscopes out of Syracuse's Post Standard or playing church on the altar I created in front of the fireplace in *Nonna* and *Nonno's* front room, I never would have guessed for a nanosecond that my intrigue with the metaphysical world would have led me to become a Healing Touch Practitioner.

As far as I was concerned, I was a creative artist, writer, and teacher. For some reason, my interest in metaphysics surprised me in my wisdom years with this ability that had been tucked inside of me for decades. Once the Spirit started moving, I was driven into the arms of Healing Touch.

Chapter 27
Reflection

Before this whole journey began, I had been drawing images of angels for close to ten years. After getting involved with Healing Touch, the drawings around the outside of the angels expanded into the various colors of the chakras that I had learned about in my Healing Touch program as well as in various energy books, including Barbara Ann Brennan's book, *Hands of Light, A Guide to Healing Through the Human Energy Field.*

In the autumn of 2004, a trinity of three significant practices came together. Healing Touch, art, and writing! I could never have pulled these three together randomly. There was certainly something greater at play.

In October, I became a Certified Healing Touch Practitioner. One month after that, I had a one-person art exhibit of my angel drawings in an old brick SoHo-looking building in my small North Carolina town.

I gave Well of Mercy a suite of signed angel prints, *Unique Impressions*—each background having a distinctive layering of techniques I had developed using gold leaf.

The angels still hang in a small room, the sisters called the Living Room, off the main sanctuary in the large-hexagon shaped Chapel of Mercy built the year after I'd completed Level 5.

During the same season, my first poetry chapbook, *In This Dream Everything Remains Inside*, was published. My Spiritual Director had helped me to prepare for the release of my book on a rather personal journey on childlessness.

During a meeting one day with Betty, she said to me quite emphatically, "Once that book leaves your hands, what others have to say and what they do with your writing no longer belongs to you."

Betty knew me and my sensitive nature well. When I was younger, I thought that feeling sensitive about anything was a weakness. But it was that very sensitivity that drove me to write and create in various genres—poetry, memoir, essays, drawings. And now, there is Healing Touch, which certainly requires a level of sensitivity to pick up on what energy I feel over each chakra, as well as what is in the energy field around each person's body. All of these have become a part of my life. And so to be doing this work, I obviously needed to be sensitive.

Fortunately, what I learned by discovering my sacred contracts were my own archetypal strengths and weaknesses, which helped me to see the purpose of my life. Even though my commitment had been there all along, I had not recognized that what I'd been doing was exactly what I was meant to do — art, writing, and now Healing Touch.

Although not technically my mentor, dear Sister Brigid had prepared me to become a healer by offering me the experience of her own hands-on healing over all those months. To have had Brigid and so many other helpers along the way was a gift.

After being certified, I continued practicing Healing Touch. I also found myself using Healing Touch while teaching memoir classes. I've paid attention to the energy and listened to my own inner voice about whatever was happening in the classroom with my students, as I've helped them tell, uncover, and craft their stories.

I've followed the inner guidance that surfaced, even when there was resistance—a scowl on someone's face, the shake of a head back and forth, an adamant reason as to why the words they wrote did not need revision.

I've gently pushed a bit harder, pointed out that maybe it wasn't the word I was pointing to, but rather the words around it (somewhat like the fields around the body). I've followed my intuition by asking more questions, nudging a little deeper, encouraging each writer to stretch a bit more one way or another.

Having gone through years of being gently pushed and pulled in my own writing and poetry groups, I understand resistance. After all, I've had my own creative struggles of what to leave in and what to take out.

Healing Touch became such a significant part of my life, I couldn't imagine living without all the information and awareness that my dive into energy work offered.

I did stop driving to Well of Mercy for Healing Touch from Sister Brigid and exchanged sessions with other energy workers, Healing

Touch practitioners, and Reiki Masters, who lived in my area. I would touch base with Brigid and even saw her periodically, when attending a special event that she would be a part of for Well of Mercy or other associations that crossed our paths.

I will forever be grateful for what she did for me during all those months of Healing Touch. She had my back emotionally, even when I silently questioned what was going on.

Right alongside Brigid, I also had the maternal guidance of Betty. She had given me more than the scheduled hour in Spiritual Direction as she pointed me back to myself again and again. Betty listened to my journey—all of my paths—while guiding me to a place where I had no idea I would be heading.

As I'd moved through the Healing Touch program, Brigid and I stayed in touch. Sometimes it was a brief encounter, or even just a short email. A word or two was often all I needed to be reminded of what I had learned under her loving guidance.

We were energetically connected. It certainly helped to have completed my two advanced Healing Touch Levels 4 and 5 right there at Well of Mercy, where Brigid was present and where I felt enveloped in a canopy of comfort and trust.

How far I had come from those early days when I thought what happened in our sessions was about Sister Brigid. Instead, I came to the realization that my thoughts and experiences were and always had been about *me* and what I was meant to learn and grow into. Brigid was one of the conduits that led me to the Divine within myself.

The September after I graduated from the program, I flew out to Boulder, Colorado, to attend the annual Healing Touch Conference, where I was pinned as a *Certified Healing Touch Practitioner*. My Level 1 instructor, Joanne, was there and joyfully said a few words that have continued to live in me and still help me manage my way through some of the more challenging times.

"Certification is just the beginning," Joanne said, "and it just keeps growing from here."

While I was literally there in the Rocky Mountains of Colorado, I felt as if I were at the top of a metaphorical mountain. I'd been handed a storehouse of tools to help me through what life would bring.

And I would also learn that not even Healing Touch or any form of energy would stop the course of life: births, deaths, moves, health concerns—my own and those of people I love—job worries, political upheavals, change in culture, ways of being and more.

New information was now at my disposal to help me maneuver through continued challenges. The trials would not stop, but knowing about energy helped me navigate them a bit more easily. With all these new sources, I could look at the world and explore my archetypes in a way that I'd never consciously done before.

Through the next several years, I continued seeing Betty. She helped me stay grounded and clear about my intentions and desires, not only in Healing Touch but also in other aspects of my life—my profession as a creative writer, poet, artist, instructor; as a wife, daughter, sister, aunt, cousin, friend. My roles have continued to unfold.

Like my grandfather, *Nonno* Stagnitta, I've performed energy on people. My personal tool has been Healing Touch. I have not reached out to find clients. I knew if it were meant to be, we would connect. I've used the techniques that Sister Brigid had used on me, as well as other techniques I'd learned along the way.

It helped tremendously to have been a part of a uniquely creative mentee group led by Deborah, my mentor, during those years I drove back and forth to Winston-Salem. I've stayed in touch with some of them as well as with other healers I've met.

In one of the many sessions I'd given, I felt the presence of *Nonno*. It wasn't the first time, but it was one I've thought of often.

I started the session the way Brigid always did by calling in the person's guides and angels, asking for her highest and best good. I hand-scanned above her body and checked the chakras of the trusting soul laying on my Healing Touch table.

I started off with what seemed to be a normal healing session, although truth be told, I never really knew— nor do I know now— what might come up. I gave up second guessing way back during my early apprenticeship years, when I thought my brain knew what I should be doing.

Instead, the various ways of checking the chakras would always point out what parts of the body needed energy work.

That day, as I scanned the client's energy by floating my hands over each chakra—head, brow, throat, heart, solar plexus, sacral, root—I felt in my palms if there was any static or any spots of hot or cold. Some of my client's chakras were calm and open, some were full of static energy.

Then I used the basic chakra connection technique to disperse any congested energy as I moved from feet to head, while giving more attention to the chakras that needed an extra boost. I used additional Healing Touch techniques to clear several congested areas of the body.

It seemed to go smoothly until I went back to one area that had much more static than anywhere else: the eyes.

I spent time brushing the energy in the space around my client's eyes, before trying to rest my hands over the specific area that felt compromised. No matter what I did, I couldn't find the exact spot that needed clearing. I tried and tried again but felt I was missing the mark.

I was at a loss and couldn't even intuit what it was I needed to do until, suddenly, I felt a presence so strong, I knew the energy like I knew my own body.

"*Nonno*," I said to myself, so as not to alarm my client. "*Nonno*, is that you?"

As if he wanted to let me know it was him guiding and helping this session, I felt as if my hands had been taken from me and directed over and above the person's left eye rather than the right where I'd been lingering.

I brushed the space above the left eye and then held my hands still, sending love and energy directly into a certain spot. After working on that precise area, I could feel the static slowly subsiding until eventually the space felt smooth.

The session was complete.

Afterwards, when my client was off the table, she said, "I forgot to tell you something before we started. My left eye had been bothering me right here," she pointed, in the very spot to which my grandfather's energy had directed my hands.

That's how it has been. There were times I've had no earthly idea, when I began an energy session, where my hands would be directed. I've learned to follow the energy and let the sense of hot, cold, static, and other sensations, along with a quiet internal voice, lead me instead of me leading the energy.

The process has been healing not only for the person receiving, but also for me. As a practitioner, I've always left my Healing Touch room feeling centered and calm, as if I had just received energy myself.

Ever since 9/11 I'd been on such a spiritual quest and am so thankful for my desire to journal, write, create the angels, and experience energy practices of all kinds. This quest and work kept me grounded as I came face to face with physical, emotional, and spiritual challenges.

Whenever I think of my initial awareness around energy during those early years, I am back to my first Healing Touch session on Sister Brigid's massage table …

I am off somewhere. I don't know where
it doesn't matter.

I'm floating around in a fog, a very, very, very comfortable,
gray, soothing, serene fog.

In time, I see it around, above, and over my body.

A diagram.

Small dotted lines — green, I think.

It's like a graph, a grid, a grid of lines connecting parts of me from
one spot to another.

I am a diagram of energy swirling around and through
and in between.

Am I a hologram? I wonder.

No matter.

Whatever I see,
feels perfectly right.

PART II
AFTERWARDS

"Healing may not be so much about getting better, as about letting go of everything that isn't you – all of the expectations, all of the beliefs – and becoming who you are."

—Rachel Naomi Remen

I

In the Era of the Second Decade of the 21st Century

There have been many changes in the twenty years since my spiritual journey began after 9/11. Sister Brigid stopped doing Healing Touch, and another practitioner is offering energy work at Well of Mercy. I have periodically seen her and love the memory of those early months of the healing we worked on together. Brigid will always mean a great deal to me.

Betty had to stop giving Spiritual Direction, and our relationship grew into a friendship. I would drive to her home so that we could talk, go out to lunch, be together.

When she was taken to a nursing home a couple of hours away, closer to her daughter in the North Carolina mountains, I was devastated, even though it was in Betty's best interest. I drove to the mountains a few times to visit her. After a couple of years, Betty was moved back to a center closer to her home, and I've had the chance to see her again.

It took me a number of years to finally reach out to another Spiritual Director. I am fortunate to have Carol in my life. She is perceptive and sensitive to my innermost thoughts and feelings. Carol is an amazing listener who always brings the Divine into the room by acknowledging the insights, hers and mine, that I need for this time in my life.

I've also learned, just as my first Healing Touch instructor Joanne had said would happen, that life would continue to change and challenge and surprise beyond the newfound knowledge I'd acquired through the Healing Touch Program.

The ever-changing challenges of life never stopped just because I became a Healing Touch Practitioner.

The destruction and tragedy of the Twin Towers on 9/11 sent me in search of something greater than myself. If it had not been for Healing Touch, Spiritual Direction, and the discovery of my purpose in life through my sacred contracts, I don't know how I would have moved forward after the cultural changes that followed, including the Great Recession of the late 2000s precipitated by the banking crisis of 2007 to 2009.

The housing bubble of those years resulted in the loss of wealth for many, especially the middle class. Plus, it triggered cuts in consumer spending, among other economic woes.

Many Americans struggled to climb back to financial security, available housing, accessible health care, and all levels of affordable living. I believed that during those following years, we Americans were pulling ourselves back up, becoming stronger, being more responsible about spending.

There also seemed to be a sense of concern for others in greater need and an acceptance of those different from ourselves.

Throughout this time, I was grateful for having gone through the Healing Touch Program. It not only left me more aware, it also inspired me to continue to learn about other complementary treatments and healers with unique ways of operating outside of mainstream medicine—Neural Depolarization, The Body Code, Emotional Freedom Technique (EFT), and more.

As a nation, I believed we were becoming increasingly understanding of others no matter their color, sexual orientation, or place of birth. I even had this optimistic notion that Americans were maturing. We had stretched beyond ourselves and elected our first African American president.

Being a female baby boomer, I'd waited for years to see a woman in the office of president—a bright, intelligent, cognizant woman from my generation—like Hillary Clinton.

Despite my sense of loss and deep disappointment when having a woman chosen to run in the highest position in the land was not successful, I grew to appreciate the integrity of President Obama, his wife and family, and the people with whom he surrounded himself.

Perhaps our nation was evolving to a point that we could treat others with respect and fairness. All wasn't perfect, but another level of caring for people was budding.

At least that was what I perceived in the world I lived in of writers, poets, artists, humanitarians, scientists, educators, energy workers, and caring human beings.

What I had learned in studying Healing Touch and working with energy was that this new way of being had become a part of my life. I read more books on spirituality and metaphysics, went to talks and workshops on new and various healing and energy techniques, met different healers who either came to the area where I lived, or whom I would drive hours to see.

Given the positive energy around me, I was not prepared for what was to come in the second decade of the 21st century—the election of 2016. I went to bed the night of the election with a sick feeling in my stomach. When I awoke and saw reality, I didn't know what to do with myself.

I was confused and disconcerted. How did Hillary Clinton not get elected? Should I stay under the covers? Avoid turning on the television? Cancel my morning class? Was I entering another 9/11?

Texts from students who could not bring themselves to attend memoir class that day started coming in. If I was not the instructor, I wouldn't have gone either. Despite my meandering from bedroom to kitchen to bathroom and around again, I managed to get dressed and slowly move out the door.

After all the candles I'd lit, after all the prayers I had sent up to whatever God existed, after all the beliefs I had about it being time for the feminine to play an equal role in our society, my messages had not been heard. Something major had gone awry.

Even my self-proclaimed Republican husband was surprised. Like many, he had his issues with both political parties, but my calm, accepting spouse understood that it was time for an intelligent, capable woman to be elected president of the United States.

After many decades of marriage, Stu and I were finally on the same page politically. But given the way the election had gone, being politically aligned was not consoling.

In the end, I was glad I had my class to attend the morning after November 8 because there were students who needed to be there. One came early to talk. Another stayed late, concerned about her children, knowing that one of them, a young teen, was already struggling with his sexuality.

She was afraid the results of this election would have a damaging effect on her young son's already shaky place in this world. She acknowledged that the former secretary of state was supportive of young people as they struggled to find acceptance and a path for themselves.

That day after I received emails from friends and relatives here in the United States, and in Italy. Even a young American mother living in Germany for six months with her husband and two babies contacted me, along with writers I had met in Canada and elsewhere.

The young mother in Germany especially wanted to know what other Americans were thinking and feeling about the outcome of the 2016 presidential election. When 9/11 hit, the assault came from foreign terrorists. But now it felt as if something were shaking beneath the ground we lived on.

As time wore on, many women shared with me that they could not get out of bed the morning after the election. So many felt the result deep in their gut—the same body parts where I'd experienced such discomfort, the solar plexus down into the sacral.

A cousin told me she sat in her bed and sobbed. Many women and men I knew felt wronged—family, neighbors, colleagues, students, friends. Each would share their experiences of a response from something deep within themselves—a warning call, a cry from beyond.

When we—women or men—touch base with our intuitive, feminine nature, we have an internal compass that feels Mother Earth's discontent. The hurt was agonizing for far too many, and, because of my own sensitivity, I seemed to be feeling not only my pain but others' pain too.

I had waited years for a woman to become president. A woman from my era—the 60s generation. In my eyes, Hillary Clinton was a brilliant, well-educated individual who had experience in running a government and ample ability to participate in both foreign and domestic affairs.

I had actually met Hillary Clinton in Seneca Falls, not far from where I was born and raised. I was there with lifetime friends—my sister Nicki, and my two dear friends from kindergarten, Jackye and Rosemary (also known as Rose).

It was the weekend of October 7-8, 2005, when Hillary was inducted into The National Women's Hall of Fame with nine other women.

That Friday night the four of us attended the Gala Welcome Reception with rooms full of people who had traveled to Upstate New York to honor the inductees. That was when Hillary walked through the same space we were standing in at the Hall of Fame.

Each one of us four gals stood face to face with her at one time or another and said hello in a crowded gallery room. I was dumbfounded, really.

My words were minimal at best, something like, "Hello, Hillary. I really appreciate the work you've been doing for women and children," thinking about how meaningful her book, *It Takes a Village And Other Lessons Children Teach Us*, published in 1996, had been to me. Hillary smiled and thanked me just before Rosemary was about to say something.

Now being 2005, Hillary was the senator from the state of New York while George W. Bush was still in office. At that time whenever any news broadcaster asked Hillary if she would run for president, she would dodge the question and focus on her job as senator from the State of New York.

But within seconds after I complimented Hillary, Rosemary spoke right up, "Hillary, are you going to run for president?" she asked in her decisive tone.

Three of us, Nicki, Jackye, and I, were shocked, since Rose had not committed to Hillary, or any Democrat, at that point in time. We made faces at Rosemary, but that didn't affect her in the least. Instead, she stayed talking with Hillary and even showed her a greeting card that poked fun at Bill.

I had seen it earlier and my body began to cringe until Hillary burst out in her deep-set, loud boisterous laugh. Then she gave Rose her autograph on that very card.

Rosemary also asked her if Bill was going to be at the luncheon the next day. Hillary smiled and said "yes" before turning slightly in a different direction, and Rose began a conversation with one of the Secret Service agents standing nearby, who, I could see, had both eyes on Hillary and anyone in her vicinity.

Hillary then came face to face with my sister. Although she did not know it, Nicki had gone to a private Catholic girl's high school in Syracuse with a few people who would later attend college with Hillary. Some guys from the brother high school would also become Hillary's friends.

"Let's go out for a glass of wine later," Nicki said in jest, and they both laughed. Although that was not what happened, we would certainly have another experience with Hillary before the night was out.

But right then, Jackye spoke up. "What are your thoughts on *No Child Left Behind?*" she asked Hillary about George W's education legislation and policy.

That's when Hillary took a direct turn and looked seriously into Jackye's face and asked, "What are you thinking?"

Jackye was the director of Editorial Policy and Publishing at the U.S. Department of Education at the time, and would eventually work in the department for twenty-six years. And it appeared Hillary sensed from her question that she would get some solid, intelligent, and important information out of my friend.

Jackye would later remind us that she had just finished college tours with her daughter and became aware of the prioritizing of math and science over the arts at the college level. It was then she realized that with *No Child Left Behind's* favoring of math, science and English, instruction in history, arts, language, and music at the K-12 levels had been reduced.

This was especially the case for students from lower socio-economic levels and was what led to Jackye's findings at the higher ed level.

Jackye and Hillary stood and talked for quite a while, which supported our on-going anecdote we had created years before that Jackye was the Brains, Rosemary the Bold, and I—well, when we went in search of a label for me, I ended up with Beauty only because it began with a B. (It had been challenging to figure out what to call me, the one who has always preferred to live in a metaphysical state of mind.)

My sister Nicki, who had been one year ahead of us in elementary school, high school, and college, wasn't part of this narrative when it first began. We all thought that Nicki was certainly one of the Brains, from the class ahead of us.

While we were standing in Hillary's little alcove with Secret Service around, Rose spoke out again, "Hillary, you need to run for president."

Hillary smiled and said something like, "My job right now is working for the people of the great state of New York."

After all, Hillary was still a senator in 2005. And it was at that moment in time, I called Rose over and within seconds we pulled a quick photo shot together—the four of us ladies with the person whom we thought and hoped would be the first female president of the United States.

Shortly after, The National Women's Hall of Fame organizers of the weekend announced it was time for our next event. We stepped out into a predicted downpour and pushed open our umbrellas. One of the Secret Service folks handed Hillary an umbrella and there we were walking side-by-side with her to the next venue.

Hillary was open and friendly as everyone from the event marched down the street in the rain. We were lucky to be with Hillary again. I was directly on her right and the other three were close by. Everyone seemed to be enjoying the march with the women and supportive men in attendance.

Hillary seemed just as happy to be marching by our sides as we were with her. She chatted with us as if we were old school friends, and was kind, and smart, and real—everything people over the years tried to pretend she wasn't.

"You have to run," Rosemary insisted, and Nicki, Jackye, and I looked at each other and rolled our eyes. And don't you think for a minute we didn't call Rose on her obvious support afterwards.

As my mind moved back to the present, I knew there were others who felt differently about Hillary's loss in 2016. Since the experience had been fresh and raw, I had to do whatever was necessary to protect myself from those others.

When January 2017 came around, I began to prepare myself for Stu's annual Super Bowl party that we'd been hosting since the 1980s.

I stated in the invitation, "Please leave all political opinions outside the door." I know there were those who didn't want to do that but, in the end, they showed up, and everyone, Democrat and Republican alike, honored my request.

Without someone like Hillary at the helm, we would, in a short period of time, see working immigrants pushed out of our country, parents and children who showed up at our borders for asylum detained, long-time allies criticized and alienated.

How immigrants were treated, whether they were already here or trying to get in, was tough for me to see. I came from a family of immigrants.

My father immigrated here from Sicily at the age of fifteen to meet up with his father already living and working in Upstate New York. My mother was the first in her family to have been born in the United States, after my *Nonno* Francesco had been able to call for *Nonna* Egidia and Mom's older brother, Uncle Joe, to come to the United States. Dad's mother and two sisters were finally able to come and be with Dad and my *Nonno* Morina only after World War II ended.

I felt the pain the present immigrants were experiencing. My relatives had come in under a different status in the early and mid-20th century, but they were still immigrants. So was everyone else who came to this country—except for the Native Americans. And we know what happened to the indigenous people from this country whose land we now live on.

I've always seen myself as first-generation American, only a short span away from the hardworking, responsible people from other countries who arrive here, live here, try to stay here, lead productive and giving lives here in the United Sates.

I remember, a few decades ago, when flying back from California to the East Coast on a red-eye, seeing a group of young men from south of the border being brought to our country by, what I assumed were, business men looking for cheaper labor.

Before these young guys even boarded the plane, I saw a person handing them papers and explaining in Spanish where they would be going. Those young men did not speak English, had no awareness of what to do on the plane, what food to accept, or what facilities to use.

They sat perfectly still in their seats, looking back and forth at each other, their eyes wide open, as if in fright.

When C.E.O.s needed workers ready to do manual labor and couldn't find enough people in the United States willing to work for low wages, allowing immigrants to cross the border to get their work done was perfectly acceptable. After these young people were used up by business owners for their own gain, many of the same hard workers were sent back or left here to fend for themselves—as if human beings were expendable.

Besides my unease for the immigrants, I, along with others, were deeply troubled about the environment, something being dismissed by people in power. No wonder Mother Earth began rebelling with more intense tornadoes, earthquakes, hurricanes, storms of all sorts.

Then trade wars began, huge tax breaks were given to those who already had more money than entire classes of people. American citizens in the U.S. territory of Puerto Rico were ignored, receiving only limited aid after Hurricane Maria caused one of the deadliest U.S.-based natural disasters in many decades. Concern for the people began to disintegrate.

I was clearly not ready for the total upheaval of our American culture and society after the 2016 presidential election, nor did I understand the causes of and, in turn, the results that would ensue from many of the changes that had begun so quickly.

Different quotes came to me almost daily, including what I learned years ago in Catholic school as the seven Corporal Works of Mercy (attributed to Jesus): feed the hungry, give drink to the thirsty, give alms to the poor, shelter the homeless, visit the sick, visit the prisoners, and bury the dead.

In my mind, that would have been the direction Hillary Clinton would have followed. I was sure of it, especially after having met her, felt her caring energy and her concern for others, and walking down the street with her in the pouring rain.

Hillary would have been the one who would have cared for the people and the earth like a mother would care for her offspring.

Although she has never been overt about her United Methodist religion, there is a line that came from her faith tradition that I've heard her humbly use a few times, "Do all the good you can, for all the people you can, in all the ways you can, as long as ever you can."

Many, not all, who lived in the United States and kept up with the press, national or international, suffered over the challenges we were bumping up against. The shift in consciousness, for which I had advocated and many Americans imagined, was now gone. And I was thrown back into a life of high stress and anxiety.

I kept wishing I could return to the calm state I'd been in after having moved through the Healing Touch Program. As time evolved, separating my body, mind, and soul from the turmoil of what was going on in our country, became my greatest longing.

No matter how many energy sessions I was receiving, no matter how many Spiritual Direction appointments I went to, no matter how much I meditated, journaled, and prayed, I wasn't able to stop worrying about the changes taking place around me

The day before the 2017 presidential inauguration on January 20, I drove to Washington, D.C., and stayed with my friend, Jackye, and her husband, Carl. Together the three of us attended the Women's March.

Even though there were those who tried to talk me out of going, I followed my own yearning. Luckily, I drove with a writer friend and colleague who was meeting up with a friend of hers in D.C. We shared the same convictions and the same anxiety about the 2016 election.

I lived through the Viet Nam war era and then there were the Gulf wars. These wars were challenging enough, never mind Stu losing his only nephew in the War in Iraq.

I couldn't help but be aware that what was going on now was on our shores, in our faces, an upheaval taking over the country from within.

Once again, just like after 9/11, I was in need of something bigger than myself, something I remember feeling when I went in search of a Spiritual Director, then entered into Healing Touch.

Back in 2004, my fellow mentees, mentor, practitioners, and I had been warned by one of the visiting healers that something big was going to hit one day, and we in America would never be prepared.

Could all the chaos and dissention occurring in our country be what the healer had warned us about?

The grit that sent me to Washington for the Women's March made me realize I was now a person on a mission. But I had no idea what that mission was or could be. I started with the march and continued when I returned home with phone calls to my senators.

My messages against restricting immigrants from particular countries, including those from the Middle East, from entering the United States, against building a wall between us and our southern neighbors, against huge tax cuts to the wealthy, warning about climate change and more—none of those messages ever appeared to make a difference.

Any suggestions I or any of my friends made were not even minimally included in any decision made by my United States senators in Congress.

There were actually times when whoever answered the phone at one of my senators' offices would argue with me about my concerns that I had typed up on a Word document. I did that so as not to go off track and into one of my rants about the state of our country.

Being as persistent as I've been about fairness for all, I would speak my piece and disagree right back. After all these years as a woman believing in equality, I would not be shut down.

One day on the phone, a young man, perhaps an intern, asked, "What are you reading from?"

"I'm reading what I wrote so that I don't go off track and let you have it."

"I don't believe you," he said. "I think some group told you exactly what to say."

"You do, do you?" I responded raising my voice an octave. "Well, be prepared because now you're going to hear even more of what I think about how many of the senators and their colleagues are handling this country so poorly."

His comment was all I needed. I let him know what I thought about the new education secretary and how little she knew about students and teaching.

I shared my critique about the cutbacks on health care, my disgust over the closing of the borders, detaining parents and children there, my frustrations over the lack of gun control, limiting immigration from certain countries, the rise of attacks on Black communities and other minorities, and the delusion that white people are superior to other ethnic groups.

As the list went on, that young man could not get off the phone fast enough.

After I had returned from that earlier trip to D.C., I also attended local marches hoping that one or another of my senators would at least attempt to hear the other side. Having been an educator most of my life, I was distraught over the Parkland shooting. But nothing was being done about the rising gun violence.

Again, neither of my senators ever made an overture toward any suggestions I and other like-minded friends called or wrote in to them about. In fact, my concerns were squelched by a controlled, callous, heartless, and cruel GOP Congress that seemed determined to allow America's democratic way of life to be disrupted or squelched.

Just five weeks after the horrendous school shooting in Parkland, it was the students from Marjory Stoneman Douglass High School, along with others, who had the courage to stand up and protest—not only for their lives, but for the lives of many other young people.

On a gray Saturday, March 24, 2018, my husband, once a teacher, joined me and some of our friends in uptown Charlotte for the *March For Our Lives* protests against the violent acts happening in our schools and to the children of the United States.

We joined in support of the young people who were marching in Washington and other cities around the country.

Two young survivors of Sandy Hook Elementary School, now in high school and living in our area, were among some of the speakers we heard in Charlotte, as was a relative of a recent victim of the Parkland shooting in Florida. All three spoke about the desperate need for gun control. As the students and other supporters around the country clearly stated, and I felt deeply about, these young people were truly marching for their lives.

I thought the Florida shooting would have done me in, but when members of our government directed workers at the border to take immigrant children away from their parents and put them into cages, my heart felt it was being torn from my chest.

Why, after all these years of Healing Touch and Spiritual Direction, workshops and energy classes, why after listening to other healers, why after years of meditating, journaling, helping others write their stories, why had I come to a place where I was as stressed as so many others in this country?

How could that be? I should have been able to center myself, get clear, be strong. After all, I was a Healing Touch practitioner, wasn't I?

Like many others, I felt immobilized. Was I at my wits end? Or was I being called to take some form of action, something different than I'd ever done before? What action would that be? I wanted desperately to find a way to make a difference.

II
The Second Decade Continues

All the while, I meditated and walked, journaled and wrote, took steps to get myself back to feeling more centered, the way I'd been after those years of studying Healing Touch. I thought about earlier times at Well of Mercy as I did my best to handle the anxious feelings that had now surfaced. I was still receiving energy work regularly from a colleague who lived close by, as well as meeting with Carol, my current Spiritual Director.

During each visit, I would be sure to write down any awareness or clarification that came to me. Afterwards, I would continue writing more thoughts and revelations. Of course, it was my Writer archetype—in my 1st astrological House—that drove me to always have a pen or pencil in hand.

And now, my Mystical Seeker archetype in the 9th House of travel, philosophy and other higher mind activities was about to take me out of the country for a break.

In October 2017, Stu and I, along with nineteen other travelers, flew to Italy and Sicily for a tour entitled *Following in The Footsteps of My Father's Daughter*, based on my first memoir about traveling to Italy with my parents. I organized the trip with a company out of Boston, Stu's and my old stomping ground. (It's where we met.)

We followed the same path we had taken with Mom and Dad in the fall of 2000, the year before 9/11. My husband and I were looking forward to revisiting the route we'd once followed, and taking a pause from the struggles we had been experiencing back home in the United States.

Many Italians asked what we thought about our current political scene, and I expressed my disgruntled outlook as did the travelers with us who felt the same way. But there were a few, like some folks at our annual Super Bowl Party, who supported and believed there was hope for what was going on back home.

Like we did at the party earlier in the year, Stu and I were sensitive to those who had different beliefs and, when necessary, directed the conversation elsewhere.

While traveling through Italy and Sicily, I remembered the stories my father told when Stu and I were there with him and Mom. I couldn't help but think of Nazi Germany and Hitler, of Mussolini and my grandmother, Dad's mother, my other *Nonna*, and his two sisters.

They were the women of my father's family still in Sicily waiting for their husband and father to get their papers from our government so he could call for them to come to the United States.

But before that could happen World War II broke out, and my grandmother and aunts not only took care of themselves, but they also helped other women and children—my grandmother's sisters, her nieces and nephews, cousins, and those in their small village who needed assistance.

In the 1940s, my female relatives, especially my *Nonna* Morina, became a force in a culture where the men, off at war or overseas, had always been in charge.

Even before my father had emigrated at fifteen years old, before being called to the United States by his father, there were elements of fascism throughout his homeland.

Some people I knew suggested that my feelings about the 2016 election were rather exaggerated, but they backed off after the immigration ban, children held in cages at the border, gun violence in schools, and numerous other inhumane actions occurred by the day.

It all brought back so much of what Dad had said about his years growing up in pre-World War II Italy.

When we were younger, Dad would tell my siblings and me, "There is going to be a revolution in this country one day. (He was referring to the USA.) I want all of you to remember what it is I've taught you."

There were lots of things Dad had taught us, and finally one day we pressed him on what exactly it was he wanted us to remember.

"Pray the Rosary," he said.

We looked around at each other. His response—totally unexpected. A few of us older teens, including me, guffawed under our breaths and even rolled our eyes at each other when Dad wasn't looking.

My father was always the one, not my mother, who insisted we do a family rosary each evening after dinner during Lent and possibly other times of the year, especially if he had a special intention in mind.

The day Dad told us the way to protect ourselves was to pray the Rosary, we didn't take him seriously. We were young and invincible— so we thought.

But now as adults, my siblings and I have talked about Dad's prediction, especially after his death in 2015, the year before all the changes in our country began. Not one of us eight kids had ever forgotten our father's message.

Although I never said it aloud to anyone, there were times at night when I was not able to sleep, worrying about the state of the world and where our country was heading.

In the dark, I would reach over to my bedpost where three sets of rosary beads hung: a blue-crystal pair of *Nonna* Egidia's that she had given me when I was a teenager, a pair made of small silver metal beads that had belonged to my *Nonno* Stagnitta, and the brown pair with carved wooden beads I had bought at the Vatican in Rome when Stu and I were there with Mom and Dad.

I would never know which one would end up in my hand. But I could feel the shape of the beads with my fingers and realize which pair I held before I'd began the opening prayer, "I believe in God …."

Back in Italy on the *Footsteps Tour*, Stu and I thought of my parents. My mother was still living, and no doubt thinking of us. And we imagined my father watching over us in Spirit, as we followed the same itinerary that we had taken with them in 2000—flying into Rome for three days, before heading south by train to Sicily.

I had so wished I could have taken another trip with my parents before 9/11 happened, the trip during which I had wanted to return to Linguaglossa and get inside of St. Egidio's church and visit the cemetery that we had not seen last time.

I'd felt a strong pull to go back there for a reason I couldn't understand myself. I had wished Mom would have gone with us, but there was no way she would have ever traveled abroad again without my father.

I never imagined we'd have as good a time as we did when traveling with my parents to our ancestral homes. But, despite Mom and Dad's absence, Stu and I had an amazing time with four of my five sisters, Nicki, Fran, Teresa, and Jo Anne. (Bridget, the youngest, had already taken the same journey with her husband and two children a few years earlier. And my two brothers would in time go with their families).

A number of my cousins came too. Having a number of relatives present, just like there had been in the book, made the experience come alive. And there were other courageous travelers, including my dear friend, Rosemary, willing to visit the towns I'd written about in *My Father's Daughter, From Rome to Sicily.*

While in my mother's family's village of Linguaglossa in the region of Mount Etna, we ate lunch in the same restaurant, *Gatto Blu* (Blue Cat), where Stu and I had eaten with my parents and Mom's cousins. There we were again, with three of those cousins, eating the town's traditional meal of pasta, the *prima piatta*, and the *secondo*, second course, the homemade Italian sausage for which Linguaglossa is famous.

We chatted and talked, and the language was easy since we had a guide and translator with us, along with my cousin Joe, and my sister Nicki. They both spoke Italian better than I did. Mom's cousin Nino and his wife, Elena, also spoke some English and understood whatever we said.

During dinner, my sister Fran—the third daughter in our family— asked Nino if he knew about his uncle, our grandfather, *Nonno* Stagnitta's ability to do healing work.

"Of course, I know about it," Nino said in a firm voice, as he held his hands up in amazement.

Of course, he would know such a thing, I thought!

My sisters—Nicki, Fran, Teresa, and Jo Anne—looked over at me and we looked around at each other. Our mouths dropped open.

"It comes from his mother's side, *il matriarcale,*" Nino said emphatically, and then began to list names of relatives and ancestors in my grandfather's family who had practiced forms of healing work— saying names of people going back generations.

The five of us sisters were amazed, speechless really. As we continued to look around at each other, our eyes widened with curiosity.

Later, when Nino took us to the cemetery, he pointed out gravesites that housed the many healers from the Stagnitta side, which he stressed came down through the Manganos, *Nonno's* matriarchal-ancestral line. If I understood Mom's cousin correctly, there were a few in his and my mother's generation who had practiced not only healing but also medicine there in Sicily.

Here I was in late October 2017, with my sister Nicki, a nurse by profession, who has strong Therapeutic Touch abilities. I was never in the medical profession, but I was thrilled to have been approved by a board of nurses through the Healing Touch Program.

After me, the next woman in our family was my sister Fran. She had given up work in the corporate world to become a Pilates and Yoga instructor, and would eventually become a Certified Professional Coach.

Fran was named after my grandfather, Francesco Stagnitta. Fran, short for Francine, had recently begun studying Reiki, another healing energy modality.

And in my heart I knew there were others, a number of others, who showed signs of this intuitive ability—I suspect another sibling or more, including my youngest brother, Gerard, whom we almost lost over a medical mishap the same year I'd become a Certified Healing Touch Practitioner.

While in Intensive Care, he would later tell us, our grandfather, *Nonno* Stagnitta, already dead for over thirty years, had been there by his side comforting him.

We had now found a longer family line, the missing link, to the origin of our ability to do energy work.

After we left the restaurant, Mom's cousin Nino directed our bus driver to the area of town where my grandparents lived before moving to the United States a century earlier. *Nonno* emigrated first and eventually *Nonna* would follow with their first-born child (our Uncle Joe), a young family starting their life together on foreign soil in the United States.

The one place I had hoped to get into this time was the church in the area of town where my mother's family had lived. I had been to Linguaglossa three other times and the doors there were always locked solid.

When planning the trip, I begged the tour company to do all they could to get us inside. Our tour guide told me that if we arrived at the church before three in the afternoon the doors would still be open for us.

We drove down a narrow road on the left side of the church. The driver stopped the bus at a spot where everyone could get off safely. We walked back a few blocks, crossed the street, and approached the church from behind.

I headed around to the front of the Early Gothic structure and found myself standing in the small triangular *piazza* in front of the *Chiesa di Sant' Egidio Abate*. After having tried multiple times over a number of visits to get inside this church, the colossal wooden doors were now open.

I walked up the stairway, entered through the portal. In front of me, a red carpet covered the diamond-shaped marble floor of the nave, which I walked down, passing remnants of frescos peeling away from the surface of the thick Gothic walls on either side of me.

Ahead lay the altar I moved towards. Finally, I was in the church where generations of my mother's family worshipped. I thought of Mom and wished she could have been here with us. But something else grander about Mom surfaced even though she was always the quiet parent, listening to what Dad had to say. Here in this church I began to remember something my sister, Nicki, had said to me.

"I've been thinking about Mom and her ability to heal."

I had never thought about that before. Never. It wasn't Mom, it was her father, my *Nonno*. And then it was Nicki, who showed promise, and Fran, and my cousin Frank, and then me with Healing Touch.

But Nicki had reminded me one day about Mom and her soothing touch when rubbing our backs, tending to a wound, or gently taking water in her hand and flowing it over an injured part of our body. Mom was always so subtle.

Oh my goodness, had my own quiet and humble mother had the healing gift, too? Whenever I asked if I could practice on her, she always jumped at the chance. Being the gentle soul that she was, Mom must have minimized her own ability that she inherited from her father's line, used it on all of us, but kept it to herself.

On this trip, I ultimately learned what was hidden in Linguaglossa that I was so curious about uncovering before 9/11 happened and all possibilities of travel with my parents were crushed. I knew there was something back in the shadows of Mount Etna. And now I realize why I wanted to return with my mother. There was something I would eventually discover about Mom and something else I was meant to learn first.

Following the journey into Healing Touch allowed me to discover my own ability to do energy work before learning that the healing arts had been deeply rooted in my ancestry and passed down through my maternal grandfather's matriarchal lineage to *Nonno*, and now, I suspect, to my unassuming mother.

III

Back in the U.S.A.

After we arrived home from Italy, I also thought about what my father had been trying to convey when he told us all those years ago, and many times after, to pray the Rosary.

The Rosary, a devotion in honor of Mary, Christ's mother, is a sequence of prayers following a string of meditation beads of five decades, each decade starting with one large bead, then ten small beads, ending with one more large bead. Every decade has the Our Father prayer, ten Hail Marys, and a Glory Be to God prayer.

Dad had appealed to a higher source, greater than himself.

What amazed me was that I finally saw how important it had been for my father to connect with the Divine through Mary—the feminine archetype of our family's religious tradition. How ironic it was that through the female my own father found support.

For many years, my prayers had come through journaling—writing to a higher source, posing questions, even answering back as I found clarity. Most mornings, I would meditate—hope for some form of internal communication—walk in nature, commune with the Divine.

Now back in the USA, any kind of praying or meditating or even journaling was not enough to settle me, knowing, as I did, that a woman from my generation would probably never become president. Having watched for years the good that many in our generation had done, now be undone, was painful. Little did I know how much worse everything would soon become.

Instead of praying for those running the government, each time a power-hungry politician, versus one who cared about the people, spoke on television with something that stood for everything I was against, I would jump from my chair. I would position my fingers and hands as if wrapping them around that person's throat.

I would even tell anyone who would listen, "I don't know why these guys are still around. I've been choking them on the nightly news or whenever they've appeared on TV."

The metaphorical choking continued for months, then a year, then longer. Until one day, I was at an eye, ear, nose, and throat doctor for a minor nose irritation.

"You have a nodule here in your thyroid," the doctor said, as he poked and prodded around my throat. "Have you ever felt anything there?"

Of course, I hadn't. I would definitely have had it checked. Three of my five sisters and a number of my first-female cousins were on Synthroid, but I had dodged that medicine, or so I thought. My sister Fran even had surgery on her thyroid when they discovered one of the nodules was cancerous.

I said to the doctor, "But my Ob/Gyn … she just felt around my throat three months ago."

"Except that *I'm* the specialist," he firmly replied, while I held back from rolling my eyes, aware that, whether I liked it or not, the world was controlled by males.

Yes, he was the specialist, I will acknowledge that, and I felt grateful he found the nodule. At that moment in time, all I could think of were the number of months I had pretended to choke the power-hungry who needed to be in control. With all I'd learned about the body/mind connection from the Healing Touch program, the person I was undeniably choking was myself.

When I came to that realization, I stopped and took a deep, a very deep, breath. It was time to take note of my life and how I was handling this difficult time with my disappointment that went far beyond not having a woman in the Oval Office. It was then I realized how important it was for me to start looking further into myself and my own need for healing, again, but on a different level.

I followed the medical doctor's advice about first going for an ultrasound and, if indicated, agreed I would go for a biopsy of the nodule. While waiting a few weeks for my appointment, I checked with some alternative healers, starting with the herbalist I've used.

I wanted to be sure my nutritional intake was supporting my thyroid. We talked about the few weeks I had to prepare for the ultrasound, and my herbalist encouraged me to follow a sulfur diet with fifty-plus foods to choose from, including items such as asparagus, avocados, broccoli, cabbage, eggs, spinach, and fish. I had been seeing the herbalist for years, so I was comfortable with her food choices, vitamin suggestions, and any other advice she offered.

I definitely received energy work from a Reiki Master once a month, someone with whom I've exchanged energy sessions with for years. She performs Reiki on me during one visit; I do Healing Touch on her the following week. I also started carrying a light blue aquamarine stone for my throat chakra.

I went through the medical protocol along with my own alternative care, including homeopathy. When the ultrasound showed a large nodule, I knew the biopsy was a given. It took a few weeks to get back in because there were no available appointments in the outpatient center of the hospital.

In the meantime, I had to figure out a new way of being. I told myself that I could no longer jump up and choke anyone, even if it was imaginary. I also returned to some of my books that offered wisdom on the throat, the voice, the issue of not being heard. The Reiki Master asked me questions such as, "Where do you think you're not being heard?"

I was reminded of my work with Sister Brigid in my early Healing Touch days. They were the kinds of questions she would have asked.

I told the Reiki Master that I had resolved so much of my work and family life—now and earlier. But after having made strides throughout the last number of decades, I realized as a female from the 60s generation that those in power would soon set back women's advancement.

Even the landmark decision of 1971-73, Roe v. Wade, passed almost fifty years ago, was being threatened. Little did any of us know that by June 2022, Roe would be overruled by the Supreme Court and sent back to the states, where many would strip women of more and more reproductive rights. There was now a huge push to control women's bodies, one of the things I had feared. As a woman, I couldn't help but take this personally.

Also as a woman, not being heard at this later stage in my life after having believed in and supported women's rights, these challenges were a huge struggle for me.

During the Reiki session where we focused on my thyroid, I realized that I had much more work to do and felt a shift toward a new direction. With this cultural, societal, and political swing, my course was still unfolding and transforming.

No matter what my focus turned out to be, the energy practitioner pointed out that I had, for a few years at the least, been telling her that I needed to get back to a place I had been during and after my Healing Touch Program.

Fortunately, I had a Spiritual Direction appointment with Carol just before I began my medical tests. Of course, I talked about my thyroid and my awareness and about my imaginary choking of autocratic politicians on television.

I told Carol that it would be in my best interest if I turned the TV off when I found myself so irritated. I also talked to her about my years of studying Healing Touch and that I wanted desperately to get back to focusing on energy in a deeper and more involved way.

These thoughts and feelings had all started surfacing before the 2016 election. Something was stirring inside.

Turning the television off was not an easy task. I wanted to be aware of what was going on in the world I lived in. But when I kept it on, I'd often feel agitated. I needed to return to a different source, and I needed some kind of portal to take me there.

The day before Stu and I were leaving to go up to Connecticut for my nephew's high school graduation—my sister Fran's youngest, the last of my parent's eighteen grandchildren—there was an appointment available for the biopsy of the nodule in my thyroid. I wanted to get the procedure over with. I did and it went well.

Unfortunately, with all my sensitivities, the medicinal soap they had used created a red, itchy rash—but not until after Stu and I got on the road. Over-the-counter suggestions by the medical doctor I spoke with by phone didn't work. So, I called my homeopath, and the rash slowly began to go away with the remedy he suggested, *apis mellifica*.

In Connecticut, I was busy with my family—Mom, all seven of my siblings, a number of their spouses, as well as my cousin Ann Marie who had lived with us growing up. Many nieces and nephews also made it to the graduation. Being with them over the weekend had been a great distraction while waiting for the biopsy results.

After my nephew's graduation, Stu and I headed up to Boston to spend more time with my sister Nicki and her husband, Ed. While there, Nicki and I went to see Karen, a healer my sister knew. Nicki's appointment was on a Tuesday. While I was there, I made one for the following day. We chose to sit in on each other's sessions and take notes.

Nicki and I had pursued our interest in metaphysics decades ago, when we were roommates in Boston. We'd gone a number of times to see an astrologer, whom we both liked.

To this day, we still remember some of Mrs. Lynde's astrological predictions that have gotten us through some challenging times, including an old warning that one day we would wonder whether those who brought children into the world were better off than those who did not. At the time it felt odd because neither one of us were in a serious relationship, nor did we know that I would not be able to have children.

The night before my appointment with the healer, the assistant from the doctor's office called me on my cell from North Carolina to tell me that my nodule was benign. The doctor had noted that I should come back in if I felt any changes.

I knew that my plan was to go full steam ahead with energy work, herbology, homeopathy, prayer, meditation, and a heavy dose of working out ways to stay connected with divine love versus anger, choking, and chaos.

When Nicki and I were with Karen, she sensed both of us had healing abilities, and that they were different from each other's and also from hers. We smiled and explained that Nicki did Therapeutic Touch and I did Healing Touch.

Karen also talked to me about my need to let go of whatever it was that was choking me. She didn't put it in quite those words, but she came pretty close. This healer suggested I consider sending love into the places where I felt resentment.

LOVE? That was hardly what I'd been feeling.

The next morning, I told my sister that if I was going to send love to anybody across the energy field, it was going to be tough love. I believe each of us is accountable for our own behavior.

When I arrived back home from New England, I continued journaling about my frustration and anger toward the administration now running the country. I thought of my initial conversation with Sister Donna years back at Well of Mercy about my struggles with a male-dominated church. It wasn't just the church.

The patriarchy that prevailed had been a challenge for me for a good part of my life. I always blamed Dad for any feelings I had about men being in control. But it was bigger than my father, even though he did perpetuate the patriarchal system. Dad, like me, came from that structure—the cultural, religious, and governmental system in which men hold most of the power.

I used to say, "Why would Dad give up his control? The whole patriarchal setup is in his best interest."

My uncles and grandfathers acted the same way—men were heads of the household in my Italian American culture. When I went out into the wider world, I experienced similarities. Eventually, I took my resistance back home where it started and began to fight the system, starting with Dad and working on it one small step at a time.

When my father wanted something, like a cup of coffee, he'd ask one of us girls or Mom to get it for him. When I learned to start challenging Dad by responding to his "Supreme Commander" attitude (a title he gave himself), I would retort, "Do you not know how to pour a cup of coffee yourself?"

Often, he'd lash right back with the same line, "Why do you think God gave me a wife, six daughters, granddaughters, and a niece?" Dad, of course, was insinuating that our role was to wait on him whenever he pleased.

As time went on, we pointed out to Dad that God gave him six daughters and the other females in the family so that there were enough of us to stand up to him and the male energy that he supported.

When my generation of women hit the 1960s, the conventional archetypes of the patriarchy started being questioned and bantered around our kitchen and dining room tables often.

Now in this early part of the 21st century, the truth came out about the shadow side of our so-called land of the free as white supremacy, fascism, and racism resurfaced. The truth was especially poignant not only for women and women's rights, but also for people of color, citizens in lower socioeconomic classes, immigrants from particular countries, disability discrimination and those with gender differences.

All the agitation that so many of us were feeling began to surface in the *MeToo movement, Black Lives Matter, Mothers Against Gun Violence, March For Our Lives, Environmental movement,* and other social and awareness campaigns.

It wasn't just women who resisted. I think of my husband, my brothers, brothers-in-law, male cousins, friends, and colleagues. These men, who also believe in the equality of all people, including women, act with concern.

I continued journaling and writing and recognizing where all the disturbance and resentment stemmed from. It is so much bigger than one household, one culture, one political tenure.

In taking myself back to that time in my Healing Touch program and afterwards, I opened up to the truth of what had surfaced for me after Hillary's loss, and what I continue to experience in our American society, where most in power are white males—both public features, and those wheeling power from behind the scenes.

By exploring the depths of my feelings, I was on a mission to find my way back to what I'd learned through Healing Touch, Spiritual Direction, and my sacred contracts, so that I could move forward to a place that would help me enter a different world, a world of compassion, caring, and love.

Doing so would guide me deeper into my purpose and make a difference in my life and in the world where I lived.

IV
Back to Well of Mercy

In 2018, Sister Brigid and Sister Donna retired from directing the retreat center. Well of Mercy continued to be alive and flourishing. The team of people overseeing Well followed Brigid and Donna's mission to offer a place for those in need of "a temporary respite from daily demands, expectations and stresses or (for) those who simply wish to move apart for a time of prayer, rest and renewal."

The Sisters lived on the land but in their own home, tucked away from the center of the guest houses, chapel, grounds, creek, and other areas for visitors and staff. Because of teaching memoir writing and workshops, and because I had three books published, I was contacted by a board member at Well and asked if I'd be interested in teaching a Soul Writing Workshop in 2015. Of course, I would.

Doing the work I've loved on the land I've loved was a gift. Again in 2018, I led another Soul Writing Workshop at Well. Both events were held in the rustic, octagon-shaped chapel with expansive windows from which we looked out over lush-green vegetation surrounding the building.

Participants and I sat around a circular, altar-like table. Each person was invited to bring with them their own personal object, keepsake, or memento to put on the altar. We placed woven prayer stoles over our shoulders honoring the sacred chapel where we gathered.

Everyone wrote from prompts I had created specifically for soul work. Those who wished to do so, shared their memories.

There were meditations, music, sparks of energy, conversations of how it felt to capture thoughts and feelings on paper—feelings some folks had been holding onto, in many cases, for decades. There were discussions about how to continue writing after the workshop ended, how to pay attention to what stories surfaced, how to make journaling part of one's spiritual practice.

I closed both workshops with the song I had first heard in my early Healing Touch days, "Return Again" by Shaina Noll. The lyrics reminded me of the importance of returning to the land of my soul.

Return again, return again
Return to the land of your soul
Return again, return again
Return to the land of your soul

Return to what you are
Return to who you are
Return to where you are born and reborn again[12]

After the second workshop, I stayed overnight and spent time with my own journaling, which I had been doing more of as I wrote about my struggles during these last number of years, after the 2016 election.

Getting what was inside of me out and onto paper always helped, along with meditating, walking, and focusing on staying centered. All of these techniques I'd learned over the years crept back into my life and helped me handle the anxious feelings I'd been experiencing in the midst of the chaos of the times.

The morning after the workshop ended, I arose early to walk the grounds as I had many times before. After a brief saunter along Hunting Creek, I veered off to the left. A short way ahead, I saw a site that stopped me in my tracks. I was thrown back to a time in 2003 during my Healing Touch Level 4 training.

There had been a number of rites and ceremonies throughout my program but now, nearly fifteen years later, a memory of one particular day surfaced. I approached the site as if entering sacred ground and climbed a short incline to a natural area with sunlight shining above an open space. Trees and other greenery hugged the outskirts as if guarding this special piece of land.

In the middle of the natural area was a wooden sign hammered into the wide trunk of a large oak tree. Painted on the sign in black-blocked Roman type were the words **SACRED CIRCLE**. Large, dark-gray boulders lay below a canopy of trees. Beneath one of the moss-covered boulders sat a white-sculpted angel just over a foot tall with full, detailed wings extending from its body. Small stones, twigs,

---

[12] Shaina Noll, "Return Again," Track #3 on *Songs for the Inner Child,* Singing Heart Productions, 1992, Audio CD

leaves, and other natural elements lay at the feet of the angel. People who had visited the site may have placed the items there as a possible prayer request. Slowly I turned myself around 180 degrees and faced the Sacred Circle.

On the afternoon that flashed through my mind, Sister Brigid and Sister Donna were present as was my eventual mentor, Deborah Larrimore, and the founder of the Healing Touch Program, Janet Mentgen. Participants, including my soon-to-be fellow mentees, were also there.

At the time, none of us who were participating knew why that specific piece of land on Well of Mercy's grounds had been singled out. Maybe Brigid or Donna knew, but the rest of us just followed along that day as part of our program. It was not far from the chapel, yet to be built, and there was a sense of the mystical hovering in the air. Hardly anyone spoke outside of a whisper.

I believe it was Sister Donna who passed out pieces of paper, pencils, and pens. She asked us to find a spot where we felt comfortable to sit, write, and put into words what we sensed about the land, the grounds around us, any energy we picked up.

A few folks meandered over to the large oak tree in the center, sat down, and rested their backs against the trunk of the tree. Some sat on large boulders. Others began writing immediately, while there were those who seemed to wait and reflect a bit, as if thinking, meditating, maybe praying.

I watched a few moving about by themselves toward the rim of the circular space until they eventually settled in the low grass. One person moved quietly from one spot to another, stopping periodically to jot something on his paper.

Since I'd been distracted by the beauty of this place and the movement of others, it took me awhile to focus on what we were doing. I found a spot close to the middle of the circle near the oak tree.

I remember having asked someone nearby to explain again what we were supposed to write. After the person repeated what Sister Donna had said, I put pen to paper and began.

Twenty or thirty minutes later, we handed our papers to the sisters. While walking away, some whispered their thoughts about the Indigenous people whom they sensed had passed through this area of

North Carolina decades, probably even centuries, earlier, long before the land had been purchased and developed into a retreat center. Another believed there were actual Native Americans who had lived on these grounds.

I heard a whisper about troops marching, and a fellow participant told of the animals that moved through the gentle, rolling fields. One of my close companions sensed a time, even further back, when eagles, owls, and many other birds of prey inhabited earlier trees and the sky overhead.

I wish I could have kept a copy of what I wrote that day, because what I eventually began to write were words that flowed into what felt like automatic writing—the flowing of words that came from something greater than my own mind, a connection directly to the spiritual part of self, something we all have. What I sensed was that we were on ancient ground, sacred earth, consecrated land from something encompassing the collective consciousness of all living beings.

After we slowly began our walk back to the retreat center, I could not recall most of what I had written. The ideas came through me and the memory of what I had captured seemed to disappear once the words landed on the paper.

As far as I know, only Sister Brigid and Sister Donna still have what we wrote that day in what I will always think of as sacred space.

This memory of my time on the land with other Healing Touch folks filled my heart with joy, with love, with a centeredness that I hadn't felt in quite a while. And this special memory is one of the many I still hold from the numerous times I've visited Well over the years.

Life had changed long before the 2016 election, and I missed not going to Well of Mercy as frequently as I had during my Healing Touch days. That includes the times when I received Healing Touch from Sister Brigid and later the advanced levels I had participated in during my program that sent my life into a whole new direction.

It was in those years that I not only learned how to work with energy but had also discovered and became more aware of other aspects of my life's purpose: more writing, teaching/mentoring, along with what inspired my other ten archetypes that had always been a part of me, anyway.

From the time I first began leading memoir classes and workshops, I gave talks on the importance of writing our stories for ourselves, for generations that follow, and for those drawn to the writer's journey. I created a piece of art now and again, since poetry and memoir had taken center stage at this time in my life. In the midst of it all, I was fortunate to still be receiving and giving energy.

When my Healing Touch client arrives at the door, I guide her to the right toward a side table with a silver platter full of angel cards. Each card is turned upside down with a word hidden on the back side. My client picks a card for this session—the word Surrender. I pick a card, too. Energy!

I direct her to the door on the left that leads into my Healing Touch room. She sits in the comfortable red wing chair across from where I sit, on a sturdy straight-back desk chair.

"How are you?" I ask, and she shares with me her present concerns.

My client has been here before and easily tells me what is on her mind and why she has returned for more energy work. I listen carefully. Today, we talk for about twenty minutes, before her conversation begins to slow down, and I know she is ready to get on the Healing Touch table.

"Is there any part of your body you are having trouble with?" I ask.

"My head," she says. "I've been thinking too much."

It's easy to do in this busy world where we spend more time in our heads with thoughts spinning around.

As my client lies down on the table, I ask if she needs a cover. A light sheet is all she wants. I place it over her and tuck a pillow under her knees so she is comfortable and her back is not strained.

"Do you need anything else?" I ask, and she shakes her head side to side.

After lighting a candle, I cover her eyes with tissue, then lay down a rich-red, satin eye pillow that my sister Nicki had given me a number of years back. I turn on meditative music. Today *The Shamanic Dream* plays quietly in the background.

Once I see my client relaxed and restful, I stand behind her at the head of the massage table, center myself, and begin spinning each of my own chakras, visualizing them as clear and open. Even though I meditate and clear my chakras each morning, I always re-center before beginning a session so that I am prepared for doing this work.

Then I start by saying aloud, "I call your angels and guides and my angels and guides to assist me in this healing for your highest and best good."

I pause before walking to the right side of the table, hold my hands about twelve inches above my client's body, palms face down, and begin checking each chakra to see which are open and which are congested. I start with the seventh chakra, the head, and will work my way down through each chakra until I reach the first one, the root.

As I hover around my client's head and move closer to her eyes, static pinches the palms of my hands—congested. Moving to the sixth chakra, I continue sensing what energy is over the brow—the third eye. On to the fifth chakra—the throat, then the fourth—the heart.

When I feel static and prickly pinches in my palm, I stay with the heart a little extra to be sure of what I sense before moving down over the first three chakras—the third—the solar plexus—abdomen, a heavy weight settles in my hands; the second—the sacral above the ovaries, uterus, pubic bone; the first –the root, the tailbone and down to my client's feet.

I step further out beyond the Healing Touch table and into the space around the body—the field. Through my hands, I feel no static or discomfort. All is clear and smooth. I jot my findings down on the form I use and walk back to the end of the table.

When first evaluating the chakras, I go from crown to root. But when it's time to work on clearing any disturbances I've detected, I start at the feet and move up the body to the crown.

Now, I stand at the bottom of the table, hold my client's feet. Instantly, I feel as if there is a spike in my thumbs as they rest on the ball of each foot. Holding my thumbs still and my fingers around the rest of each foot, I send energy through the feet to the solar plexus, a direct connection to the third chakra.

Once the static subsides, I begin moving slowly, hovering my hands above my client's body.

If there is any static, heat, or turbulence, I hold my hands still and send energy until all sensations calm down, dissipate. I work my way up the right side of the body from feet to ankle, ankle to knee, knee to hip. I do the same on the left side letting the energy lead me.

Sensing friction over the left knee, I clear it by brushing my hands above the knee, then hold my hand on top of it until the friction subsides. My mind wanders, remembering a time on the table when I felt a shaman close by.

I couldn't help but think of that tall thin woman, dressed in white, a guide with a veil over her head. My mind is soon drawn back from the memory and back to my client's knee that I'm lingering over. Is that same shaman helping me feel the tightness on my client's knee?

My intention is to balance each chakra before moving to the next.

I float my right hand above the root chakra connected to the tail bone beneath the body. I hold still while positioning my left hand over the sacral chakra, above the lower abdomen.

Again, I hold my hands in place and send energy, waiting for the static in my palms to diminish. Many a time, Sister Brigid held her hands over my lower abdomen. I can almost feel her presence now.

I'm jarred back to the body below me, now sensing calm.

I move my right hand over to the sacral chakra while, at the same time, I move my left over the solar plexus, stomach. I stop, assess, move my way up the body.

Wherever I pick up turbulence through static or heat against my hands, cold breeze, or multiple other sensations, I brush strokes above the area of the body I am working on, hold my hands in place, and send clear energy until all unrest subsides.

I am strictly the facilitator guided by what the person's energy indicates.

I do get clues and thoughts about what may be going on as I move my hands above various parts of the body. I make a conscious note in my head to discuss these with my client afterwards to see if she had any awareness of anything during the process.

When I reach the crown, the seventh chakra, I think I have finished, but I am drawn back toward the eyes. I stop and am not sure what the static is about and where I need to be.

Within a nanosecond, I sense *Nonno* by my side. He is one of my helpers. I find myself moving one hand over the right eye, the other over the left. I stay put a good long while.

At the top of the head, I begin a full Mind Clearing, which I do using various hand positions on the crown, neck, jaw, forehead. It's a technique I learned early on.

At one point, I pull up a stool and sit, holding my hands on the crown of the head, feeling a throbbing sensation in my palms. Throbbing. Throbbing.

How does the beat of the drum in the meditative music align so perfectly with the motion from this pulsing, heart pounding, rhythmic pattern against my palms? Then it stops.

After moving myself from feet to head, I spend quiet time holding the top of the head. How did I move over my client's body so quickly?

I take a brief look at my watch and am surprised that forty-five minutes have already gone by. Being in this energy, I've been in an altered space myself.

More often than not, after the energy is cleared and settled, I realize I've lost all sense of time.

The person on the table is calm, relaxed, seemingly asleep but probably in her own alpha state. I've heard her breathe softly along the way. She'll tell me afterwards whether she fell asleep or has been in a state of peace.

Rechecking the chakras with the palm of my hands, I am pleased they are smooth, serene, open. I check the energy field around her again, and all is still tranquil. Today's session is complete.

After pressing the client's legs lightly from the knees to her feet, I walk toward the top of the table, place a few drops of zesty tangerine citrus oil into the palms of my hands, and rub them together. Then I hold my hands slightly above her nose until it starts to twitch. Her arms and legs begin to move. I hit a tuning fork that vibrates a sound through the room.

We are finished, and I remove the red pillow from my client's eyes. After I guide her carefully off the table, I hand her the customary glass of water to help ground her in the present.

We talk about what she's experienced and what I've sensed and found. What she shares with me about her experience on the table today is as fascinating as my discoveries. It's private, of course.

"No partying, bar hopping, or dancing tonight," I say with a smile, repeating what I always say to her and every other client. "Relax, take gentle care, stay in a quiet space for the rest of the day and evening."

It's hard to explain all the facets of what happens during a session. It's often mysterious even to me. But when our time together is complete, we walk back by the silver platter that holds the angel cards, and I feel as if I have received as much energy as I have given.

If I am going to give Healing Touch, I need to keep myself clear. I am grateful to have an energy worker as well as a Spiritual Director. Both help me recognize my own disturbances as well as address any uncomfortable awareness that needs to be dealt with.

If I don't face and resolve my concerns, I can't be a clear vessel to help anyone.

I am also grateful for having returned to Well of Mercy and places on the land reminding me of what I had learned those years ago. Even though I went in and out of feeling centered after the 2016 election, that peace would wear off much too soon.

I now see that my struggle to find what I had lost during and after that painful election was an internal self-preparing to do this work in a new way.

From the core of my being, I cannot take Healing Touch or any energy work for granted nor can I forget the importance of it in my life. It appeared at a time I needed support to help me navigate a world I'd never knowingly been a part of. I am fortunate to have discovered such a powerful source and must always remember that by giving or receiving energy, I am brought back to a place of acceptance, clarity, and love.

V

The Pandemic

Perhaps in writing this memoir about my healing path, I have reached another level of honesty about how I have felt during the times we've moved through in the United States since 2016. It seemed difficult when I began Part II of this memoir, until I finally had the courage to write about my distress over such a qualified woman not being able to get elected to the highest position in our country.

Little did I know at the time that there was also a pandemic in the making.

Until COVID-19 hit, I had not been aware that *Nonna* Egidia's father had actually died from the Spanish flu in 1918 in their Sicilian village of Linguaglossa the year before *Nonna* and *Nonno* got married. That's why in *Nonna's* wedding photo she's wearing a long, brown cotton dress instead of the traditional white-laced gown and veil the young women from her village wore when they married.

In respect for her father (my great grandfather), my dear grandmother honored him and their customs by wearing dark clothes during the one-year mourning period.

Before the pandemic broke in early 2020, many of us were already struggling with a government that changed by the day—not just because of one individual (although it felt that way), but also because of hidden symptoms of larger problems that began to surface in our country.

Each time I finished journaling about one thing that stressed me out, another stressor appeared—immigration, children at the border, health care, climate change, women's issues, gun violence, white supremacy, racism … and the list went on.

As if living through these times wasn't enough, once the coronavirus hit and Americans began to shelter at home, we were forced to face the reality of a global pandemic without any clear end.

I stayed sane by teaching my memoir classes on Zoom, journaling, writing, meditating, taking my sister Fran's Zoom Pilates class, walking, and going deep within, the way I had done after 9/11.

All I could think of was getting myself back to those days when I began Spiritual Direction, moved into Healing Touch, discovered my sacred contracts and lived out all three in a soulful way during both good and difficult times.

Another revelation I had during the pandemic was that both my students and I used our additional time at home to go further in depth with our writing.

With each memoir class and workshop that I've taught, in the past and now, I've encouraged participants to write *their* feelings, *their* experiences, *their* stories. I've announced in my classes, in talks I've given, and to anyone who would listen that, if we don't write our stories, they will die with us; worse yet, someone else may attempt to tell our truth.

That's what I did and continued to do—write, edit, and write some more. How else would generations that follow know how people felt and thought during these times if we didn't capture our memories on paper or in a digital document.

I also continued participating in Healing Touch and energy work, as well as Spiritual Direction. Energy work—giving and receiving—had to be Long Distance Healing. LDH is a practice of sending energy to a person by using the same techniques and imagining the person receiving the work.

It was something I had learned to do during my Healing Touch Program.

I would set up the Healing Touch table and position pillows, as if forming a person, before covering all with a blanket or two using the colors of one or more chakras. Each session began with a Zoom conversation. Then we would get offline and the client would lay down at home while I performed Long Distance Healing in my Healing Touch room.

We ended with a brief discussion about what transpired for the client and what I discovered in the process. Continuing in Spiritual Direction also took place on Zoom.

I wish I could tie my healing path up into a large yellow bow like the ones people have tied on trees to welcome a soldier home from war. While I thought I had tied that bow in 2004, once I became a Certified Healing Touch Practitioner I've learned that as long as I am alive, there will always be twists and turns, more stories and poems to write, new challenges, new revelations, maybe even more drawings of angels or other art forms. Who knows?

Like many, I spent a considerable amount of time sheltered at home, fortunately with a supportive spouse. I also continued on Zoom with my own students—professional adults who have taken my memoir classes and workshops for the sheer longing to get their stories written and, in some cases, published.

When I started teaching memoir writing, the year before 9/11, I thought I would teach for only two years. But people's lives have always been far too intriguing. Also, I did not want to stop working with those who had the same passion to get their stories written.

My own healing path took me back to places like Well of Mercy, my family home in Syracuse, New York, and to the towns of my Sicilian roots, where the DNA had been planted generations earlier, where I learned that the healing arts were part of my matriarchal line.

My time in isolation during the pandemic also gave me the opportunity to reflect on what I had learned during those Healing Touch days and the importance of making energy a bigger part of my life.

Being more introspective also gave me time to explore other ways of moving forward in this continually changing world.

Many have never had time to allow for reflection and introspection. Yet, there are people who have changed what they've done for a living or where they've worked. I've known a number of those who left one path for another.

With the pandemic, almost everyone was forced to slow down, examine who and what matters, assess what path may now be calling them to follow.

It made me think of two fellow mentees I had studied with in Healing Touch who had volunteered to hold and rock babies in the NICU (Neonatal Intensive Care Unit). Having listened to them talk about their experiences was inspirational, as they shared how essential it was for them to cuddle and rock little preemies in their arms.

A number of folks I've known over the years have changed directions, even before the pandemic, when they felt driven toward something else. One friend became a financial advisor in midlife and helped those who had resources to invest. She also assisted others who had less by helping them set up effective financial plans.

There were those who left their work at large corporations to begin small businesses: importing and selling Italian olive oil, baking and selling truffles, opening up salons and shops.

A number of people I've known entered medical fields—nursing, physician assistants, physical therapy, homeopathy, sign language interpreters, and other health-related professions that became even more needed with the coronavirus onset.

Sometimes I've wondered if something greater than ourselves led many into those health fields. I have certainly been grateful for their commitment to humanity.

I've also known those who've entered the government, education, the arts—literary, visual, and performing. And another generation of women and men have slipped into parenting and grandparenting children in their families and communities.

We can all make a difference by following what we are curious about and what we're attracted to. That reminds me of one of my state senators whom I met during her first local election season. She didn't initially win when running for office.

But when I heard her speak at our town hall about public education, health care, the environment, gun violence, and other concerns, I supported her. She was eventually elected to office and able to encourage and support the principles that I have always believed in.

During the 2018 midterm election, I participated in a postcard campaign. Women in my area met and wrote out postcards to send to those in towns throughout the country asking the recipient to consider voting for a candidate in their city or state that held their same concerns.

I was grateful to two women—a former social worker and an elementary school principal—who led this postcard project and invited a number of us to participate. That mission included pieces of my sacred contracts—writing, sketching an image on a postcard, contributing to what felt like a humanitarian cause.

When the 2020 election came and then 2022, I picked up where I left off, writing more postcards along with writing letters and notes on flyers for the candidates I supported.

A friend, who is a scientist, was one of the many researchers who began working on COVID-19 toward the development of anti-viral drugs or drug repurposing to complement a future COVID vaccine treatment. This friend has been involved for decades in research on various infectious diseases, cancers, cardiovascular disease, and autoimmune disorders.

Being able to participate in research for the development of COVID-19 vaccines or companion anti-viral drugs clearly became a priority for her within the scientific community worldwide.

Many had already committed to a path long before the pandemic appeared. Those who hadn't, being in isolation certainly provided an opportunity to reflect further on what interests we have had and have done nothing about. Each time we follow our curiosity we can make a difference.

It can take us deeper and guide us to a place we may have never thought of before. That's how energy works—we follow where we feel pulled and it creates ripples that move beyond ourselves.

With Writer as archetype in the 1st astrological House of my sacred contracts, writing was inevitable, although I didn't know that early on. It crept up on me when, over thirty-five years ago, I had this passion to walk across the campus where I was teaching art and take a creative writing class. I was hooked.

The remaining archetypes that I chose have reflected what I've also always been drawn to in one way or another: Angels, Teacher/Mentor, Heroine, Mother, Mystical Seeker, Artist, Networker, along with the four survival archetypes of Child, Prostitute, Victim, and Saboteur.

Besides the guidance of my archetypes, energy workers, Spiritual Directors, mentors, and others, I have had much support and guidance along the way. I joined an Astrology group that grew out of the Charlotte Friends of Jung, which I've been a member of for years. Archetypes have been one of the focuses of our astrological explorations.

I have also gone deeper into dream work. My dreams have provided me with more awareness of what my unconscious tries to tell me.

Books, articles, and programs have offered new and helpful insights. A few impactful ones that I read after Hillary Clinton had lost the election and as we moved into the early pandemic era were: *What You Have Heard Is True, A Memoir of Witness and Resistance*, by author and poet Carolyn Forché; *The Time Is Now, A Call to Uncommon Courage,* by Benedictine nun Sister Joan Chittister; *Cosmos and Psyche, Intimations of a New World View*, by cultural historian Richard Tarnas; *It Didn't Start With You, How Inherited Family Trauma Shapes Who We Are And How To End The Cycle*, by Mark Wolynn; *Crazy Brave* and *Poet Warrior* by former Poet Laureate Joy Harjo, along with countless other books, stories, and poems.

What I learned after 9/11, through the challenges of 2016, and on, including living in a global pandemic, was that life would continue to surprise. There have always been things we can't control. But what we can control is pursuing what we are inquisitive about.

Each of us will be drawn to different interests in various ways. Whatever we are pulled toward is where we need to pay attention. I think of these words from the poet Rumi: "Everyone has been made for some particular work, and the desire for that work has been put in every heart."

It's been a long winding journey since 9/11, when I went in search of a Spiritual Director to help me move through changing times and discovered much more. As I've continued through more unpredictable times, I've gone deeper, been more reflective, paid closer attention to my curiosities.

It's hard to know exactly where any of us will end up. Countless hearts have been broken after so many people lost family members, including children and friends through the coronavirus, gun violence, an insurrection, immigration policies and practices, effects of a changing climate, the war in Ukraine, and the loss of women's rights.

If we listen and trust our inner voice, live out the intentions of our heart, act with love and compassion, keep commitments to ourselves and to others, we will each be directed again and again to the deep inner voice of our soul.

ACKNOWLEDGMENTS

I have always believed that I have stood on others' shoulders throughout my creative life, and A *Healing Journey, From 9/11 Beyond the Pandemic* is no exception.

There are so many to be grateful for, starting with my grandfather, *Nonno* Francesco Stagnitta and his matriarchal line, the Manganos, from Linguaglossa in the region of Mount Etna, Sicily. It was there that the healing first began. The gratitude flows on to others who have passed on, including my grandmother, *Nonna* Egidia Stagnitta; my parents, Mary and Nick Morina; my baby sister, Mary; my Morina grandparents, *Nonno* Antonio and *Nonna* Nicolina; and my many aunts, uncles, and cousins, some who have made an appearance in the pages of this story

Of course, I could never write a memoir without thanking my siblings, whom I love dearly, and who patiently travel with me through this journey of awareness: Nicki, Anthony, Fran, Teresa, Gerard, Jo Anne, Bridget, and Ann Marie, as well as their spouses and my nieces, nephews, and cousins, including those who traveled back with my husband, Stu, and me to Sicily and our family's origins.

And Stu, ah Stu! What would we all do without him, especially me? He has been the one to drive me up and down the East Coast and beyond. Stu, who I've placed right in the heart of my acknowledgments, has been the calming influence of my-sometimes anxious temperament. He makes me laugh, soothes my worries, accepts whoever I am on any given day. He's been there for almost five decades. It is no wonder my family often call him Saint Stu.

Much gratitude to the women who were instrumental in guiding me through this journey: Betty Pendle White, my first Spiritual Director and Sister Brigid McCarthy, my first Healing Touch practitioner and a mentor throughout. More gratitude to Sister Brigid McCarthy along with Sister Donna Vaillancourt, the Foundresses of Well of Mercy Retreat Center, a seat of much of my healing and the place where the truth of my ancestry, unbeknownst to me at the time, surfaced.

Grateful acknowledgment to those who have continued to keep my energy flowing: my present Spiritual Director, Carol Hassell, and my energy worker, Karin Sawhill; along with Charlotte Friends of Jung Astrology group for listening so carefully to my heart; and to the expansive Healing Touch Community members, you know who you are; as well as to my Inclusion Community, who have helped me live the questions.

A huge thank you to those wonderfully kind souls who read drafts of my story and offered supportive, caring, and valuable feedback: Dannye Romine Powell; Sister Brigid McCarthy; Sister Donna Vaillancourt; my own sister Francine Morina Levato; Jackye Zimmermann, who has been a part of my life since kindergarten; and my dear friend and colleague, Ann Campanella, who not only read a draft of my story but who was my hot line for any unexpected awarenesses that surfaced.

I also cannot thank my endorsers enough for their words of support, kindness, and understanding of a journey that takes us into other realms: Lisa Mentgen-Gordon, Dannye Romine Powell, Judy Goldman, Joseph Bathanti, Ann Campanella, Maureen Ryan Griffin, Delia De Santis, David Figura, and Laura Ponticello.

There is a writer, poet, colleague, and friend who has been there since our writing journeys intersected in the mid-1980s. This amazing writer, in her own right, is Maureen Ryan Griffin. "I don't know how you cannot tell this part of the story," she said one day, referring to Part II that eventually became my new 9/11. I put my forehead on the table, hoping when I looked up, she would have changed her mind. Her face was stoic, solid, and warm. She continually helped me birth that part of the painful story that I knew others feared I was writing, which I was. Maureen remained my rock throughout the telling of this journey. Thank you, dear friend.

To the members of my writing groups who have lifted me into this amazing literary community that I live amongst: Tootsie O'Hara, Irene Blair Honeycutt, Mary Wilmer, Naomi Myles, Ann Campanella, Brenda Graham, Suzanne Baldwin Leitner, Don Carroll, Larry Sorkin, Dede Mitchell, Allison Elrod, Lisa Williams Kline, and my incredible memoir-writing students who have studied with me over the last twenty-three years. They continue to be an inspiration.

Thank you to the Healing Touch Program for the scholarship at the 2016 Healing Touch Worldwide Conference in Charlotte, North Carolina, to the editors of *Quiet Diamonds,* published by The Orchard Street Press, where the poem, "The Spring Before 9/11," was first published, and to the co-editors of *People Places Passages, An Anthology of Canadian Writing,* Longbridge books, in which the story "Healing" appeared, albeit in different form. I have been gifted in my relationships with the Italian Canadian writers and the Association of Italian Canadian Writers (AICW).

I have so much appreciation for the two publishers who have combined efforts to send *A Healing Journey* into the world. Ann Campanella and Laura Ponticello have believed in my stories since first reading them. I was elated when both The Bridge and Divine Phoenix teamed up to get my story out into this ever-changing world.

The talents of Ann and Laura have complemented each other, and I have been the grateful recipient of these two warm and caring women. Thank you both for all that you have done in support of my writing.

Much gratitude to my early copy editor, Linda Vespa. I also have great appreciation for the creative and knowledgeable book designer Chris Moebs. It was a joy to have you back on board for *A Healing Journey.*

Much gratitude to you, my readers. We've passed through a journey together, from different locations. In truth, we are all on this path, continuing the work of the people who have held us firm on their shoulders so that we can carry forward the contracts we're here to fulfill.

ABOUT THE AUTHOR

Gilda Morina Syverson, an award-winning writer, poet, artist and teacher, has taught memoir-writing classes and workshops for over twenty-three years. She is the author of the award-winning memoir, *My Father's Daughter, From Rome to Sicily,* and two collections of poems. Gilda's work has appeared in numerous literary journals, anthologies, magazines, newspapers, and online sites in the United States and Canada. She has discussed and read her work on podcasts and for programs in the United States, Canada, and Italy. Her essay, "Healing," was published in *People Places Passages, An Anthology of Canadian Writing.*

Gilda is a Healing Touch Practitioner and was awarded a scholarship for the *Healing Touch Worldwide Conference, A Healers Retreat* during the writing of this book, *A Healing Journey, From 9/11 Beyond the Pandemic.* Gilda lives outside Charlotte, North Carolina, with her husband, Stu. Connect with Gilda at *www.gildasyverson.com* and on social media.

Also by Gilda Morina Syverson

NONFICTION

My Father's Daughter, From Rome to Sicily

POETRY

Facing the Dragon

In This Dream Everything Remains Inside

A medium that transports
story from inspiration to creation.
Our desire is that authors and readers
will be affirmed through
creativity and the written word.